The Psychology of Overeating

The Psychology of Overeating

Food and the Culture of Consumerism

BY KIMA CARGILL

Bloomsbury Academic
An imprint of Bloomsbury Publishing Plc

BLOOMSBURY

LONDON • OXFORD • NEW YORK • NEW DELHI • SYDNEY

Bloomsbury Academic

An imprint of Bloomsbury Publishing Plc

50 Bedford Square
London
WC1B 3DP
UK

1385 Broadway
New York
NY 10018
USA

www.bloomsbury.com

BLOOMSBURY and the Diana logo are trademarks of Bloomsbury Publishing Plc

First published 2015

British Library Cataloguing-in-Publication Data
A catalogue record for this book is available from the British Library.

ISBN: HB: 978-1-4725-8108-2
PB: 978-1-4725-8107-5
ePDF: 978-1-4725-8109-9
ePub: 978-1-4725-8110-5

Library of Congress Cataloging-in-Publication Data
Cargill, Kima.
The psychology of overeating : food and the culture of consumerism / by Kima Cargill.
pages cm
Includes bibliographical references and index.
ISBN 978-1-4725-8108-2 (Hardback) – ISBN 978-1-4725-8107-5 (Paperback) –
ISBN 978-1-4725-8109-9 (ePDF) – ISBN 978-1-4725-8110-5 (ePub) 1. Eating disorders–
Psychological aspects. 2. Eating disorders–Social aspects. I. Title.
RC552.E18C36 2015
616.85'26–dc23
2015019646

Typeset by Integra Software Services Pvt. Ltd.
Printed and bound in Great Britain

For Carsten, my culinary muse and the one I can count on for thrift, moderation, and joy.

Contents

List of Illustrations

Preface

Growing up in the American South, I was raised on an extremely sweet and indulgent diet. My dad ate the cattleman's breakfast of eggs, bacon, hot cakes, maple syrup, and hash browns at the Cattlemen's Cafe in Oklahoma City every weekday morning for fifty years. As kids we woke up on Saturday mornings and like many American children watched cartoons while eating cereal. My dad fixed us great big bowls of Fruity Pebbles with half and half. For laughs I recently calculated the nutritional content of our Saturday morning breakfasts. Two large bowls of Fruity Pebbles contain around 550 calories. A cup of half and half is 315 calories (the nutritional information is given by the tablespoon since it's not intended to be used as well, milk). My estimate is that our entire Saturday morning breakfast was nearly 900 calories, 45 grams of sugar, and 28 grams of fat. We were under 10 years old.

Candied desserts such as pralines, fudge, divinity, nut brittles, and an Oklahoma specialty called Aunt Bill's were extremely popular in my growing up. These desserts, if you've never had them are simply different variations of caramelized sugar and butter, and they were a staple of our diet. I have heard a number of people over the years taste something and say "that's too sweet." I myself have never, ever had that thought about anything. I have never tasted anything that I thought was too sweet.

Trying to understand and manage my intense liking for sweets eventually led me to the study of nutrition and overeating. In the course of my career, I've been surprised to find that unraveling the determinants of overeating has required me to consider psychology, philosophy, economics, neuroendocrinology, history, labor, and government regulation. What I share with you here is the culmination of nearly two decades of research, clinical work, and contemplation.

Acknowledgments

In 2001, I was completing a clinical residency which was the final requirement of my doctoral program in psychology. My dissertation was finished and I was on the academic job market. As was my custom, I had gotten everyone at work caught up in various food competitions, taste tests, and nutritional debates. One day at a meeting, Marie van Tubbergen offhandedly suggested that I should teach a class on the psychology of food. Our supervisor Linda Vincent chimed in saying it was a fantastic idea. I scoffed at the suggestion, saying that there was no such thing as "psychology of food." After the meeting, I went to my office and Googled "psychology of food" and to my surprise found a modest, but well-respected literature to which I had never been exposed. It was a cruel irony to discover in the final days of my graduate training that three of the things I was most passionate about: psychology, nutrition, and food were connected in ways I had never thought about.

A few weeks later, I was at a job interview at the University of Washington–Tacoma. One of the questions I was asked was what I might teach as a "dream class." I hesitatingly answered that someone had recently suggested I teach a course on the psychology of food. The interview committee went bananas over the idea. Later I was offered the position of Assistant Professor. When I arrived on campus the next fall, everyone kept asking when I would be teaching Psychology of Food. I started developing the class, thinking that it was somewhat of a lark, never expecting that I would be conducting any research in the area. In short order, however, I found myself far more passionate and interested in food studies and slowly it began taking over my research agenda. Many university departments would not have been supportive of an early career shift in research focus, but the colleagues and dean of my interdisciplinary department were behind me 100 percent.

In those early days, many people literally burst out laughing when I said that I studied the psychology of food and eating. Little did I know then that the study of food was about to explode. I discovered a small group of interdisciplinary food scholars in the Association for the Study of Food and Society (ASFS) and began attending their annual conference. The folks in ASFS were and are tremendously inspiring and supportive. Warren Belasco and Ken Albala in particular were incredibly welcoming and encouraged me in my early work. Now thanks to them and the work of people like Marion Nestle, David Kessler, Robert Lustig, David Ludwig, Michael Moss, and Michael Pollan, food studies is a well-respected critical field of inquiry. Those scholars are the giants whose shoulders I stand on.

I also thank Ricardo Ainslie for his mentorship during graduate school. Rico taught me the interpretive art of psychoanalytic inquiry and how to bring the rich history of psychoanalysis into cultural, political, and ethnographic analysis. I am also very grateful for the work of Tim Kasser, Irving Kirsch, and Allen Frances, none of whom I know personally, but whose work has profoundly shaped my thinking about psychology.

I owe much of my career success to my friend and mentor Cynthia Duncan, who helped me navigate the politics of academia, has been a staunch supporter of my work, and has provided countless laughs along the way.

There are so many people at the University of Washington Tacoma who have supported my work and offered encouragement: Nita McKinley, Jennifer Sundheim, Leighann Chaffee, and Bill Kunz have been especially supportive.

I appreciate the folks at Zoka Coffee in Tangletown for letting me camp out there for a year and a half, especially Morgan Johnson and Sandy Metzger who were always keen to talk about nutrition when I needed to run an idea by someone.

Finally, I could not have written this book without Allison as a clinical case study. She has my deepest gratitude and compassion.

To consume:[1]

a   To eat or drink; to ingest

b   To use up (esp. a commodity or resource); exhaust

c   To purchase or use (goods or services); to be a consumer of

d   To spend (money), esp. wastefully; to squander (goods)

e   To ruin oneself through excessive spending.

Consumption:

a   The action or fact of eating or drinking something, or of using something up in an activity.

b   Wasteful expenditure (of time, money, etc.).

c   The purchase and use of goods, services, materials, or energy. Freq. opposed to production.

d   The amount of goods, services, materials, or energy purchased and used.

Consumption:

a   Polit. Econ. A doctrine advocating a continual increase in the consumption of goods as a basis for a sound economy.

b   Excessive emphasis on or preoccupation with the acquisition of consumer goods.

---

[1]Definitions from *Oxford English Dictionary* (*OED* Online, 2014).

1

Introduction

FIGURE 1.1 *Sea-Tac Airport Shop 'n Fly advertisement. Leslie Mikkelson, Prevention Institute.*

In 2012, Sea-Tac International Airport installed four water bottle refilling stations throughout the terminals. Such stations encourage the drinking of water, save money for travelers, and reduce the waste of single-use water bottles, of which Americans currently purchase 50 billion per year (Royte, 2008). A year later, as part of their "Shop and Fly" campaign, Sea-Tac posted large advertisements directly above those stations, depicting a Frappuccino-style drink topped with whipped cream and chocolate syrup, likely clocking in around 700 calories and 90 grams of sugar (Starbucks, 2014). The copy reads "You deserve better than water" and directs travelers to nearby Starbucks and Coffee Bean and Leaf. This picture-worth-a-thousand-words represents the paradox of "be healthy and reduce waste" vs. "consume more because you deserve it." It is this paradox that defines the crisis now faced by the entire planet as affluent consumption has reached a tipping point resulting in increasingly dire psychological, physiological, and environmental consequences.

The word "consume" and its variants "consumption" and "consumerism" have multiple definitions, which over time have gradually shifted from referring to the object that is dissipated to the human need that is fulfilled in the process (Williams, 2011). Traditionally, the study of consuming food, drink, drugs, material goods, and natural resources was separated into the different disciplines of nutrition, addiction studies, environmental ethics, and ecology, to name a few. Meanwhile, broader studies of consumerism, which had long been the domain of economics and sociology, have now flourished and developed into the interdiscipline of "consumption studies" (Campbell, 1991; Goodwin, Ackerman, & Kiron, 1996). The psychology of overeating, however, has received little attention within these broader studies of consumption, which is why I aim to better contextualize this psychology within the cultural and economic framework of consumerism by means of this book. As a departure from traditional psychological models, examining all types of consumption as a unified construct, and as part of the culture of consumerism, offers a far more sophisticated understanding of the multiple determinants of overeating. Clearly, each type of consumption has its distinct desires, histories, consequences, and mechanisms, but my central argument is that many of the same psychological mechanisms drive and regulate all forms of consumption. At the individual level, there are neurochemical, neuroanatomical, and evolutionary origins which in turn exist within a complex constellation of economic, historic, and cultural factors responsible for the rise of consumerism in the United States and the industrial West over the past several decades.

Of course, to live is to consume (Borgmann, 2000); however, overconsuming and in particular overeating is a behavior that is relatively new to humankind, at least on the frequent basis seen today and with the highly fattening, largely non-nutritious foods of the global industrial diet. This pervasive overeating with which many of us struggle exists within a broader context of consumer capitalism in which production and consumption regulate our lives, often without us realizing the magnitude of their impact. As this consumption of material goods and resources has increased, so, of course, has overeating and obesity, now paradoxically coexisting with hunger in many parts of the world (Delpeuch, 2009; Patel, 2008). The "fat cats" of capitalism, once only the kings of industry, are now arguably all of us. In fact, no country in the world in the past three decades has been able to stem its tide of obesity

(Ng et al., 2014), such that when we consider the massive consumption of goods, resources, and food, as well as the consequences of waste, greenhouse gases, and obesity, it is clear that we are eating ourselves alive.

Using a clinical case study, let me preview the forthcoming arguments in this book by illustrating how these complex determinants converge in overconsumption.

Allison

For the past several years, I've worked with a patient whom I'll call Allison.[1] Formerly a competitive athlete, Allison slowly put on about fifty pounds after getting married, then suffered a serious bout of clinical depression, and finally discovered a treacherous infidelity that resulted in her husband leaving her for one of her friends. She came to me for treatment of depression as her marriage was crumbling. Allison was raised in a wealthy family with a surgeon for a father and a mother who stayed at home. Growing up she was encouraged to find a tall, wealthy, handsome husband and she received powerful messages that this was an important life task, as well as a fate to which she was entitled. Now as the only divorced and overweight person in her family, she feels like she has failed at her primary life goal and fears that she will be relegated to the life of a "fat and lonely spinster," to use her words. After her weight gain and divorce, she has understandably felt lonely, isolated, embittered, and cheated. She is daunted at being on the marriage market again and believes herself to be struggling financially even though she is a successful attorney, earning $100,000 per year.

By her report, Allison drinks several bottles of wine a week, frequently dines in fancy restaurants, eats fast food, smokes, and rarely exercises. She is demoralized over her weight and believes that it keeps her from meeting a desirable partner, as well as prevents further career advancement. Sadly she may be right. Researchers have demonstrated that women's weight can diminish their opportunities in both the romantic and professional spheres. Overweight and obese women have lower rates of marriage than thin women (Averett, Sikora, & Argys, 2008; Conley & Glauber, 2007; Fu & Goldman, 1996), and when they do marry, it is with men of lower levels of education (Garn, Sullivan, & Hawthorne, 1989), lower earnings (Averett & Korenman, 1996; Conley & Glauber, 2007), and who are shorter and less physically attractive (Carmalt, Cawley, Joyner, & Sobal, 2008; Oreffice & Quintana-Domeque, 2010).

---

[1]Names and identifying information have been changed throughout the book.

Since her divorce Allison has redoubled her professional efforts, but she perceives her weight to be an obstacle for her career advancement. Although most of us would view anyone with an advanced degree and a $100,000 annual salary as a success, research shows that women are sixteen times more likely than men to perceive weight-based discrimination in the workplace (Roehling, Roehling, & Pichler, 2007). Moreover, workplace weight discrimination against women tends to occur bimodally at the highest and lowest status levels, that is, entry-level positions and managerial positions (Haskins & Ransford, 1999). Some researchers have estimated that even a woman of average weight will earn $389,300 less than a thin woman over a 25-year career (Judge & Cable, 2011). Allison wants me to reassure her that weight won't get in the way of finding a desirable partner or earning a promotion at work, but it would be false of me to offer that reassurance. One of the challenges I have as a clinical psychologist is whether or not to help overweight patients accept their weight and try to improve their body image (without changing their lifestyle or eating habits) or to help them with behavioral changes in their eating and activity levels, that is, to lose weight. Research from the so-called "fat acceptance" movement has suggested that helping women to accept their bodies might lead to diminished feelings of body shame, increased confidence, and better sex lives (Gailey, 2012), but this is limited interview-based research without controlled studies to validate the hypotheses. Even if helping patients accept themselves as fat had some positive outcomes, if excess weight leads to poorer health outcomes, diminished romantic possibilities, lower salaries, and fewer job prospects, not to mention the increased health care costs to society, then I am not sure it is ethical for me to help my patients accept being fat. I usually present this dilemma to them and simply ask if they want help in accepting their current body or if they want help with nutrition, lifestyle, and behavioral change. I also make it clear that I am biased toward the latter for all the reasons I discuss in this book. Of course it is possible to do some of both, but I think it's best to be transparent about those goals from the outset.

Allison often tries to get into shape, but like many of us she suffers from numerous misconceptions about diet, exercise, and behavioral self-regulation due to the many conflicting messages in mainstream media. The simplest and most scientifically valid message of "eat less" (Nestle, 2002) is unappealing to Allison, who is vulnerable to advertising and gimmicky products. She is far more likely to follow the latest fad diet and spend a lot of money on useless systems, treatments, and products. For example, when she is "being good" she visits a nutritionist weekly, juices, eats five meals per day to "stoke" her metabolism, and goes running. While these behaviors are well intentioned, they will never work. Let me explain why.

Like many Americans, Allison is intensely focused on consumption of all types. She is constantly in battle with herself over indulgence vs. restriction, stimulation vs. boredom, fullness vs. emptiness. She struggles with a diffuse sense of purposelessness and dysphoria and has trouble identifying how to make meaning for herself. She drives a new luxury car, wears expensive clothes, shops frequently, goes to expensive wine tastings, and is many thousands of dollars in credit card debt despite her ample salary. Something I've observed to her many times is that virtually any time she decides to do something new—for example, organize her closets, take up a new hobby, plan a trip—there is a flurry of consumption associated with it. Organizing her closets doesn't simply mean throwing out stuff and hauling it off to Goodwill. It involves hiring a personal organizer, going to the Container Store or IKEA to buy closet organization products, and purchasing new clothes and shoes to replace those discarded. Experimenting with a new hobby like kayaking involved outfitting herself with thousands of dollars of specialized clothing and gear before determining if it was an activity she enjoyed or would stick with. While I generally encourage my patients to invest money (if they have it) in sports and outdoor activities, in this particular case Allison had not even tried kayaking enough to know if she would enjoy it, so the investment was risky and expensive. These purchases seemed to be more about sating an appetite to spend and consume rather than an eagerness to be active and in the outdoors.

When she first decided to try and lose weight, which fundamentally should involve reducing one's consumption, Allison went out and purchased thousands of dollars of branded food, goods, and services. She hired a nutritionist and a personal trainer, purchased a Jack LaLanne juicer, a Vitamix blender, a Nike Fuelband, new running shoes, Lululemon workout clothing, an exclusive gym membership, numerous diet and exercise books, DVDs and iPhone apps, and large quantities of diet foods, such as energy bars, yogurt, cereals, sports drinks, and most disturbingly, something called "Goo," a sweet, packaged gooey concoction that's meant to give athletes energy. In other words, she began consuming more.

Eating these "special" foods, like juice or energy bars, allows Allison to feel as though she is reducing her weight because they are imbued with a false dietary magic created very deliberately by food manufacturers with logos and packaging. These "healthy" packaged foods are wolves in sheep's clothing—they are just junk food in disguise. Not only that, but going on a buying spree for diet foods is very likely to increase how much we eat, much in the same way that shopping at warehouse stores increases our overall spending (Wansink, 2006). I suspect that Allison's overall calorie intake actually went up when she went on a diet because her underlying belief is that consumption solves rather than creates problems. Don't get me wrong: many of the things she did together or separately can contribute to weight loss and improved health; the problem is that Allison does not use these tools as a means to reduce overall consumption or to locate purpose in her life. Shopping, spending, and eating are all part of the frenzy of consumption that has overtaken our culture, such that Allison's attempts at solving her overeating through more consumption are efforts that mistake the disease for its cure, perpetuating an empty and baffling pursuit for meaning that plays itself out in the world of food, alcohol, luxury goods, and materialism.

Invariably after a few days or weeks of "being good," Allison slips, to borrow a term from AA, usually when she is drinking and then starts overeating. A common scenario is that if Allison has a bad day at work, no food at home, and no dinner plans, she'll go to McDonald's and overindulge. Afterwards she feels horrible and goes home and makes some freshly pressed juice as a way of doing penance for the bad eating. Psychologically what is happening is that she wants to undo the bad behavior by following it with a good one. *Undoing* is a psychological defense that is an unconscious effort to counterbalance guilt or shame with a behavior that will magically erase it (McWilliams, 2011, p. 127). As another way to understand undoing, consider that many religious rituals involve atoning for one's sins and are a spiritual version of the same defense. Overeating and undoing go hand in hand for many of us. How many times have you eaten too much and wished you could turn back the clock just a few minutes to turn down that second helping? How many times have you hit the gym after overindulging? In fact, the purging seen in bulimia is undoing taken to its extreme. In other areas of life, undoing can be an adaptive strategy or a healthy psychological defense. For example, if we treat someone poorly, we can partly undo that behavior by apologizing to them or bringing them flowers. If we are late to lunch with a friend, we might pick up the check as a way to make amends and alleviate our guilt. Never, however, does consuming more food undo or remediate having already overeaten.

If Allison's behavior strikes you as somewhat like the behavior of an alcoholic or drug addict, you are correct. The reason I use the AA term "slip" is because research increasingly shows that overeating functions very much like other diseases of addiction (Gearhardt, Grilo, DiLeone, Brownell, & Potenza, 2011b). In fact, fMRI scans have demonstrated that some foods, especially sugary, fatty, and salty foods, activate the dopamine reward system—the same part of the brain implicated in drug and alcohol addiction. Recently, Yale psychologist Kelly Brownell (2012) and his colleagues have ushered in an entirely new way of looking at food through the lens of addiction and this area of research holds tremendous promise for individual treatment, as well as the potential to impact regulation of the food industry.

I once asked Allison what went into the juice she made after she went to McDonald's. She used a mango, an apple, a banana, some berries, yogurt, and a beet, totaling approximately 650 calories, or about 1/3 of the calories most women in their thirties ought to consume daily. Consuming this many calories just before bed after consuming over 1,000 calories of fast food isn't doing anyone any favors. Not only is the juice a lot of extra calories, but it's all sugar, which will have a specific negative effect on the hormone system that regulates appetite and fat storage. Part of what likely makes juice appealing to Allison as a means of undoing is that juice is blessed by what Pierre Chandon and Brian Wansink (2007) call a "health halo," which refers to when people infer nutrition, as in the case of fresh fruits and vegetables, and have a false confidence in what they are eating, ignoring the actual nutritional content of that food. Even if Allison were at or under the number of calories she needs in a day, the glass of juice is still a bad idea. Neuroendocrinological research has shown that different types of calories activate different hormones and neurotransmitters, signaling whether or not calories should be stored or used, and also stoking or sating appetite. In our current culture of consumption, the type of refined sugar and carbohydrates found in many branded, packaged foods are especially likely to be stored as fat without making us full, and in fact, they often increase our appetites. Failure to understand how sugar and carbohydrates work on the body and brain, and instead focusing solely on aggregate calories is a tremendous mistake, and one that has likely derailed our country in its health efforts. This does not mean that calories don't count at all. They do. Unfortunately, some of the peddlers of Atkins-type low-carb diets have wrongly told people that they can eat unlimited calories with low or no carbohydrates and lose weight. No one can consume excess calories without getting fat, but what newer research shows is that weight loss and weight maintenance hinge on both the quantity and quality of calories.

Even though Allison and I have talked about it, she will not accept that juice is unhealthy. Sometimes in our sessions when she mentions juicing she starts with, "I know you don't like juice, but…" Allison is what's known among psychologists as a "help-rejecting complainer" (Frank et al., 1952). While asking for my help, she simultaneously rejects it, or in this case, interprets it as a personal preference of mine rather than scientific information that might apply to her behavior. Help-rejecting complainers can be difficult to work with because they view themselves as powerless victims and have trouble taking on the sense of agency necessary for therapeutic change. Or it may be that Allison simply does not see nutrition as the domain of a clinical psychologist. Due to a long-standing Cartesian mind/body dualism, psychology has historically claimed the sphere of mind or emotions, whereas the science of brain and metabolism are in the purview of medicine and nutrition. Yet treating the problem of overeating often requires training in nutritional education and dietary intervention, as well as expertise in the powerful psychological mechanisms of willpower and behavioral change.

While I have some expertise in food studies and overeating, I simply do not have the rigorous training in dietary intervention that nutritionists have (nor do nutritionists have the clinical training to intervene with most psychological disorders). This divide between clinical psychology and clinical nutrition makes it difficult for patients to find clinicians able to effectively work with them in both spheres. Increasingly, I have come to believe that it is a disservice to public health to maintain this separation between the two disciplines, and I hope to see a subfield of nutrition and psychology emerge in the near future.

Returning to Allison—she works with me to help her with her mood and emotional problems and concurrently with a professional nutritionist for her diet. The nutritionist provides her with daily meal plans; however, I've seen them and these plans are not consistent with the most current research on metabolism and weight loss. For example, when she is closely following the plans, Allison eats five small meals per day, believing that numerous meals will stoke her metabolism and therefore burn fat, even though this is not supported by scientific findings (Cameron, Cyr, & Doucet, 2010). She has also been advised that she should eat something before bed at night *even if she's not hungry* in order to keep her metabolism stimulated. She will often have a piece of whole wheat toast with peanut butter around 9:00 at night with the idea that it is somehow therapeutic. Much like her belief that juice is undoing the consumption of fast food, here we can see the same faulty underlying belief: that consuming certain foods at certain times of day has some kind of medicinal or therapeutic effect. Peanut butter in particular is a very calorie dense food and when it has been salted and sugared, it then has the trifecta of fat, sugar, and salt, which is so alluring, addictive, and dangerous (Kessler, 2009; Moss, 2013). In fact, it is likely this combination of salt, sugar, and fat that is activating the dopamine pathway and setting up a cycle of addictive behavior with food and eating.

Allison chronically engages in magical thinking about diet and exercise and her ideas are often sold to her by her nutritionist and personal trainer, both of whom she trusts greatly and pays a lot of money. For example, she recently told me that she was embarking on an innovative workout program called "waterfall" with her personal trainer, in which there were special numeric combinations of exercises that had to be performed in a precise order for optimum weight loss. She described performing five sets of one exercise, then two of another, then one of the first exercise, and then four of another, and so on. Her belief was that performing the exercises in these special, intermittent sequences was superior than the simple drudgery of doing each exercise in a row. While there may be some benefit to providing variety in workouts to prevent boredom, there is no research whatsoever that shows that these methods contribute to increased weight loss. These questionable meal plans and workout routines serve to reinforce Allison's misunderstandings about food and metabolism. They promote the magical thinking that there is a secret, complicated path to health that must be purchased. These secrets are the bread and butter of the food and supplement industry, personal wellness consultants, and the industrial fitness complex. Not only that, but in both the areas of nutritional counseling and psychological counseling there has been a huge proliferation in recent years in the number of practitioners, often people with poor credentials and training who are selling quick fixes to desperate individuals—another cog in the wheel of consumerism which I will address in this book.

Finally, Allison often describes herself as someone suffering from a serotonin imbalance. She perceives this imbalance as the cause for her depression and views her weight gain as a symptom or secondary effect of depression. A serotonin imbalance, however, is not a diagnosis per se, nor can we prove in any one person that it is the cause for their depression. More importantly, the chemical imbalance theory of depression has mixed evidence for it (Kirsch, 2010) and is an explanatory model that has been largely promoted by pharmaceutical companies, who along with the food manufacturers are some of the major perpetuators and beneficiaries of consumer culture. In spite of some validity to the chemical imbalance model, it is nevertheless a unidimensional explanation that ignores cultural forces, hormonal dysregulation, addictive behavior, and a personal value system predicated on vociferous consumption of luxury goods, services, food, and alcohol. Missing the more nuanced neuroendocrinological explanation and entirely ignoring the existential explanation for her troubles keep Allison in a self-perpetuating and mystifying cycle of misery and overweight.

No matter how many different ways I try to present Allison's difficulties as a partial consequence of overconsumption, she becomes defensive and often angry. She quite simply does not want to give up or simplify a life defined by shopping, luxury, and materialism. To be fair, I am not suggesting she give this up entirely. The reality is that almost any of us, just by virtue of being American or Westerners, are living some version of this life—it's a matter of degree and a matter of being aware of where we reside on the continuum. In Allison's case, the prospect of giving up parts of this lifestyle is terrifying to her because she has imbued it with identity meaning. A life absent of these luxury and consumer behaviors looks empty to her, which is understandably anxiety provoking. Essentially, her core belief is that if she were not spending money or consuming, there would be nothing there—an existential vacuum (Frankl, 1963). She is not able to imagine a more modest lifestyle that would be rich with experiences instead of luxury goods; populated by caring individuals, nature, and cultural experiences instead of shopping; and characterized by simpler, smaller, tastier meals prepared in the home by and for cherished individuals.

What repeatedly defeats Allison in her weight loss efforts are the many powerful messages that say that better eating habits are simply a matter of discipline and willpower. By contrast, there are the opposing messages which say her genes are making her fat, or her neurotransmitters are hijacking her well-intentioned plans with powerful food cravings. These conflicting messages represent the very same epistemological divide that's plagued philosophy and psychology since the beginning: nature vs. nurture or free will vs. determinism. We can further see this divide in the way that most of the research literature on food and overeating resides in one of three spheres: (1) the medical sphere of nutrition, endocrinology, and exercise physiology; (2) the policy sphere of food science, regulation, and industry; or (3) the psychology of the individual, which usually rests on cognitive, behavioral, and evolutionary theories of choice and activity. What is missing from this framework is thinking about all types of consumption as a unified construct: culturally, economically, existentially, and biologically; that is, thinking about food and overeating not just as a dietary issue, but as one that resides in the context of the consumption of material goods, luxury experiences, alcohol and drug use, evolutionary behaviors, and all forms of acquisition. Overeating, which most of us occasionally struggle to manage (irrespective of being fat or thin), is part of a single phenomenon of pursuing and consuming highly stimulating experiences that is part of urban life in the West and is now spreading rapidly around the globe in developing economies highly focused on consumption.

In the pages that follow, my intention is to bring a new philosophical voice to the discussion on food and overeating that is bolstered rather than isolated from the natural sciences. The original data I use in this book is the clinical case study typical of the psychoanalytic/existential psychology tradition, along with qualitative data such as food industry white papers, interviews, and archives. This book is decidedly ambitious: Rather than advancing my original ideas on consumption in isolation, I have instead embedded them in a far-reaching synthesis of the multidisciplinary research so that readers across disciplines can engage with a way of thinking about food and culture in the context of multiple explanatory models. Figure 1.2 is a schematic which depicts the complex forces at work in overeating to illustrate how the many forces that influence overeating fit together.

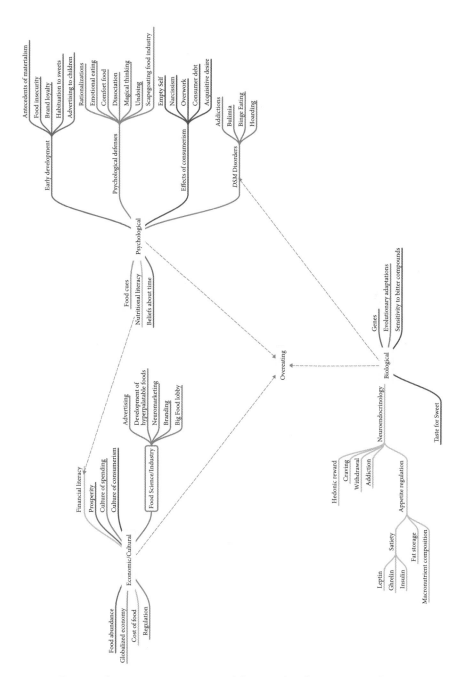

FIGURE 1.2 *Schematic representation of the complex determinants of overeating.*

An interdisciplinary treatment of any topic by necessity compromises depth for breadth. While I nest my cultural and clinical arguments in medical, historical, and economic contexts, at its core this book is about philosophy, psychology, and culture. Many of the issues I take up in this book have their own extensive literature of theory and research, and in particular, for the areas outside of psychology in which I am less fluent, I point the reader to primary sources at every opportunity. Any scientific mistakes or misunderstandings are my own and I invite the many excellent researchers whom I cite to chime into the conversation and set the record straight. I have also tried to write the book in a way that speaks to the applied clinical value of this information, so that practicing psychotherapists and nutritionists might apply these ideas to their work with clients. In terms of tone, I enjoy the art of storytelling and I firmly believe that scientific writing needn't be dry and boring to be rigorous or serious. Narrative is powerful and the telling of stories is part of the human condition. Admittedly, my tone can be strident at times. Because I tend to dislike my own consumerist instincts, self-criticism sometimes drives my indictment of consumer culture.

Finally, I should be clear that this is not a book about obesity. Overeating, which is the focus of my work, does not always lead to overweight or obesity. Many, if not most of us, struggle to some extent with resisting the powerful forces that lead us to overeat. Obesity is only the visible tip of the iceberg of the bigger problem of population-wide metabolic dysfunction. Up to 40 percent of the population is now "metabolically obese, normal weight": that is, suffering the same ill effects of obesity, including cardiovascular disease, high blood pressure, altered insulin sensitivity, higher abdominal and visceral adiposity, but maintaining a normal weight (Conus, Rabasa-Lhoret, & Peronnet, 2007; Ruderman, Schneider, & Berchtold, 1981; Thomas, Frost, Taylor-Robinson, & Bell, 2012). In other words, people who are suffering from overweight and obesity are only a subset of the population dealing with the challenges of overeating. This is a book about consuming—consuming food, electronics, drinks, drugs, cars, clothing, and natural resources.

2

The Rise of Consumer Culture

I t is not just individuals, but nations and cultures too that have psychologies. These cultural and national psychologies serve to acculturate citizens and shape economic and social policies. For us to explore the individual psychology of overconsumption in later chapters, we must first understand how the collective psychologies of consumerism shape the ways in which nations and cultures have experienced consumption historically, politically, and economically. While this chapter is the furthest afield from psychology, its purpose is (1) to briefly examine how and why consumerism has flourished in the United States and the industrialized West, and (2) to examine the trends in overeating and overspending that are the consequence of this culture.

British cultural theorists Yiannis Gabriel and Tim Lang (2006) identify five understandings of consumerism, which I use to frame the arguments throughout this book.

1 consumerism as *a moral doctrine*—consumer choice and acquisition are the vehicles for individual freedom, happiness, and power for developed countries.

2 consumerism as *a political ideology*—in contrast to the nanny state and its paternalism, the modern state protects transnational corporations and the consumerist ideology exalts choice and freedom for the consumer to acquire glamorous and stylish goods.

3 consumerism as *an economic ideology for global development*—in contrast to the austerity of communism, consumerism is seen as the driver of free trade and the nurturing of new consumers is seen as the key to developing economies.

4 consumerism as *a social ideology*—establishes class distinctions such that material commodities fix the social position and prestige of their owners.

5 consumerism as *a social movement*—consumer rights are characterized by advocacy for the protection of value and quality for the consumer often through regulation.[1]

Let us begin with consumerism *as a moral doctrine* in which consumer choice and acquisition are the vehicles for individual freedom, happiness, and power. As this form of consumerism has flourished, the psychological centrality of consumer choice has displaced the production-based economies of the past, in which work rather than consumption was the central organizing principle of identity (Bauman, 1998). In today's consumption-oriented society, our identities are tied more to what we consume than what we produce. Life in a consumption-oriented society is further characterized by the use of leisure time for spending money and the belief that owning things is the primary means to happiness (Goodwin et al., 1996). Not only is material consumption viewed as gratifying, but consumerism *as a moral doctrine* promotes consumption as a means for self-development, self-realization, and self-fulfillment (Kaza, 2005, p. 4). In other words, in this form of consumerism, acquisition becomes deeply psychological as we come to organize our interior world and our very selves around consuming.

Consequently, this centrality of consumption stimulates constant economic growth, such that we lose sight of whether it is demand generating supply or supply generating demand. Philosopher David Loy (1997) argues that with this economic growth, the Market has become a global religion teaching us what the world is and what our role in the world is, replacing traditional theistic religions. He identifies market capitalism as a force that has destroyed community fabric with the resulting collective reaction as the need for growth. He states that

> From a religious perspective the problem with market capitalism and its values is twofold: greed and delusion. On the one hand, the unrestrained market emphasizes and indeed requires greed in at least two ways. Desire for profit is necessary to fuel the engine of the economic system, and an insatiable desire to consume ever more must be generated to create markets for what can be produced (p. 281).

---

[1] I place each of these understandings in italics here and throughout the book as I continually refer to this framework in each chapter.

This desire, he further argues, can never be satisfied because once we identify as consumers we can never have too much. Similarly, William Leiss (1978) argues that today's market economies are governed by the principle that they should expand steadily, but that the consequent orientation of personal needs toward commodities makes it impossible to ever satisfy individual desires. In related research, studies have demonstrated that religious commitment is lower in individuals who use brands to express themselves (Cutright, Erdem, Fitzsimons, & Shachar, 2014), further suggesting that economic forces such as market growth and branded products have replaced the traditional role of religion.

The drive for constant growth is considered so important that economic growth is commonly used as a measure of a nation's happiness by many economists. While research does in fact show that the rich are happier than the poor within any given country, paradoxically, average happiness levels change very little as people's income rises (Frank, 1999). Despite spending twice as much per capita as they did in 1957, Americans have shown no increases in those who report being "very happy" (Durning, 1997). Equating GDP with happiness, however, has the consequence of further entrenching the cultural belief that all growth is good and that happiness is equal to growth. It should not be surprising, then, that with the unrelenting message of growth, our bodies would eventually grow along with GDP, resulting in the widespread overweight and obesity we see today.

Global hyperconsumption and hyperproduction

As this insatiable desire to consume creates more markets, more goods are produced, and a cycle of hyperconsumption and hyperproduction ensue. Daniel Bell (2008) argues that the tension in contemporary capitalism is between the discipline and asceticism required of production and the wanton hedonism and waste of consumption. While there is tremendous production and consumption of food, food consumption has historically been thought of differently than other forms of material consumption, simply because we need food to survive. Indeed, it is easier to see hedonism and waste in industries of nonessential products, such as clothing, furniture, and electronics, so we shall look at those first as a means to understand overconsumption very broadly before looking more specifically at the overconsumption of food.

One example of this hyperproduction and hyperconsumption is the world of cheap "fast fashion" by retailers such as Zara and H&M, in which companies manufacture and sell low-cost merchandise at a breakneck pace. Americans now purchase 20 billion garments a year (American Apparel and Footwear Association, 2008) and the Spanish fast-fashion retailer Zara alone processes a staggering 1 million garments *per day* (Graham, 2011). In her book *Overdressed*, Elizabeth Cline argues that this disposable clothing is damaging the environment, the economy, and even our souls, and she presents a sobering body of evidence to support her thesis (Cline, 2012). Similarly, stores like IKEA encourage high-volume consumption by offering rock-bottom prices on household furniture and accessories with limited lifespans. When asked about an IKEA table which retails for $69, a master furniture maker said, "It's mind-boggling. I couldn't buy the wood for that price, let alone build the thing" (Shell, 2009, p. 128). In her book *Cheap: The High Cost of Discount Culture*, Ellen Ruppel Shell argues that IKEA's suspiciously low prices are maintained through a combination of tax evasion, illegal logging, and child labor. With much of the world's economy now predicated on consumption, these "subsidies" of cheap labor, low quality, and toxic materials involved in the production of clothing, food, furniture, fuel, electronics, and other products allow us to mindlessly consume because we don't know the real price of things.

While such acquisition is often driven by individual desire, consumerism *as an economic ideology* refers to the transformation of consumption from an individual act of freedom or indulgence into an act of patriotism because spending fuels economic growth for the country. Shortly after September 11, for example, President George W. Bush addressed the stunned and bereft nation and said that the best thing we could do in the wake of the tragedy was to spend money. "Get down to Disney World in Florida," he urged just over two weeks after 9/11. "Take your families and enjoy life, the way we want it to be enjoyed" (White House Archives, 2001). To many, there was no connection between individual spending and the health of the nation; however, in the intervening decade we've now heard countless messages about spending money as a new form of patriotism. During and after the economic recession, for example, the prevailing political message was that we had an obligation to spend. In fact, the economic stimulus package of 2009 gave us money not to save, but to spend.

This stimulation of free trade, the nurturing of new consumers, and the developing of economies rest on a belief of superiority and instrumentalism that has dominated the West's geographic expansion and political economy for several centuries, culminating in the globalized economy we see today. Its origins are in the same ideology which drove colonialism and slavery, and it continues to drive a world market in which high consumption by the affluent depends on cheap labor and materials in the developing world. An accompanying belief that is part of the collective psychology among many in the developed West is that this type of consumerism and market capitalism are "natural"—a notion that was reinforced by the fall of communism (Gabriel & Lang, 2006). This acceptance of the superiority of market capitalism and its inevitable inequalities reveals a sense of cultural superiority and instrumentalism on the part of those who hold power, wealth, and intellectual capital. Of course a new fly in the ointment is that developing countries, now part of the increasingly global culture of consumption, have come to share in the voracious appetite for meat, fast food, and electronics that was once exclusively the domain of the industrial West. It is becoming a case of "this town ain't big enough for the both of us," as the affluent West grows increasingly alarmed about the environmental impact of consumption now that countries like India and China have joined the party.

The psychopathology of consumerism

To put these economic ideologies into more psychological terms, the superiority and instrumentalism we see in the nationalisms that drive consumerism are not unlike the features we see in the clinical diagnoses of Antisocial and Narcissistic Personality Disorders. If it's not entirely clear what the connection is among psychopathy, narcissism, economic development, and overeating, it will become increasingly clear throughout this book as we see how these exploitive personality and cultural traits have created and sustained a food industry in which the aggressive drive for profits encourages overeating and ill-health at every turn. These traits are at the heart of food makers' resistance to regulatory efforts, drive the exploitive marketing to children and the poor, and perpetuate the questionable labor practices in many areas of food production.

In his seminal work on psychopathy (now called antisocial personality), Hervey Cleckley (1941) argued that the psychopath can appear normal and even engaging, but is fundamentally characterized by a disregard for the rights of others. The psychopath may have an inflated and arrogant self-appraisal and be excessively opinionated, self-assured, or cocky. The organizing drive of the psychopathic personality is omnipotent control or the need to exert power through the domination and exploitation of others (McWilliams, 2011). Coupled with the desire for omnipotent control, it is the psychopath's famous lack of conscience that allows him or her to use others for personal gain. Contrary to popular belief, psychopathy needn't involve any physical aggression. Although psychopathy is characterized primarily by these maladaptive traits, some authors have conjectured that other features of this personality style, like fearlessness and interpersonal dominance, are adaptive in certain occupations, namely leadership and executive positions (Babiak, 2000). In fact, the world's leading researcher on psychopathy, Robert Hare and his colleagues have argued that many politicians, attorneys, and CEOs often exemplify nonviolent psychopathy in their quest for fame, power, and wealth (Babiak & Hare, 2009). Other researchers have argued that the modern corporate world in which high risks equal high profits attracts and rewards psychopaths (Dutton, 2012). In one study, for example, researchers asked historical experts to rate US presidents on certain personality traits. Unbeknownst to the historians, *all* of the listed traits were actually associated with psychopathy. The results showed that "fearless dominance"—which reflects the boldness associated with psychopathy—was associated with better rated presidential performance, leadership, persuasiveness, crisis management, and Congressional relations (Lilienfeld et al., 2012). In other words, nonviolent psychopaths often typify what it is to be a successful American: wealthy, ambitious, confident, and charming.

In the related Narcissistic Personality Disorder, we see a pervasive pattern of grandiosity, need for admiration, and lack of empathy. Individuals with this disorder have a grandiose sense of self-importance, believing that they are superior, special, or unique. This sense of entitlement, combined with a lack of sensitivity to the wants and needs of others, results in the conscious or unwitting exploitation of others. Narcissists expect to be given whatever they want or feel they need, no matter what it might mean to others. Like psychopaths, these individuals also generally have a lack of empathy and have difficulty recognizing the desires, subjective experiences, and feelings of others. Interestingly, some scholars have argued that Narcissistic and Antisocial Personality Disorders are nothing more than a slight exaggeration of culturally sanctioned (and gendered) personality traits (Ford & Widiger, 1989). In other words, these individual diagnoses are simply the natural manifestation of a psychopathic and narcissistic culture.

In *The Culture of Narcissism*, Christopher Lasch argued that narcissism has become both widespread and culturally desirable (1980). "After the counter-culture movement of the sixties Americans have retreated purely to personal preoccupations. Having no hope of improving their lives in any of the ways that matter, people have convinced themselves that what matters is psychic self-improvement: getting in touch with their feelings, eating health food, taking lessons in ballet or belly-dancing, immersing themselves in the movements of the East .... Harmless in themselves, these pursuits elevated to a program and wrapped in the rhetoric of authenticity and awareness, signify a retreat from politics and a repudiation of the recent past (pp. 4–5)." Similarly, psychoanalyst Paul Wachtel argues that "personal growth" is simply another manifestation of a growth-obsessed society. He writes, "psychology [itself] is a psychology of or for economic growth, with the same images of conquest and expansion, and the same highly individualistic assumptions that characterize the rest of our culture (p. 112)." Here I assume he is referring to clinical psychology and more specifically to the practice of psychotherapy which often holds personal growth as its goal, most especially in the nonclinical populations of the worried well which fill the private offices of American psychologists and therapists. In other words, psychology is part of the engine of narcissism that has shifted Americans or Westerners to hyperconsumers. To be fair, we cannot place the blame squarely on the discipline of psychology because in all likelihood its development over the past 100 years is as much a reflection of the culture as the cause of it.

Returning to the traits of narcissism and psychopathy, however, the larger point is that these traits are essential to both the supply-side and demand-side of consumer culture. As we shall see, producers, marketers, and advertisers often ruthlessly elevate profits above public health and well-being, while consumers often justify and rationalize the negative impact of their consumption—a seesaw of pathology, if you will. Environmentalist Paul Hawken has a slightly more forgiving view of the individual consumer: that our heedless consumption is because we don't see most of it: "it is offshore, and in mines, stockyards, slag heaps, landfills, and wastewater treatment plants" (Kaza, 2005, p. viii). In other words, Hawken argues that it is neither entitlement nor arrogance which fuels consumption but rather ignorance and denial. Perhaps there is a bit of both? I shall argue that persisting in voracious consumption involves a complex set of defense mechanisms including rationalization, denial, and dissociation, in which we justify our behavior to ourselves and others, ignore its consequences, and numb ourselves to the cognitive dissonance we experience from it. These psychological defenses are overlaid on the fundamental sense of entitlement and instrumentalism that has been the cornerstone of the West's imperialism and colonialism, together creating the blind hubris that drives consumerism.

In Chapter 6, we will further examine this symbiotic relationship between the exploitive culture of consumerism and the individual consumer by looking at the story of sugar, in which we will see that our voracious appetite for sweets was initially fed by slavery and continues to be fed by what many regard as modern-day slavery in the Americas (Campbell, 2008; Haney, Rhodes, Grunebaum, Christopher, & Paul, 2007). The multinational corporations running these sugar operations are well protected by US laws and are cozy with Congress, as is much of the rest of food industry. It will become clear through the story of sugar and many other examples how the Western practice of consumerism *as a political ideology* creates a circular relationship between consumerism at a political level and consuming at an individual level, ultimately causing overweight, obesity, and addiction, as well as generating further demand for cheap production of foods on a global level.

From thrift to anti-thrift

The US Bureau of Labor Statistics' Consumer Expenditure Survey found that between 1901 and 2003, the average US household's income increased 67-fold and during the same period household expenditures increased 53-fold (2006). Adjusting for inflation, that's a tripling of purchasing power for the average household over the past century. This increased prosperity followed by the postwar advertising boom, easy consumer credit, and technological advances in household appliances, computers, and electronics transformed the US economy to a consumer goods economy in which spending has become the largest component of gross domestic product (2006). In the United States alone, there are now 45,000 shopping malls and an average American family of four metabolizes four million pounds of material every year (Kaza, 2005, p. vii).

As a consequence of this increasing prosperity, we are in the grip of what economist Robert Frank refers to as "luxury fever," which is an uninterrupted rise in the past three decades in luxury consumption, independent of inflation and economic recession (Frank, 1999). Using a similar language of disease and infection, John de Graaf and his colleagues called the resulting phenomenon *affluenza*: a painful, contagious, socially transmitted condition of overload, debt, anxiety, and waste resulting from the dogged pursuit of more (De Graaf, Wann, & Naylor, 2001). In previous economic booms, such excesses were associated with only the superrich. Today, however, luxury by global standards is more accessible than ever to a large proportion of those in developed nations. Increasingly, working and lower-middle-class families are able to acquire private cars, cable television, and designer clothing—items that are now thought of as basic by many. Ever-rising affluence, however, distorts our views about which of our needs are "natural" vs. "artificial," with past luxuries coming to seem like necessities (Crocker, 1996).

While consumption patterns in middle and lower income earners have, to a certain extent, mirrored consumption increases by the wealthy, the difference is that median earners' incomes have decreased in real dollars since 1979, thus luxury spending is largely maintained in working and middle-class families through decreased savings, increased credit card debt, and increased hours at work—a phenomenon that economist Juliet Schor calls the "work and spend cycle," which comes at a heavy psychological cost. Not only are we now accustomed to much higher levels of affluence, but through media we are increasingly exposed to the lifestyles of those whose incomes are three, four, five, even twenty times our own, resulting in a national culture of "upspending" (Schor, 1999). This exposure distorts whom we think of us our "reference group," that is, people who occupy similar social and economic strata which was historically friends, family, and neighbors (Merton, 1957). In other words, why keep up with Joneses when you can keep up with the Hiltons?

For much of the twentieth century, the United States had "pro-thrift" policies and regulations which gave nearly all Americans access to institutions such as credit unions, savers' clubs, labor unions, and bond programs that helped people save (Institute for American Values, 2008). Additionally, the pro-thrift sector of the financial service industry limited the amount of debt that consumers could take on and had strict rules for savings and creditworthiness which borrowers had to meet. Those who borrowed heavily, gambled, or pawned their belongings were outliers and were viewed as disreputable and of questionable morals. Government deregulation, industry consolidation, and changes in tax laws, however, led to the demise of the pro-thrift culture and have in fact ushered in a decidedly anti-thrift culture in its wake, discouraging savings and encouraging over-indebtedness.

The rise of the anti-thrift culture would not have been possible without a widespread willingness to take on personal debt (Nocera, 2013, p. 20) and such willingness would not have emerged without the development of the credit card (Kiron, 1996). Between 1958 and 1970, 100 million credit cards were distributed across the United States in what turned out to be a profound shift not only in purchasing patterns, but in how Americans began to experience themselves and their desires (Nocera, 2013, p. 20). The credit card ushered in an ease of use in a new age in which hard cash was not necessary to back up purchases, consequently leading to the widespread desire and expectation for instant gratification among consumers. This ease came in contrast to the social, natural, and economic environments which had historically regulated instant gratification by providing obstacles to it. Over the past century. then, our culture has shifted to one in which there are often very few behavioral obstacles to immediately getting what we want, resulting in the elevation of impulsive consuming instincts over the careful evaluation of the wisdom of such consumption.

As more and more consumers became credit card holders, the natural consequence was for the practice of layaway to slowly decrease to the point of extinction. If you are young enough to have never heard of layaway, quite simply it was a policy once common in many stores that allowed people to reserve and make payments on a product if they did not have all the money to pay for it at once. Paying for something through layaway, in which one paid for the product in full before receiving it, was the very opposite of today's credit card purchases, in which the object is now received first and paid for later, often with hefty interest fees. To put something on layaway represented a commitment to that object and told us that discipline, patience, and methodical budgeting were essential to reward. It was part of a psychology of personal finance in which sums totaled to zero. By contrast, the current cultural messages about not needing to pay for things before we get them parallel the phenomenon of overeating because they encourage impulsive consumption without reflection. By the end of this book, I shall try to show how excess calories and consumer debt are the same thing: the surpluses of consumption.

The rise of overeating

As consumer spending has steadily increased over the past several decades, so has individual daily caloric intake. Over the past forty years, caloric intake has increased for everyone, not just for those who are overweight or obese. In 1960, the USDA's Economic Research Service estimated that the aggregate food supply in the United States provided 3,200 calories per person/day (2002). Of that, approximately 1,000 calories were lost to spoilage, plate waste, and other losses, placing estimated average daily caloric intake at just under 2,200 calories per person per day. Forty years later, the same survey found that the adjusted average daily caloric intake per person per day was 2,700. That is a 29 percent increase over a forty-year period, comprised mostly of refined grain products (USDA, 2002).

In addition to eating more overall calories, we are also eating more frequent meals. Recent research shows that Americans now consume food hourly or every hour and a half (Popkin & Duffey, 2010), a practice which may be undermining our physiological basis for hunger on a population-wide level (Popkin, 2012). Not surprisingly, this widespread increase in caloric consumption has lead to increased rates of overweight and obesity. In 2000, the National Center for Health Statistics found that 62 percent of adult Americans were overweight, defined as a BMI[2] between 25 and 29, up from 46 percent in 1980, with 27 percent of those adults classified as obese defined as a BMI greater than or equal to 30. Researchers Drewnowski and Specter (2004) found that the highest rates of obesity occur among population groups with the highest poverty rates and the least education, an effect that was more robust among women than men. By analyzing the cost of foods and their energy density (calories), they also found an inverse

---

[2]Many researchers have questioned the accuracy of body mass index (Okorodudu et al., 2010; Romero-Corral et al., 2008). I refer to BMI only when reporting on studies which used that in their measurements.

relation between price and calories, such that energy-dense foods composed of refined grains, added sugars, or fats represented the lowest-cost option to the consumer. In other words, less expensive food is more fattening or obesogenic. These findings were a major breakthrough in obesity research and served to significantly impact public perceptions and food policy. Several misunderstandings emerged from those findings, however, and have shaped public perception that the poor are disproportionately overweight and that nutritious food is always more expensive. A more complex picture of the relationship between poverty and obesity has emerged more recently that includes three key facts: (1) there is actually no correlation between the prevalence of overweight and poverty status, but the *severity* of overweight is much greater for the poor than the nonpoor (Jolliffe, 2011), (2) while gaps in obesity rates remain between high- and low-income groups, they have been closing with time as those with higher income levels become more obese (Food Research & Action Center, 2014), and (3) nutritious yet inexpensive foods do exist, but are often rejected by the consumer (Maillot, Darmon, & Drewnowski, 2010), a finding which we will return to in later chapters.

To further elaborate on differences in overweight across income groups, the National Health and Nutrition Examination Survey (NHANES) shows that between 1971 and 2006, there were no statistically significant differences in the rates of overweight (BMI > 25) between the poor and nonpoor, but when the criterion was changed to obesity (BMI > 30) the data revealed a 5–7 percent higher prevalence rate among the poor. After 2006, however, there was essentially no difference in obesity among the poor and nonpoor. To put this in simple terms, there *was* a higher obesity rate among the poor than the nonpoor in the recent past, but that gap has now disappeared. There are currently no statistically significant differences in the prevalence rate of overweight or obesity between the poor and nonpoor, but poor people suffer more severe overweight (Jolliffe, 2011, p. 354). To put this even more simply, almost everyone is fat, but the poorest are the fattest.

This is a good place for a reminder about the important distinction between obesity and overeating. Much of the recent research on food consumption has focused on obesity because it is a major public health problem; however, it is important to note the difference between the *behavior* of overeating vs. the *status* of being overweight or obese. Most, if not all of us, struggle to some extent with resisting the powerful forces that lead to overeating. The most common outcome of overeating is weight gain, but scientifically speaking, overeating and overweight are not equivalents. Some people overeat, but have a healthy metabolism or lifestyle that mitigate the excess calories. Others overeat and use unhealthy compensatory mechanisms that prevent significant weight gain. There are also a very scant few who do not overeat and are nevertheless overweight or obese due to genetic conditions. Overeating is a very broad problem that nearly all of us face, whereas we should think of overweight and obesity as the extreme clinical manifestations of overeating.

Food spending

Americans' eating habits and food spending have changed dramatically in a very short time, such that even the act of grocery shopping has changed tremendously in the past few decades, going from a household chore to a shopping experience. The very notion of going to a store and buying food, rather than hunting, growing, or foraging it, would of course be foreign to some of today's world and certainly to our ancestors. My maternal great-grandparents, only two generations ago, were not even part of the cash economy. They were subsistence farmers in Oklahoma and traded for the goods and services they needed. The number of products, including clothing, vehicles, and goods, they consumed during their entire lifespans was extremely small. They certainly did not overeat, at least not chronically. Even when they had an opportunity to overindulge, minimalism and thoughtful consumption were part of a larger ethos that regulated their behavior. Self-regulation was effortless, probably because it was so well-ingrained in the context of a widely shared belief system, as well as because of a restricted economy.

Rises in income capital have also been associated with more frequent dining out. In fact, the proportion of total food expenditures spent on food-away-from-home increased from 34 percent in 1972 to 49 percent in 2006 (Lin, Guthrie, & Frazão, 1999; Stewart, Blisard, & Jolliffe, 2006). Eating at restaurants and fast-food chains almost always involves consuming food that is served in large portion sizes, has been trucked long distances, and is therefore loaded with preservatives, fat, and salt to retain flavor and preserve food. Moreover, this highly palatable restaurant food is increasingly trademarked or bestowed with a luxury name or region (Kobe or Waygu beef, Outback Steakhouse's Bloomin' Onion, Taco Bell's Dorito Loco tacos) as part of the broader frenzy of consumption that includes branded clothing, automobiles, and consumer electronics. Aggressive marketing and branding is such an integral part of the consumer marketplace that even fruits and vegetables, such as the SweetTango apple, are now branded and trademarked (Seabrook, 2011).

In short, the steady rise in American consumerism and American caloric intake has been well documented by the USDA and the Bureau of

Labor Statistics. These increases in eating and spending are part of the same phenomenon: an insatiable appetite for consumption that shows no sign of tapering. These data also show that a large portion of the increased calories went toward the consumption of grains and refined carbohydrates (USDA, 2002), and a large portion of consumer expenditures went toward luxury and discretionary goods (Bureau of Labor Statistics, 2006). Much like the global shopping landscape is littered with cheaply made clothing and furniture which encourage high-volume consumption, the food landscape is littered with low-quality packaged sweets and refined carbohydrates which also encourage high-volume consumption. I think of this consumption of empty calories and the consumption of unnecessary goods as remarkably similar. I've come to use the term "sugar" to describe them both literally and metaphorically. That is, the sugar that we consume in the form of sweets and highly processed foods is toxic to our bodies and the "sugar" we consume in the form of disposable clothing, luxury watches, and soon-to-be obsolete gadgets are toxic to our psyches when consumed in large enough quantities and without mitigating healthful behaviors.

3

The Psychological Effects of Consumer Culture

Freud argued that the fundamental paradox of civilization is that it is a tool we created to protect ourselves from unhappiness, yet it is simultaneously our largest source of unhappiness (1930). Society gratifies desire or the pleasure principle, but neurosis is caused by the frustration which society imposes in the service of its ideals. In the culture of consumerism, the ways in which we can gratify the pleasure principle are virtually unlimited, and yet the psychological, physical, and environmental consequences of such gratification, as we are now coming to see, can be devastating. To say that we consume more than ever is to say that the sky is blue. But what are the psychological antecedents, justifications, and consequences of that consumption? We need to think both about the external culture of consumerism and how it provides the illusion of protecting us from unhappiness, as well as the internal ways we experience, think about, and consume food and material culture that ultimately cause us unhappiness.

My work is influenced by a long line of existential psychologists who somewhat unlike Freud generally believed that psychological distress originates in conflicts surrounding the givens of existence, such as mortality, freedom, and authenticity. Under the shadow of the Holocaust and in the beginning days of widespread talk therapy, early existential psychologists and psychiatrists such as Viktor Frankl, Eric Fromm, and Karen Horney spoke to questions of loss, suffering, and unprecedented individuality. Theirs was a depth psychology that departed both from the earlier sexualized doctrine of Freud with its focus on repressed sexual drives and early childhood experiences, and from the contemporaneous explanations of the reductionist behavioral school.

Eric Fromm, in particular, was the one of the first psychologists to argue that the capitalist economy of the modern industrial West created an acquisitive society responsible for disturbances in mental health (1955, p. 83). More recently, contemporary psychologists Phil Cushman and Paul Wachtel, both strongly influenced by existential psychology, as well as the counterculture movements of the 1960s and 1970s, addressed the psychological effects of affluence and consumerism. In his article *Why the Self is Empty* (1990), Cushman argued that Westerners have what is a historically unprecedented notion of ourselves as individuals. He wrote that "during the beginnings of the modern era in the 16th Century, the Western world began to shift from a religious to a scientific frame of production, from a rural to an urban setting, and from a communal to an individual subject" (p. 600). He noted that we have come to view ourselves as self-contained and highly individualized beings, characterized by free will and mastery over the environment, rather than as a small part of a collective entity with perhaps a predetermined destiny. It is quite difficult for us to see that our notion of ourselves—of what it means to be human—is so culturally and historically specific. Our very proximity to ourselves creates a blind spot. It *feels* as though people might have always thought of themselves as having free will, as being highly individualized and unique, but this is a relatively new development in the course of human history. In just the past century or less, " ... Americans have slowly changed from a Victorian people who had a deeply felt need to save money and restrict their sexual and aggressive impulses .... to a people who have a deeply felt need to spend money and indulge their impulses" (p. 600). This shift coincides with the move away from the production-based economies of the industrial era, as well as the shift from a culture of thrift to anti-thrift. Social theorist Zygmunt Bauman argues that the protestant work ethic which gave rise to industrialism has now been displaced by a "consumer ethic" in which "consumption, not only expands to fill the identity vacuum left by the decline of the work ethic, but it assumes the same structural significance that work enjoyed at the high noon of modernity" (Gabriel & Lang, 2006, p. 84). We can think of the Empty Self then as embedded in and caused by a capitalist, consumer-driven society which encourages impulsivity and indulgence, while also discouraging self-regulation, discipline, and thrift.

Contrary to the reigning biological explanations for overeating and obesity, if we begin with this philosophical approach in understanding the configuration of selves and how we imagine our own selves in this specific place and time, we then have a more nuanced tableau to understand our relationship with food, material culture, nature, technology, and other living beings. In other words, this historic shift in the Western self-concept to that of maximizing one's individual needs and desires was a key element in paving the way for the heightened consumption of food and material goods that typifies the age of affluence. It was also a key component in the development of *consumerism as a moral doctrine*, in which consumer choice and acquisition are the vehicles for individual freedom, happiness, and power. As Cushman argues, "…our terrain has shaped a self that experiences a significant absence of community, tradition, and shared meaning. It experiences these social absences and their consequences 'interiorly' as a lack of personal conviction and worth, and it embodies the absences as a chronic, undifferentiated emotional hunger. The post-World War II self thus yearns to acquire and consume as an unconscious way of compensating for what has been lost: It is empty" (p. 600). That we can experience these *cultural* ills, such as loss of community or shared meaning, as *individual* deficiencies, such as anxiety or depression, is one of the prerequisites for widespread overconsumption. As we increasingly have come to believe that our problems, ranging from clinical disorders to more diffuse feelings of emptiness, are housed within our bounded selves, we have turned toward the individual consumption of pills, consumer goods, and food to "treat" those ills.

Limitless desire

In the culture of consumerism, supply generates demand by presenting seductive options to consumers who are primed to slake unmet desires. The assumption by many economists has been that consumer wants and desires are both unlimited and insatiable because there is an endless array of products available and forthcoming to provide ephemeral satisfaction (Slater, 1997). Recently this assumption has been challenged by scholars who argue that the insatiability of such desires stems from problems created by their very pursuit (Wachtel, 2003). In what Colin Campbell calls "imaginative hedonism," the modern hedonism of desire rests on the daydreams of novel products. He argues that individuals construct daydreams populated by images and narratives of consumer products as presented by media and advertising (Campbell, 1987), yet find themselves disappointed that the actual consumption of these products does not satisfy the imagined desire.

The recent and surprising popularity of so-called "unboxing" videos perhaps illuminates the regressive fantasies of such imaginative hedonism. Usually posted on YouTube, these videos most often depict the disembodied hands of someone unwrapping a newly purchased consumer product. There is a vaguely pornographic undertone to the unwrapping that is remarkably like a striptease. Many of these videos are geared toward toddlers and depict the unwrapping of Disney toys and Play-Doh sets. I was particularly interested in why these videos might appeal to toddlers who have very little experience (relatively speaking) with consumer purchases and their associations. In one video viewed over 92 million times, a woman known as "DisneyCollector" slowly opens a series of plastic eggs with her brightly colored long fingernails, crackling their cellophane wrappers in seductive high-definition and cooing her narration in the background. Such "egg videos" dominate the unboxing genre, so much so that *New York Times* columnist Mireille Silcoff wrote, "Fascinatingly, surprise eggs—oblong plastic casings holding tiny trinkets usually destined for the garbage—are the powerhouse plaything in children-oriented unboxings, the videos that seem to really go viral. Searching 'surprise egg unboxing' feels like pressing an elevator button and seeing the doors open to a vast alternate universe beyond" (Silcoff, 2014).

I began to wonder more about what made these plastic eggs so fascinating to toddlers. My own free association was to a personal memory of how my youngest sister used to play an imaginary game she called Hatch during her toddlerhood. In Hatch, my sister would cocoon herself inside several blankets or afghans and ask someone in the family to use their body to envelop her in a kind of incubation. The rules were that the family member was supposed to then hypnotically whisper, "hatch, hatch, hatch ... " until she would slowly and victoriously emerge from the blankets, pretending that she was a freshly hatched chick. This imaginary play had a powerful hold on her and she never tired of it. I later came to think of her game as a regressive fantasy of being born and the desire on her part, now a conscious being to reexperience that existential triumph of birth. Interestingly her own son, now a toddler, is fascinated with the photos and videos of himself in the hospital that were taken immediately after his birth and he views them almost daily with rapt fascination. I believe that these egg unboxing videos engage toddlers in a powerful way because toddlers are at a developmental stage in which they've begun to question how they themselves came into existence, grappling with the question, "How does one come to be?"

Unboxing videos for adults follow a similar pattern of seductive unwrapping, but instead usually feature high dollar electronics or fashions. Just as sexual pornography suspends the viewer in preclimactic tension for as long as possible, this consumer pornography allows the viewer to occupy the moment of anticipation, just before the climax of satisfaction and the inevitable refractory period of disillusionment or denouement which follows. These unboxing videos seem to activate a regressed fantasy space in which erotic tension, birth, and sexuality converge with consumer desire. Pop artist Andy Warhol toyed with this same kind of anticipatory sexuality of consumerism with his phallic bright yellow banana that adorned a Velvet Underground album and invited the consumer to "peel slowly and see." Of course, peeling slowly to see is dangerous because once the desired object is attained or seen, dissatisfaction ensues until another object of desire creates a new daydream, creating a continual longing for the new and unknown. In other words, the idealized images and narratives used in consumer culture generate feelings of inadequacy in the consumer which the products themselves are supposed to cure (Richins, 1995). These unsated desires inevitably lead to increased consumption in more desperate attempts to meet expectations. In other words, using consumerism to address psychological needs is what leads to overspending and overeating.

There is surprisingly little empirical research on consumerism and its psychological effects on well-being (Kasser & Kanner, 2004, p. 4). Using early humanistic-existential theories as the foundation of their approach, Tim Kasser and Richard Ryan are two pioneers in the study of materialism. They and others have demonstrated that focusing on luxury experiences and acquisition undermines well-being, increases depression and anxiety, and creates a pattern of diffuse and unfulfillable desire (Kasser, 2002; Kasser & Kanner, 2004; Wachtel, 1983, 2003). Using the Aspiration Index (1993) Kasser, for example, has empirically shown that not only does materialism cause unhappiness, but that unhappiness causes materialism (2002). In other words, the cultural, economic, and psychological forces which perpetuate consumerism are circular, in that they cause us unhappiness through consumption, but they also embed the message that when we are unhappy, buying things is the antidote.

Other studies have shown that past conditions of financial or material insecurity make people more vulnerable to materialism (Cohen & Cohen, 1996; Kasser, Ryan, Zax, & Sameroff, 1995), much in the same way that past food insecurity makes people vulnerable to obesity (Drewnowski & Specter, 2004); and that financial hunger is correlated to caloric hunger, such that when people feel insecure about their relative wealth they are likely to consume more calories (Briers & Laporte, 2013). These parallel findings regarding food and material insecurity are two more clues that the overconsumption of material goods and the overconsumption of food are regulated by some of the same psychological mechanisms.

In her book *Hooked! Buddhist Writings on Greed, Desire, and the Urge to Consume*, Stephanie Kaza and her colleagues argue that we are "hooked" on consumption and that our consumerist impulses function like an addiction (2005). Addicts often experience intense cravings, devote extraordinary amounts of time to pursuing the addiction, and then disappointingly find that the reward delivered diminishes over time, leaving them forever chasing the initial high. Not surprisingly, emergent research has shown that some foods especially the sugary fatty foods of consumer capitalism are addictive. In fact, the food industry is increasingly compared to the tobacco industry because of its development and sale of addictive substances, topics which I will take up in later chapters.

What is perhaps most insidious in this cycle of desire/acquisition/ disappointment is that we do not experience the psychological consequences of consumerism as the effects of a problematic social ideology. Instead, we experience them as individual failures of willpower, discipline, or neurochemistry and turn to further consumption as a solution, thereby creating more demand for products and a never-ending cycle of consumerism. This is why retail therapy and comfort food are two sides of the same coin: they are both attempts at self-soothing through consumption, ultimately leading to self-defeating consequences. As we shall see throughout this book, there are countless examples of such cycles of consumption, in which we are chasing our tails by using one type of consumption to solve the problematic consequences of another.

For the purposes of understanding overeating as a form of overconsumption, I am largely focusing on the "dark side" of consumerism and consumer culture, yet many scholars take a more positive approach to consumerism (Bloom, 2010; Watson, 2006), to which I do not entirely disagree. Here we would do well again to make a distinction between consumption vs. *over*consumption, the latter causing more problematic psychological, social, and environmental consequences.

Poverty, debt, and consumer culture

Many scholars have argued that the values of consumer society exacerbate the effects of poverty, namely by the creation of an emotional poverty driven by the desire for more (Sahlins, 1974). Sociologist Zygmunt Bauman argues that to exist in poverty in the culture of consumerism is unlike the historic experience of poverty, in which there was a direct threat to survival due to hunger, disease, or lack of shelter. In the culture of consumerism to live in *relative poverty* is a social and psychological condition in which the poor are excluded from the culture's version of a happy life. In consumer society, "a 'normal life' is the life of consumers, preoccupied with making their choices among the panoply of publicly displayed opportunities for pleasurable sensations and lively experiences. A 'happy life' is defined by catching many opportunities and letting slip but few or none at all, by catching the opportunities most talked about and thus most desired, and catching them no later than others, and preferably before others" (Bauman, 1998). He views the disenfranchisement of the poor as a function of them being "flawed consumers." "In a society of consumers it is above all the inadequacy of the person as a consumer that leads to social degradation and 'internal exile'. It is this inadequacy, this inability to acquit oneself of the consumer's duties, that turns into bitterness at being left behind, disinherited or degraded, shut off or excluded from the social feast to which others gained entry. Overcoming that consumer inadequacy is likely to be seen as the only remedy—the sole exit from a humiliating plight" (p. 38).

Economies focused on consumption foster conditions that heighten psychological insecurities and economies with dramatic income inequality, such as seen currently in the United States, even further heighten psychological distress (Wilkinson & Pickett, 2014). Income inequality in the United States is not simply a wealth gap between high and low earners, but a two-tiered institutional system. "The top tier consists of pro-thrift institutions that provide myriad ways and means for higher earning Americans to invest and build wealth. The bottom tier consists of anti-thrift institutions that provide multiple ways and means for lower earning Americans to forego savings, borrow at predatory interest rates, and fall into a debt trap" (Institute for American Values, 2008). Other research on indebtedness shows that it has significant negative physical and psychological consequences on borrowers and is associated with increased obesity, anxiety, depression, and suicide (Fitch, Hamilton, Bassett, & Davey, 2011; Münster, Rüger, Ochsmann, Letzel, & Toschke, 2009; Webley & Nyhus, 2001).

It is not just consumer debt that is associated with these negative outcomes, but even student loan debt which had historically been considered "good debt." A recent Gallup survey of college graduates found that those with more than $50,000 of student loan debt are worse off emotionally and physically than other graduates, even after they paid off the debt (Gallup, 2014). Economist Samuel Cameron argues that when consumption is tied to self-esteem, people are less responsive to borrowing costs and can more easily become problem debtors. Indeed, debt levels are greater in poor families (Wagmiller, 2003), meaning that the psychological and physical toll of debt has disproportionate effects on the poor, just as obesity, diabetes, and related disease disproportionately affect the poor. If we think about debt as both financial and caloric, we can see how the culture of consumerism encourages overeating and overspending by both manufacturing needs and offering irresistible, unaffordable, and self-defeating "solutions," such as cars, electronics, sodas, and junk food.

Many well-intended advocates for the poor believe that securing access to consumer culture and its panoply of choices will solve the troubling problem of disenfranchisement, yet other scholars have argued that poor people (and poor countries) often make self-defeating decisions about what to consume because they are enticed by seeing the consumption habits of wealthier individuals (Nurkse, 1957) and are responding to constructed desires manufactured by advertising and media (Belk, 1988; Keyfitz, 1982). Addressing income inequality is one of the most pressing social and economic issues we face; however, addressing it by guaranteeing the right to acquisition, although intended to diminish inequity and reduce disenfranchisement, serves to further entrench the negative psychological consequences that come with acquisitive desire and materialism. More specifically, guaranteeing belongingness to consumer culture by securing access to its food ultimately undermines longevity and increases mortality in the form of a psychological and nutritional Pandora's box, as we shall further see in the coming chapters.

Choice and acquisition

The staggering array of choices available in the marketplace presents an additional psychological burden to consumers who have to filter and assess information about hundreds of thousands of products to make their selections. Historically, economists have thought of consumer choice as good for the individual, healthy markets, and innovation. Recall that this is what Gabriel and Lang refer to as *consumerism as moral doctrine*, in which consumer choice and acquisition are the vehicles for individual freedom, happiness, and power. In 2004, however, psychologist Barry Schwartz challenged this notion and instead argued that too many consumer choices negatively affect psychological well-being, lead to paralysis in decision-making, and lower satisfaction with purchases (Schwartz, 2004). If we decrease or limit our consumer choices, he argues, we could achieve greater well-being because we would spend less time fretting about so many choices and reduce our risk for buyer's remorse and consumer regret. Many economists have since questioned his research because it has been difficult to replicate, and more importantly, other research has even contradicted it. Schwartz himself, in reviewing the contradictory results that have emerged, acknowledged that there is a balance that must be achieved, but defends his original argument (Schwartz, 2014). Anecdotally, I can say that many of the patients I work with in my clinical practice struggle with the sheer number of choices they face in dating, education, careers, geographic mobility, and even fertility. They are, to put it in Jean-Paul Sartre's terms "condemned to freedom."

In addition to the psychologically unfulfilling consequences of excessive choice, shopping, and consumerism, there is yet another set of ill-effects which come from accumulating so many possessions and dealing with the crushing weight of the stuff we buy. In *Life at Home in Twenty-First Century* (Arnold, 2012), social scientists using archaeological and ethnographic methods studied contemporary American middle-class families to better understand their material worlds. Among many other findings, they discovered that families struggled with the sheer quantity of possessions, stockpiles of convenience foods, and a sense of vanishing leisure time. In terms of material possessions, they found that beyond the financial burden of unrelenting shopping, the accumulation of the physical merchandise took its toll well beyond the pocketbook. Families' homes were overflowing with clutter that created intense psychological stress and increased depression for the parents, especially the mothers, as measured by the stress hormone cortisol. Of course the massive growth of the storage industry in the United States is a direct result of the difficulty we face in managing so many possessions. In fact, we might think of storage units as functioning not only as warehouses of goods, but as psychological defense mechanisms which allow us to externalize the stress of overconsuming. Putting things in storage means we don't have to face the difficult act of letting things go, but allows us to compartmentalize the problem of acquisition by keeping the objects out of sight. Similarly, we increasingly need more and more storage in the form of body fat to accommodate the overconsumption of food. Not coincidentally, the American Psychiatric Association recently added two new disorders to its diagnostic manual: Binge Eating Disorder and Hoarding Disorder, which are the focus of Chapter 8.

Consumerism: From cradle to grave

Understanding these complicated origins and consequences of materialism can give us more compassion for ourselves and for others struggling with materialistic impulses. In the case of my patient Allison, there are a number of developmental events that might have made her feel insecure and that consequently increased her vulnerability for internalizing materialistic values. By her report, Allison's family is a conservative, affluent family from the American Midwest that promoted traditional gender roles and a luxurious lifestyle. Although she was encouraged to earn a college degree and enter the workforce, she was also taught that her career should be second to her husband's and that marrying a high-status, high-earning husband was the most important goal. As a teenager and then again as a young adult she was the victim of date rape, in which she was sexually assaulted by young men whom she was dating, thereby undermining her sense of safety and security in romantic relationships. Many years later, after being abandoned by her husband she then found herself in a new city with a diminished income and a group of extremely affluent friends as her reference group. She subsequently became highly concerned, obsessed even, with her relative financial position and her perceived lower status following her divorce.

Last year, Allison decided to take a trip to Paris with a female friend. She was eager for the trip and spent a long time planning for it. Leading up to the trip there were two themes which repeatedly came up in our sessions together. The first was her intense wish to purchase something from the luxury boutique Hermès in Paris. She was aware that most of the items there were priced in the thousands of dollars, well out of her budget, but she learned that the least expensive item for sale was a scarf for $400, which she was determined to buy. In a kind of internal "unboxing" fantasy, it was the anticipation of that purchase that she most looked forward to about the trip. Of course there is nothing inherently the matter with buying a nice souvenir. Context is everything. In this case, the purchase of the scarf became a central foci of the trip and more importantly, Allison spent countless hours of fantasy anticipating the pleasure it would bring her (which she later reported it did not). The second theme had to do with her fear that it would be difficult to travel with her friend whom she considered more beautiful than her, and more importantly, thinner than her. It was often agonizing for Allison to socialize with this friend and in fact many of her female friends whom she described as thin, tall, and wealthy, making her feel "fat, dumpy, and poor" by comparison. She often sobbed in my office saying that she was tired of being the "pretty girl's friend," yet by her own admission she sought out these friends because she felt that by association they helped her project a high-status image on the marriage market.

Allison's expectations of status and money negatively impact her romantic prospects because she refuses to date anyone who is even slightly overweight or who earns less than her. Although she is quite overweight herself, she believes that she will be able to get back to her college size by crash dieting. In the meantime, she has effectively cut off all dating prospects because of her intense preoccupation with social status and weight. The disappointment of dating someone who is not a fit, high earner is impossible for her to bear and so she has spun herself into a lonely, isolating web of spending, eating, dieting, debt, and envy. Call these first-world problems, and they are, but the distress is very real to those seeking to alleviate their suffering and improve their lives. Like many of us, Allison is blind to how she is partly the architect of her own misery. In her fixation on status, money, and physique she has selected only friends who exemplify the characteristics she so desperately wants for herself, and in so doing has become prisoner in the jail of comparison. She is unable to like anything about herself because by comparison she is always fat and poor. She finds herself shopping in luxury stores and overeating luxury foods as a way both to keep up with the Joneses and to assuage her increasing feelings of distress. Allison is a consumer who lives "from attraction to attraction, from temptation to temptation, from swallowing one bait to fishing for another, each new attraction, temptation, and bait begin somewhat different and perhaps stronger than those that preceded them…" (Bauman, 1998, p. 26). As the circular model of affluence and psychological well-being predicts, she finds herself feeling worse, increasing her debt, and increasing her weight. Although she came to me for help with what she perceives as a neurochemically caused depression, I view her distress as a deeply existential battle of authenticity, mediated by capitalism, alcohol, food, beauty, men, and luxury.

Many of us are aware of these potent and destructive forces of consumerism, yet feel powerless against them or are unsure how to combat them. In 1998, the Merck Family Fund surveyed Americans about their attitudes concerning consumption and found that "People are saying that we spend and buy far more than we need. Our children are becoming very materialistic and we're spending for what we want today at the expense of future generations and our own future.... There is a universal feeling in this nation that we've become too materialistic, too greedy, too self-absorbed, too selfish, and that we need to bring back into balance the enduring values that have guided this country over generations: values of faith, family, responsibility, generosity, friendship" (De Graaf et al., 2001). Similarly, a 2004 poll by the Center for a New American Dream revealed that contrary to mindlessly living in the work-spend cycle, nearly all Americans agree that we are too focused on working and making money and not enough on family and community. In fact, 85 percent of respondents said that living in a fair and just society better describes their concept of the American dream than achieving an affluent or wealthy lifestyle. Respondents also identified numerous social problems such as consumer debt, overly commercialized children, harm to the environment, and increased stress as consequences of materialistic values (Center for a New American Dream, 2004).

This widely expressed ambivalence hardly squares with a recent Cadillac commercial, which debuted during the 2014 Superbowl. In it, a handsome and polished white middle-aged American man stands by his pool and asks the audience, "Why do we work so hard? For what? For this?" gesturing to his pool. "Other countries that work, stroll home, stop by the cafe. They take August off. OFF. Why aren't you like that? Why aren't we like that?" He walks inside a modern opulent home, where two children are playing on digital devices, he changes into a designer suit and then says to the camera, "You work hard. You create your own luck. And you gotta believe anything is possible." As he slides into his Cadillac, he says, "As for all the stuff... that's the upside of only taking two weeks off in August." In this brief commercial, we see the Empty Self lived out and articulated. The man glorifies the American bounded, masterful self by saying, "You create your own luck" and "you gotta believe anything is possible." He states that overwork is a fair price for affluence and the imagery suggests that the loss of family time and leisure are all worth it.

Advertisers are usually subtler than this, but what made this commercial bold and successful was explicitly naming and embracing materialism and luxury as worthwhile and acceptable goals. Apparently Cadillac did not see the Center for a New American Dream poll, or perhaps its executives knew that the 85 percent of respondents who expressed misgivings about affluence are not likely to be Cadillac buyers. According to Cadillac's advertising director Craig Bierley, the ad was intended to serve as "brand provocation" (McCarthy, 2014), and provoke it certainly did. Jonathan Hoenig, *Fox Business News* contributor and founder of capitalistpig.com, said that the ad "celebrates Americanism and celebrates America's essential sense of life: productivity, individualism, self-sufficiency, profit-seeking, and yes, enjoyment of the material world" (Fox News, 2014). By contrast, the *Huffington Post* said, "Cadillac made a commercial about the American dream, and it's a nightmare…. The luxury car company is selling a vision of the American Dream at its worst: Work yourself into the ground, take as little time off as possible, and buy expensive sh*t (specifically, a 2014 Cadillac ELR)" (Gregoire, 2014).

In spite of Americans' expressed ambivalence about materialistic values, advertisers persist in pushing luxury and opulence onto the public. Perhaps they suspect that it appeals to a part of all of us, in spite of our misgivings? It is arguably this unconscious or primitive appeal of acquisition that has allowed advertising and marketing to reshape the culture and to renegotiate our core values from what they were a century ago. That this commercial debuted during the Superbowl, just as the United States began to comfortably emerge from the economic downturn and as consumer spending began to increase, suggests a kind of cultural pronouncement by Cadillac that was a direct response to recent attention toward income inequality, the passage of universal health care, and the Occupy Wall Street movement. The message: working more than other industrialized nations, striving toward luxury and affluence, perpetuating income inequality, and advancing a winner-take-all economy is our cultural backbone that should continue to be the American dream.

In short, we are completely surrounded by buying and selling and it starts early. When I was ten years old I joined the Girl Scouts, something I'd wanted to do for years. It was incredibly exciting and my mom and I were instructed to go to the local department store that carried the uniforms where we spent over $50 on the jumper, the sash, the beret, and numerous accessories. It was a lot of money at that time and for our budget. I eagerly wanted to learn how to tie knots, build fires, sew, go camping, and other skills. Because of the time of year, however, our first project was to sell Girl Scout cookies. I dutifully trekked up and down my neighborhood streets, went to the local shopping mall and sold my share of the cookies. Our next project was to sell Garfield seat belt covers. Do not ask me who uses seat belt covers or why, but we were charged with selling plastic sleeves adorned with pictures of the beloved feline cartoon character Garfield that people could put over their car seat belts. Next, we were charged with selling magazine subscriptions. The scout who sold the most magazine subscriptions was to win a special grand prize, so I doubled up my selling efforts and marched around the neighborhood every day after school selling my wares. I did in fact sell the most subscriptions, winning the "grand" prize: a hardback edition of Bob Villa's *Back to Basics Home Improvement* book. Take a moment and let that last sentence wash over you. I cried when I received that idiotic grand prize, something completely inappropriate for a ten-year-old girl.

Bitterly disappointed, I quit the Girl Scouts. I was not able to understand at that age that my feelings were a response to the commercialization of childhood and the consumerization of a revered organization. Stuck with an expensive and useless uniform, a manual written for handymen and contractors, and having lost hundreds of hours I could have spent playing or doing other creative activities, I simply thought I had failed at being a Girl Scout. In fact, I had devoted myself to selling useless crap that nobody wanted in order to financially support an organization that was supposed to further the development of girls. To be fair, I know many women and girls who have had excellent experiences with the Girl Scouts. It seems that my experience was an outlier, but I have never been able to let go of my grudge against the organization, and you can only imagine what I think about their cookies.

The funnel of consumption

If now we return to the definitions related to consuming and consumption which introduced the book, we can see how the overconsumption of food is embedded in a broader pattern of overconsumption in which we are literally eating ourselves and the planet alive. In fact, if we rearrange the various definitions of consuming and consumption into the visual schematic shown in Figure 3.1, we can see the powerful funnel effect of the culture of consumerism on individual behavior.

With this is mind, in the next chapter we will turn our attention toward the food industry and the global industrial diet (the top of the funnel) and see how they exert pressure downward, creating powerful psychological impulses toward overeating (the bottom of the funnel).

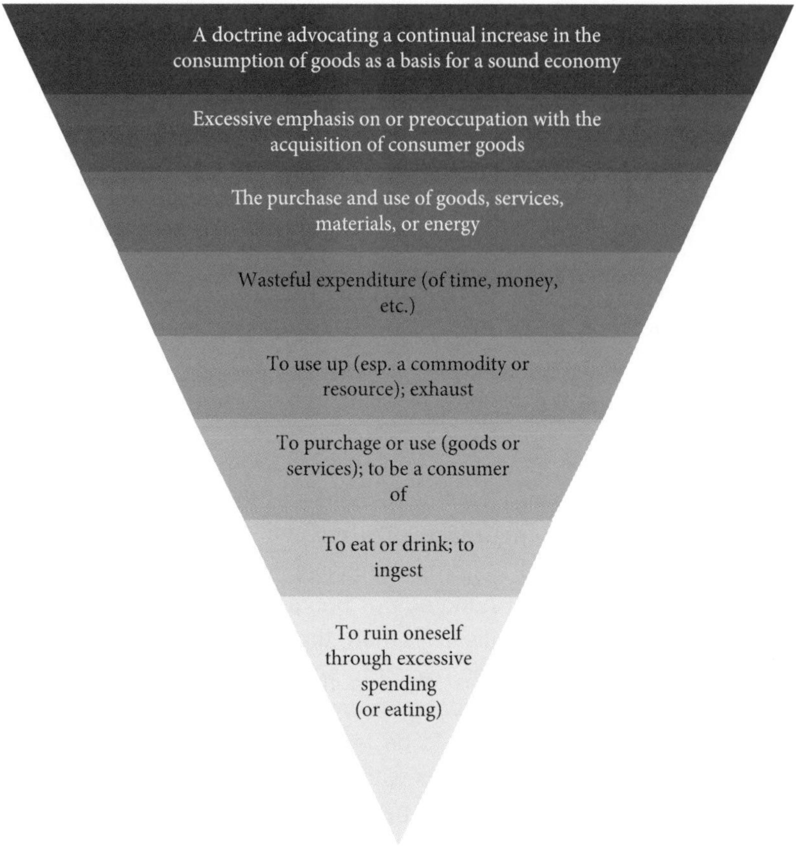

A doctrine advocating a continual increase in the consumption of goods as a basis for a sound economy

Excessive emphasis on or preoccupation with the acquisition of consumer goods

The purchase and use of goods, services, materials, or energy

Wasteful expenditure (of time, money, etc.)

To use up (esp. a commodity or resource); exhaust

To purchage or use (goods or services); to be a consumer of

To eat or drink; to ingest

To ruin oneself through excessive spending (or eating)

FIGURE 3.1 *Funnel of consumption.*

4

Food, Money, and Consumer Culture

With the rise of consumer culture came developments in food science, branding, and marketing which profoundly changed the composition of the American diet. Early food science and marketing began in earnest in the post–World War II era. It was just after the war that the food industry began developing convenience foods, and in 1954 Swanson TV dinners fulfilled two postwar trends: the lure of time-saving modern appliances and the fascination with a growing innovation—the television. More than 10 million TV dinners were sold during the first year of Swanson's national distribution (Smith, 2009). Looking at TV dinners and then later at fast food, it is clear that these new food habits expressed a changing sense of self that prioritized mobility, efficiency, and increased individualism. While these culinary developments reflected cultural and economic changes, they also became antecedents for further distance from food sources, depersonalization of food preparation, and ultimately increased consumption, overweight, and obesity.

There are a number of terms used in food and nutrition studies to describe varying levels of food refinement, processing, and palatability. I adhere to the following definitions throughout my work:

Processed food—Food that has undergone any kind of chemical or physical process that alters it from its raw state. Fermentation, smoking, cooking, and curing are all means of processing, thus there are many healthy processed foods such as sauerkraut, almond butter, smoked salmon, and plain yogurt.

*Ultra-processed food** (sometimes called hyperprocessed food)— The Lancet NCD Action Group defines this as durable, palatable, ready-to-consume products made from processed substances extracted or refined from whole foods. Such products are typically energy dense; have a high glycemic load; are low in dietary fiber, micronutrients, and phytochemicals; and are high in unhealthy types of dietary fat, added sugars, and sodium. Their intense palatability is achieved by high content fat, sugar, salt, and cosmetic and other additives which harm endogenous satiety mechanisms and promote energy overconsumption (Moodie et al., 2013).

*Hyperpalatable food**—A neuroscientific term referring to foods high in refined sugars, flours, fats, and salt which produce high hedonic reward (pleasure) and an accompanying surge in dopamine (Avena, 2015). The term comes from *palatability*, which refers to the acceptability of an item on the basis of taste (Friedman & Stricker, 1976). Note that ultra-processed foods are often described as hyperpalatable, but not all hyperpalatable foods are ultra-processed. For example, bacon-wrapped dates stuffed with goat cheese could arguably be called hyperpalatable because of their irresistible combination of sugar, salt, and fat, yet they contain only a few whole ingredients and can easily be assembled in a home kitchen, therefore they are hyperpalatable, but not ultra-processed.

(Global) industrial diet—A sociological term referring to the processed, refined, corporate-produced, mass-marketed, and simplified food supply that is high in fat, salt, and sugar and low in nutritional value (Winson, 2013). This diet originated in the United States, but is increasingly a global phenomenon. This term emphasizes the industrial production of the global food system of ultra-processed foods.

Edible commodities—The profitable, edible products of the industrial diet (Winson, 2013). This term generally refers to ultra-processed foods with an emphasis on the commodification and profitability of such products.

Junk food (vernacular)—Food that appeals to popular (especially juvenile) taste but has little nutritional value (OED, 2015). Junk food is likely to be hyperpalatable and ultra-processed.

*I use the term *hyperpalatable* when I want to emphasize the deliciousness or hedonic reward associated with a food, and I use *ultra-processed* when I want to emphasize the production and manufacturing of the food in question.

FIGURE 4.1 *Glossary of terms.*

Food science and the development of ultra-processed food

As the American consumer responded enthusiastically to convenience foods, the food scientists who invented them quickly realized that they were sitting on a goldmine. Initially these scientists focused more on food preservation, food safety, and the development of time-saving options such as instant pudding and frozen dinners, but there was a later shift toward improving flavor quality and palatability. This eventually developed into a highly competitive industry chasing the newest flavor discoveries for the hungry and wealthy American public. Today, many food scientists are locked in a fierce battle referred to as The Great Flavor Rush, (Khatchadourian, 2009) in which they are trying to predict and create the next big flavor: kiwi flavored Snapple, acai berry yogurt, or pomelo bubble gum.

I remember when I was about ten years old and was over at a friend's house. The friend's mother put out some vegetables and dip. I dipped a carrot into the white speckled dip and tasted something unlike anything I'd ever had before. It was delicious and revolutionary. I asked what it was. "It's called ranch dressing," they said. Very quickly ranch dressing became the "it" food—moms made it from a packaged mix because there were very few bottled salad dressings at that time. I didn't know it then, but these were the early days of food scientists working their gustatory magic. While certainly there were branded foods dating back to the better part of the nineteenth century, there was not the extensive library of manufactured flavors on grocery store shelves as there is today. Nowadays much of our food is created in laboratories such as Givaudan, where food scientists carefully develop and test flavors, colors, and brand names. This highly processed industrial food, sometimes referred to as "edible commodities" (Winson, 2013), is such a dominant part of the food landscape that it is virtually impossible to disentangle it from the culture of consumerism.

I once had a student ask me what I meant by the term "whole food." I realized that I had failed to define that term for the class and proceeded to describe it as food that was unprocessed or unrefined. The student was still confused, as were others in the class, so I defined it again as food that was not manufactured in a laboratory or converted industrially from its original form. Still perplexed, she said she just didn't get it. I playfully asked, "Well, have you ever seen a donut tree?" To that, she and the rest of class burst out laughing in understanding. In the ensuing discussion I discovered that many, if not most, of the students had never reflected on the distinction among whole, processed, and ultra-processed foods. Many had never considered that there were no refined or packaged foods until fairly recently in human history.

Food, poverty, and cultural belongingness

While the global industrial diet has undermined nutritional quality for almost everyone, it is now clear that the health burdens are disproportionately shouldered by the poor. Just as income equality has created a two-tiered economy in which the rich get richer and the poor get poorer, the global industrial diet has created a two-tiered system of nutritional "classes" in which the poor eat lower quality food and more of it compared to their wealthier counterparts. On its face, it might seem that this nutritional class divide is simply an extension of economic class, such that wealthier people can afford higher quality and more expensive food, while the poor must get by on whatever they can afford, namely the obesogenic foods of the global industrial diet. It is far more complicated than that, though.

Common explanations for poor dietary quality among low-income groups are that (1) healthful foods generally cost more than unhealthful foods (Drewnowski & Specter, 2004), (2) those in low-income households often live in "food deserts" with limited access to grocery stores (Beaulac, Kristjansson, & Cummins, 2009), and (3) individuals living in financial poverty also commonly face time scarcity (Mullainathan & Shafir, 2013) which exerts pressure toward consuming quick, convenience foods. These explanations are partly correct, but there is an untold story here as well. In particular, the correlation between food cost and nutritional quality has given rise to a well-accepted myth that there are no inexpensive, nutritious foods (DeSilver, 2013). Not so. There are in fact many inexpensive nutritious foods. The USDA's Thrifty Food Plan, for example, identifies and recommends foods such as eggs, ground turkey, cabbage, chickpeas, and lentils that are low cost and nutritious, yet some researchers report that these foods are not widely consumed by low-income households (Maillot et al., 2010). Why not?

Some have argued that the Thrifty Plan "ignores the current eating habits of the American population" by encouraging the consumption of foods like legumes and reducing the consumption of citrus juices, among other foods (Golan, Stewart, Kuchler, & Dong, 2008). In one study, researchers posed the following question: Are nutritious, inexpensive foods rejected by the low-income consumer because their use violates unspoken social norms (Maillot et al., 2010)? Their hypothesis was that nutritious, inexpensive foods deviate from current consumption standards, fail to meet cultural requirements, and are socially or culturally inappropriate. Notably, however, the term "culture" was never defined nor operationalized in that study. Certainly it was not defined as a set of ethnic, religious, or regional beliefs or practices that could justifiably be used to defend a specific diet. Is the culture then, to which they refer simply the culture of consumerism? If so, is there a human right or moral right to access that culture as part of a human right to food security (Chilton & Rose, 2009)? Some have argued yes and have even further argued that there is a right to eat away from home, which presumably refers to eating fast food and convenience food, as is consistent with broader societal trends (Maillot et al., 2010). These advocates argue that "good nutrition does go beyond mere survival and should include taste, convenience, and variety and be consistent with societal norms" (Drewnowski & Eichelsdoerfer, 2010, p. 2).Yet, as we shall see, it is these very hallmarks of the global industrial diet—taste (hyperpalatability), convenience, and variety (increased choice)—that cause overeating.

Note here that I am not speaking of the 5 percent of American households suffering from "very low food security" (Coleman-Jensen, Gregory, & Singh, 2013), but rather of low-income individuals and families who have sufficient food, but food that is not always desirable. Even among those with very low food security, however, there is often a paradox between their material comforts and their food security. In a striking *National Geographic* photo essay on the new face of hunger in the United States (McMillan, Cahana, Sinclair, & Toensing, 2014), we see images of families living in large, decent homes with nice appliances. They wear trendy, branded clothing like Nike Airs and have cell phones, yet they are food insecure. Their diets consist of take-out chicken gizzards, hot dogs, chicken nuggets, and tater tots. Such images tell a compelling story of paradox, although it is also important to note that these snapshots reveal the episodic nature of food insecurity in contrast to the accumulative nature of other goods which may not reflect a family's current circumstances. Nevertheless, they reveal the strange consequences of being poor in a culture of wealth, as well as the difficult choices faced by families struggling to get by, yet like most of us, inured to the commodities of affluence.

Just as branded shoes, clothes, and electronics offer a sense of social belongingness, branded foods too are even cheaper and more accessible tokens for such belongingness. In fact, these products often take on powerful emotional valence for those living in poverty, becoming valuable cultural tokens of membership. Unlike the historic experience of poverty, in which there was a direct threat to survival due to hunger, disease, or lack of shelter, to live in *relative* poverty in an affluent consumer society is a psychological condition in which the poor are often excluded from the culture's version of a happy life. Returning to Bauman's concept of the experience of *relative* poverty in consumer culture, consider that living in poverty in an affluent country often means exclusion from the "panoply of publicly displayed opportunities for pleasurable sensations and lively experiences." The pleasurable culinary sensations and lively food experiences of our culture are often chips, sodas, fast food, cookies, ice cream, and juice. In *Work, Consumerism, and the New*

Poor, Bauman argues that modern capitalism has opened up the possibility of freedom to ever-increasing numbers of people offering "the rapidly expanding, seemingly limitless, world of consumption" (p. 57), and because of the importance of this increased choice, those excluded from those choices become disenfranchised and oppressed (Bauman, 1992). In other words, consumer indulgences as simple as junk food become cheap mechanisms to experience belongingness—a means to mitigate the chronic marginalization and disenfranchisement experienced by the poor. The food industry exploits this by flaunting its products with the promise of quick and easy access to the happy life, just as zero-down loans for cars and homes also promise such access.

Further reinforcing the consumption of ultra-processed food to the poor is the system of SNAP (Supplemental Nutrition Assistance Program) benefits or food stamps. Recently the CEO of Kraft opposed food stamp cuts because one sixth of the company's revenue comes from food stamp purchases (Rappeport, 2012). Even though SNAP-eligible foods are supposed to be healthy, Pepsi and Coke also lobbied against cuts because the soda industry has managed to keep sugar-sweetened beverages (SSBs) on the approved list of SNAP eligible foods, resulting in profits of $4 billion annually in SNAP revenues (Adams, 2013; Simon, 2012). Not only that, but Big Soda disproportionately targets black children and teens with their advertisements (Harris, 2011). Black kids are more likely to live in poverty than children of any other race with a poverty rate of 38.2 percent, more than twice as high as the rate among whites (Macartney, 2011). Because of these targeted advertisements, black children and teens see more than double the number of ads than do white children and teens for Vitamin Water, Sprite, Sunny D, 5-hour Energy, and Mountain Dew, even after statistically controlling for differing rates of television viewing across groups (Harris, 2011). It is no wonder, then, that new research shows that gaps in dietary quality between higher and lower SES groups in the United States have continued to widen over time, largely accounted for by increases in the consumption of sugar-sweetened beverages (Wang et al., 2014a). Not only do these beverages cause obesity and diabetes, but research is now pointing to the addictive nature of sugar which serves to further create an endless cycle of desire and consumption. In other words, junk food, just like cigarettes and cocaine, makes us feel good and provides us social belongingness by making us look cool to other users.

Illustrating this point is a refugee family from Burma whom I have mentored for the past five years. Before their arrival in the United States in 2009, they lived in a refugee camp for fifteen years. Shortly after they were relocated here the parents and two children were underweight and likely suffering the effects of years of malnourishment. They initially stocked their American kitchen with fresh produce, milk, chicken, rice, and frozen fish, acquired through public assistance programs and several area food banks. A few months after their arrival we went to the public library for an afternoon. It was a cold, rainy day and we wound up at the library cafe. Because of the language barrier I did not know what they might like to eat or drink so I ordered them four hot chocolates, thinking that was a safe bet. As they each took a first sip of the hot chocolate, they spluttered, staggered, and exchanged horrified looks with each other. I instantly realized my mistake. They had never tasted anything so sweet. At that time they were the poorest of the world's poor and had never been exposed to the global industrial diet. Much to my chagrin, I was the first to offer them a taste of the poison apple.

Now five years later, one of the parents has a stable minimum-wage job and the family has joined the ranks of the working poor. They all have iPhones and their kitchen is filled with jugs of orange soda, chips, cookies, ramen noodles, and fast-food wrappers. Three of the four of them have gained considerable weight and the mother is now clinically obese. The two kids recently told me that before 2009 they had never seen or tasted a Coke and now they drink several each day. What do we make of their story? On the one hand, their safety and religious freedom are no longer under threat as they were in their home country. They have health care, free education, and the opportunity to work. They have shelter, electricity, clean clothes, and running water. Most importantly, their subjective or lived experience is vastly improved. The price for these freedoms and material comforts is that they live in an urban housing project with few parks nearby and no access to nature. They have stopped wearing their native clothing which were beautiful woven tunics that signified their ethnic affiliation. The little boys have very little fluency in their native language and one of them now refuses to speak it altogether. They have a long list of consumer goods they want to purchase. They overeat and overspend. Because of their poverty and lifestyle, they are at risk for obesity and type 2 diabetes, with the mother of the family already considered prediabetic. They have high-interest payday loans as well as bad credit reports due to their misunderstanding of cell phone contracts. I worry about the psychological effects of losing their native culture, being disconnected from the natural world, and looking for happiness and meaning through acquisition. For their first year in the United States their extreme poverty combined with their naiveté to consumerism paradoxically functioned as a protective factor, but as their incomes increased they understandably wanted to join in the culture through the established tokens of membership: fast food, electronics, sodas, and sweets.

As we are beginning to see, the financial and nutritional regulatory failures which characterize the culture of consumerism serve to maintain the poor in both poverty and obesity by creating insurmountable obstacles to upward mobility. Certainly those in poverty should not have to eat undesirable food, any more than they should have to live in crime-ridden neighborhoods or near toxic waste plants, but we should also question the ways in which social policies meant to help the poor do so by securing the right to consumerism and consequently have the potential to undermine psychological and physical health.

Reckoning

I had a patient in my practice several years ago who was nineteen years old at the time. Chloe was about 100 pounds overweight and referred to herself as obese. At her young age, she had already struggled with drug and alcohol abuse and had a problem with overeating. A bank had just issued this young woman a credit card with an outrageously high interest rate and a credit limit of $1,000. After just a few weeks of having the credit card, she quickly maxed it out buying clothes and cosmetics. She mentioned to me in passing that she wanted to buy an expensive new mobile phone and was waiting for the next billing cycle to buy it. Knowing that she didn't have much money and was unlikely to pay down the card balance, I asked her how she would have enough available credit to buy the phone. She was puzzled by my question. When I clarified it, remarking that she'd have to at least partially pay off the card balance in order to garner enough credit to buy anything else, she was astonished. "I thought it just started over every month," she said. This smart young woman thought that she would magically have $1,000 every month available to spend and had never considered where that money came from or how it was paid for. After I explained to her that the money she charged to the card was a loan that she would have to pay back, she burst into tears.

Chloe was from a middle-class background with two loving, gainfully employed parents. Like many Americans they were living high on the hog and paycheck to paycheck with staggering credit card debt, a huge mortgage, two brand new cars, and no savings. She had never actually seen someone truly pay for something, nor had she internalized any messages about careful consumption. Consume what you want, whenever you want, was the cultural and familial message of her life. What chances did Chloe have when these forces were likely working in tandem with the powerful hormonal and neurochemical forces that put her at risk for substance abuse and overeating?

This reflects the prevailing American mind-set and the one that drives the consumer economy: that you don't have to pay for things in advance, or at least you don't have to know exactly how you will pay for something when you purchase or consume it, can be seen in myriad ways across the culture. The subprime mortgage phenomenon was about selling homes that were beyond the reach of consumers. In many cases, the homes were larger and more lavish than necessary to meet the families' needs, and the loans involved predatory practices that depended on scant financial savvy on the part of the consumer. The subprime lending fiasco likely could not have happened in a culture like Japan or Germany where government policies created and reinforced a widespread cultural belief that you must live below your means and save aggressively (Garon, 2012). Notice how there are similar mechanisms at work in the food industry as there are in the lending industry, all pressing us toward consuming more while obscuring the real cost of things. We can see this, for example, in the unrelenting food branding using the word "free." There are thousands of products branded as sugar-free or fat-free, all of which discourage accountability with the promise that consumption of the product somehow does not count.

The idea that everything must be paid for was lost in the transition from a pro-thrift to anti-thrift culture. History and accounting professor Jacob Soll (2014) has argued that stable, sustainable capitalism requires that individuals know how to do double-entry bookkeeping, that is, balance financial credits and debits in parallel columns. Tracing the history of this idea back through Weber and to the Italian Renaissance, he notes that this practice not only was fiscally sound, but was part of a larger moral accounting to God. Soll frames the rise and fall of great nations as a story of accounting. "At crucial moments accounting and accountability break down, adding to financial and political crises, if not creating them. The success of a society, at least financially, is, in great part, the mastery of accounting, accountability, and the ensuing struggle to successfully manage them" (p. xiv). I would expand on Soll's thinking and argue that the current accountability breakdown in the United States caused not only a financial and political crisis, but also a public health crisis by discouraging nutritional accountability. Caloric and financial reckoning are something we must all do to remain financially solvent and physically healthy—a kind of self-regulation governed by accounting principles that is in opposition to the powerful forces of consumer culture.

The entire development and marketing of hyperpalatable food could be thought of as another form of predatory "lending." With the predatory lending of subprime mortgages, the loans were sold to lower-income and less-educated folks who often had a history of material insecurity coupled with low financial literacy. Similarly, low-cost hyperpalatable foods are marketed and sold to many of the very same people who often have a history of food insecurity coupled with low nutritional literacy. With subprime mortgages they were sold an attractive product without fully realizing the long-term consequences of their consumption. The banks won by selling more and the consumers lost through mass foreclosures and the loss of their homes. In the case of hyperpalatable foods, the food industry wins by selling an enormous volume of their product and the consumer loses by becoming overweight, diabetic, and obese. That the food industry makes extraordinary profits while taxpayers and the government pay for the consequent public health crisis is simply another case of privatizing profits and socializing losses, just as we saw when the government bailed out the financial industry in 2008.

Those saddled by consumer debt and excess weight have been blindsided by thousands of cultural messages they've received in their lifetime. Countering these forces is incredibly hard work requiring vigilance, reflection, and impulse control, as well as a high level of knowledge of nutrition and finance. I do not dismiss the personal responsibility in the equation, but it would be a mistake not to identify the systematic cultural and regulatory failures that lead people down the road to financial and nutritional ruin. Such ruin has been disproportionately shouldered by the poor who inhabit the lower rung of the two-tiered economy, an experience of near-constant desperation mediated by a profound sense of scarcity that drives poor nutritional and financial decisions.

Not surprisingly, researchers have found a relationship between obesity and the likelihood of declaring bankruptcy, such that obese individuals are 22 percent more likely to declare bankruptcy than normal weight individuals (Guettabi & Munasib). The medical industry and the legal system have both created mechanisms for people who fall prey to the extremes of overeating and overspending: bariatric surgery and bankruptcy. The surgeon's knife or the judge's ruling can absolve us of from excess, but both of these interventions intervene at the individual level for problems that were created by the failures of consumerism *as an economic ideology* and *moral doctrine*. While these interventions serve as an extreme reset for those teetering on absolute ruin, neither solves the larger problem of the cultural and economic forces pushing us toward overconsumption. Not only that, but with both bariatric surgery and financial bankruptcy the individual is likely to experience incredible shame and stigma, and is also likely to experience the failure as personal or individual rather than as societal.

Again we see the effects of the post–World War II shift to the highly bounded Empty Self, in which problems are experienced and treated interiorly as individual pathology when in fact the disease infects the culture. If, however, we think about individual psychopathology as the final outcome of all that is wrong with a culture (Henry, 1963), then we can see that the extreme sufferers of bankruptcy and obesity serve as proxies in a struggle against widespread cultural toxicity. Philosopher Susan Bordo wrote, "I take the psychopathologies that develop within a culture, far from being anomalies or aberrations, to be characteristic expressions of that culture; to be, indeed, the crystallization of much that is wrong with it. For that reason such culture-bound syndromes are important to examine, as keys to cultural self-diagnosis and self-scrutiny" (1986, p. 229). We will return to this relationship between cultural and individual psychopathology in Chapter 8, examining how Binge Eating Disorder and Hoarding Disorder may be culture-bound syndromes which crystallize the ills of overconsumption.

Nutritional and financial illiteracy

Another contributing factor to today's widespread nutritional and financial illiteracy may be the demise of home economics and shop class as standard parts of the curriculum for young people. Gender-neutral home economics classes, when taught well, teach financial and nutritional literacy, cooking skills, prudent grocery shopping, and personal and household stewardship. Meanwhile, shop class connects people to their material culture by teaching how objects are designed, constructed, and repaired, as well as promoting a sense of agency or internal locus of control through the use of tools. There is evidence that both cooking and the use of tools have deep psychological importance to humans. In his recent book *Catching Fire: How Cooking Made Us Human* (2009), primatologist Richard Wrangham argues that cooking food, which began probably about 500,000 years ago, is what originally separated humans from apes and from our nonhuman ancestors. Our ancestors discovered that the control of fire could be used to cook food which offered crucial biological advantages, such as maximizing energy, impeding food spoilage, and improving overall food safety. The advantages to cooking food were not just biological. The social changes to human life were revolutionary. Gathering around a fire required socializing, and it calmed the human temperament, fostering cooperative living. Not only did cooking food become biologically and culturally important some 500,000 years ago, but it seems that it also became psychologically important to our species. As cooking, nourishment, and community became intertwined, the act of cooking and sharing meals likely became archetypal for humans. In other words, taming fire and using it to cook food not only had profound evolutionary consequences, but profound psychological consequences as well. We need to cook food to satisfy a deeply instinctual and uniquely human desire because cooking is what civilized the species (Lévi-Strauss, 1969).

Needless to say, the ultra-processed foods of the global industrial diet undermine the instinctive process of cooking and puts us out of touch with this essential human activity. The other facet of cooking besides fire is of course the use of tools, another behavior deeply embedded in human evolution and, I would argue, archetypal. In his book *Shop Class as Soul Craft* (2009), Matthew Crawford argues that the slow takeover of the intellectual economy and the outsourcing of most production have together conspired to withdraw us from the built material world. He writes, "A decline in tool use would seem to betoken a shift in our relationship to our own stuff: more passive and more dependent" (p. 2). In other words, buying prepared foods and objects rather than making and fixing things was part of the shift from an internal locus of control to an external locus of control in which we became consumers rather than creators and producers. When we relegate the assembly and production of consumer goods and foods to unseen others, we no longer know where things come from, whose hands they've passed through, what exploitation has been done to others, or what damage might be done to ourselves in consuming them. Over time, that has positioned us to passively and mindlessly metabolize the products presented to us, creating wealth for others while undermining our own health and agency.

At the same time, many of the calls for home cooking and eating whole food have rightly elicited criticism that such urgings are elitist and insensitive to the time scarcity and limited resources faced by the poor (Freedman, 2013; Heffernan, 2014). Certainly I agree that there is an undercurrent of elitism in many nutritional messages, but I simply don't buy that because someone is poor they can't prepare food at home. Cooking beans in a slow cooker and heating up some frozen vegetables requires less than ten minutes time to prepare and even less than that for cleanup. Even accounting for the tremendous time scarcity faced by many Americans, the argument that the poor cannot complete simple cooking tasks is both false and patronizing. Ultimately it creates a myth which encourages helplessness and serves to increase profits for food companies, all the while further entrenching an external locus of control in a great many people who feel powerless against the forces and conventions of consumerism. To that end, it is worth considering the many calls to revitalize gender-neutral home economics and shop class curricula (Bosch, 2012; Graham, 2013; McKenna, 2014; Phipott, 2013; Traister, 2014) to address some of the problems of nutritional and financial illiteracy.

Affluence, food, and consumer culture

In contrast to the poor, middle- and upper-class Americans have access to far higher quality food, but are by no means protected from overeating and overindulging. Not only did food science and marketing profoundly influence everyone's vulnerability to buying much of the wrong kinds of foods, but marketers have now developed highly sophisticated techniques to sell different brands to different income demographics. Just as the beverage industry markets cheap sugar-sweetened sodas to black children and teens, they market high-end versions of the same products to wealthy adults in the form of coconut water and cold-pressed juices. All of these branded products are access points into the culture of consumerism and act as status and identity markers. For the middle class it might be Doritos Locos, Yoplait yogurt, or Snickers ice cream bars. For the affluent, it may be Vosges chocolate, candied nut mixes, imported cheeses, or Italian gelato. It is this kind of consumerism *as a social ideology* in which products establish class distinctions such that material commodities fix the social position and prestige of their owners, or what Veblen (1899) referred to as "conspicuous consumption."

For much of the twentieth century, outside of immigrant-dense locations such as New York City, Americans across income strata ate very similar foods and shopped at similar grocery stores, which stocked mostly similar products, excepting for slight regional differences. A Piggly Wiggly in Louisiana might have carried more hot sauces than an IGA in Massachusetts, and the IGA might have carried Old Bay Seasoning or real maple syrup, but once supermarkets began to sell nearly 70 percent of America's food, almost all stores had a very similar inventory to each other (Humphery, 1998), thereby homogenizing the American refrigerator in most parts of the country and across most income groups. More recently, however, increased prosperity, increased spending, and a new face of urbanization have changed grocery stores and consumers' expectations of them.

Increasing income inequality has led to highly concentrated geographic concentrations of wealth called "Superzips," that is, zip codes that are comprised of residents in the top 5th percentile of education and income (Murray, 2013). This demographic has created a huge market for luxury foods and luxury food stores, such as Dean & DeLuca, Williams-Sonoma, and Whole Foods Market. There are now 882 Superzips across the United States that enable these luxury markets, which explains the expansion of Whole Foods Market into places like Boise, Idaho. The proliferation of such stores as part of widespread "affluenza" has resulted in the inevitable outcome of what I call "luxury food fever" among wealthier Americans.

Whole Foods Market is an excellent case study by which to examine luxury food fever, and it is a store I know well. I grew up a few blocks away from the original Whole Foods Market at 12th and Lamar in my hometown of Austin, Texas. In the 1980s, Whole Foods was a modest health food store, smelling of patchouli and populated by hairy Birkenstock-wearing men and women. There was a vegetarian cafe that served unappealing green juice and every food dish was served with an obscenely high pile of alfalfa sprouts atop. There was no sugar or salt to be found anywhere. Fast-forward to 2014 and the flagship Whole Foods Market, a few blocks away from the quaint original location, is 80,000 square feet and is colloquially referred to as "whole paycheck," referring to its very expensive prices.

FIGURE 4.2 *The original Whole Foods Market (1980) at 12th and Lamar in Austin, TX.*

It would have been very difficult to get fat, or even to overeat anything from the original Whole Foods Market—the "whole" foods they sold simply did not have the right components to trigger overeating. Today's Whole Foods, however, sells extraordinary amounts of luxury junk food such as candy coated nuts, kettle chips, and chocolate covered pretzels. In fact, I would

FIGURE 4.3 *The flagship Whole Foods Market (2014) at 12th and Lamar in Austin, TX.*

argue that the very name Whole Foods has become a misnomer, given the large quantities of ultra-processed and refined foods they now sell. The health philosophy on the website for Whole Foods Market states that they "provide food and nutritional products that support health and well-being," that they are "committed to foods that are fresh, wholesome and safe to eat," and that they "define quality by evaluating the ingredients, freshness, safety, taste, nutritive value and appearance" of all of the products they carry. However, a visit to any Whole Foods Market reveals that it sells just as much junk food as conventional grocery stores—often presented as expensive items in fancy packages.

Food sold by these luxury food stores tends to be packaged as small special foods, so quality over quantity is emphasized as part of the luxury experience, appealing to cultural narcissism and elitism. The branding and status connotations might change but the main ingredients in the foods are the same: sugar, refined grains, fat, and salt. These shoppers are often not looking to stretch their dollar, but to indulge in a status food experience. In a recent blog post, the market research firm The Hartman Group asked whether Whole Foods Market should move "downmarket"? Noting that the chain has more recently tried to appeal to shoppers in midmarket zip codes, it asks whether this practice is "diluting a brand long associated with affluence and high quality," and cites the success of Trader Joe's as proof that "you can go deep into midmarket households while sustaining a quality, upmarket halo" (Hartman Group, 2014). In theoretical terms, what this market research firm is asking is whether or not Whole Foods can increase sales without compromising the store's ability to offer a salient means of class distinction, social position, and prestige for its primary consumers (Bourdieu, 2010; Veblen, 1899).

In their interviews with Whole Foods Market shoppers, Canadian researchers Johnston and Szabo (2011) found that in spite of Whole Foods' stated mission, consumers were motivated by "traditional consumer pleasures," such as convenience and product selection. Interviewees cited the aesthetic appeal of the store, describing it in terms of luxury and indulgence. The researchers noted that while some participants identified ethical consumption as a reason for shopping at Whole Foods, this was overshadowed by reasons that fit conveniently with existing consumer habits, such as accommodating car-centered lifestyles and selling prepared foods for busy professionals. The metamorphosis of Whole Foods Market is an illuminating case study in what has happened in the United States in the past several decades in terms of increased spending power, luxury fever, food marketing, and the emergence of food as a class marker. Whole Foods Market as we now know it simply could not have existed forty years ago.

There weren't enough people with the right tastes and the deep pockets needed to support such a store.

While certainly Whole Foods does sell many healthy items, and very importantly they screen their products for unsafe ingredients, they may be just as guilty as any other grocer for promoting the hyperpalatable foods that make us fat. By contrast, truly encouraging people to eat whole foods would serve to *decrease* overall consumption, something no store wants, simply because by eating whole foods we feel full sooner and have fewer cravings (Clark & Slavin, 2013; Flood-Obbagy & Rolls, 2009; Slavin, 2005; Slavin & Lloyd, 2012). In fact, stores that only sold fresh fish, meats, produce, dairy, and few packaged foods would have trouble competing with these luxury "natural food" stores. That is essentially what farmers' markets are and they certainly come nowhere near the level of profitability that the luxury supermarkets do. Instead, Whole Foods Market along with most of the food industry uses sophisticated and clever packaging, marketing, language, and advertising to manipulate people into consuming more. How they do that and why we let them is the story of the next chapter.

5

How the Food Industry Uses Psychology to Trick Us (and Why We Let Them)

There is a voluminous literature on the methods used by advertisers and marketers to sell products, ranging from early accounts of Madison Avenue ad men to the current study of neuromarketing. Many such accounts portray market researchers and advertisers as nefarious manipulators, but that's only half the story. Certainly it is true that the food industry in particular creates, markets, and brands seductive and addictive products, but we also collude with them via self-deception, allowing ourselves to be "tricked" so that we can have what we want. With the notable exception of children, no matter how little education someone has, no matter how little nutritional literacy one has, there is still common sense. None of us is forced to eat junk food and it doesn't take a college degree or even a high school diploma to know that an apple is healthier than a donut. It is with this in mind that this chapter explores the tension between the manipulative, often deceptive practices of the food industry and how our psychological defenses allow us to be led down that path of seduction.

The tricks

Taste, variety, and convenience

The food industry must constantly convince people to eat more in order to satisfy its stockholders (Nestle, 2002), and to accomplish this they use the work of both market researchers and experimental psychologists to study class demographics, effective branding techniques (Gabriel & Lang,

2006, p. 32), and the contextual and environmental cues that increase eating (Logue, 2004; Wansink, 2006). I focus here on only a small fraction of these techniques, namely the creation of irresistible convenient foods, the increase of variety and choice, the creation of public confusion about nutritional science, and the appeal to class, gender, and age-based desires.

Palatability

Palatability refers to the pleasure or "hedonic reward" provided by foods or fluids, and it is the strongest predictor of food choice (Aikman, Min, & Graham, 2006; Drichoutis, Lazaridis, & Nayga, 2006). Until the 1980s, most food researchers studying palatability examined only sweetness as the single factor, then Adam Drewnowski began to look at how the combination of sweetness and fat increased hedonic reward (1983). More recently, the newer term "hyperpalatability" has been used to refer to the high sugar, high fat, and often high salt foods manufactured by the food industry (Moss, 2013), which inevitably makes us eat more foods high in sugar, fat, and salt (Kessler, 2009).

Related to the concept of "hyperpalatability" is "bliss point," a construct developed by experimental psychologist Howard Moskowitz. Moskowitz optimizes the flavors of foods through sophisticated taste tests and mathematical modeling and has discovered that desirable tastes like sugar have a threshold or tipping point for most people, after which point continuing to add more of that ingredient diminishes the food's palatability (Moskowitz, 1981). With his market research and modeling techniques, Moskowitz is able to determine the exact point at which sugar, salt, and fat reach the ideal convergence of hedonic reward, a neurological point which he termed "bliss point." Using the incredibly sophisticated science of bliss point, food scientists now devote their professional lives to creating the irresistible flavors and mouthfeel of chips, ice creams, chicken nuggets, and energy drinks. This is of course why so many food commercials use slogans such as "I can't believe I ate the whole thing!" Usually when we can't believe we ate the whole thing it's because our brains registered a portion size that looked too big, but once we started eating the bliss point was activated and we consumed more than imaginable. Eating the whole thing also usually means that we never willingly stopped eating—we stopped because the food was gone, suggesting that it never made us feel full or that it tasted so good we didn't care that we were full.

Variety

Not only do these manufactured foods taste really good, but there are so many to choose from. Recall that one of the hallmarks of modern consumer culture is the vast expansion and glorification of choice—the more choice, the more freedom, the more happiness (Schwartz, 2004). Choice is one of the key contextual factors in overeating. People eat less when they have fewer food choices due to "sensory-specific satiety," that is, when our senses become numbed after continuous exposure to the same stimuli (Inman, 2001). By contrast, we eat more when we have more choice, even when those choices differ only visually and not in actual flavor. For example, Dr. Barbara Rolls' team at Penn State showed that if people are offered an assortment of yogurt with three different flavors, they're likely to consume an average of 23 percent more than if offered only one flavor (Rolls et al., 1981). Similarly, Brian Wansink and his colleagues found that when people have more M&M colors to choose from they will eat more, even though all M&M's are the same flavor (Kahn & Wansink, 2004). Needless to say, the proliferation of ultra-processed flavors and products provides a staggering variety of choices, colors, and flavors, with the average grocery store now carrying over 43,000 items (Food Marketing Institute, 2012). In other words, grocers, advertisers, and food scientists increase consumption by undermining the power of sensory-specific satiety in their offering of so much variety.

By contrast are the many cultures with less variety and fewer choices. For example, a few years ago I went on a university trip to Cuba. Our first meal after we arrived was a simple lunch of roast chicken and beet salad. I absolutely love beets and hadn't had any fresh ones for some time. "Beets!," I exclaimed when I saw them and quickly decided I would just eat beet salad and nothing else for lunch. They looked so delicious that I didn't want to miss out on having as many as possible. At dinner, beets made another appearance. Wow, twice in a row! Thinking myself very lucky, I ate quite a lot of beets again, only to find them on the breakfast table the next morning. And at lunch the next afternoon. Of course Cuba is an island that engages in very little trade due to the US embargo. Because of its fecundity and tropical location, it produces a bounty of fruits and vegetables such that Cubans eat only local seasonal produce as all humans once did. So when beets are in season you will eat a lot of them, as I surely did when they continued to appear at breakfast, lunch, and dinner for the entire two-week trip. Although I knew about sensory-specific satiety in theory, I quickly learned experientially that when you eat the same thing at every meal you are far less likely to overeat because of the decreased variety.

Convenience

Another factor that makes us eat more is our sense of time scarcity. Along with reconfiguring our sense of selves, modernization and industrialization have resulted in powerful changes in our concept of time. In his essay on American cuisine, anthropologist Sidney Mintz argues that Americans do not, and likely will not, have a cuisine of our own in the traditional sense of the term, largely because of our notion of time (1996). He argues that Americans are repeatedly told (and strongly believe) that they are so busy that they have little or no time to spare. In turn, this serves to increase aggregate consumption with the astonishing variety of time-saving products and foods. "Most convenience food," he writes, "is successful because of prior conceptions about time. But most such food would not succeed if Americans cared more about how and what they ate" (p. 121).

Buffets, fast food, and ultra-processed convenience foods respond to and sustain the myth that there is no time.[1] In fact, the aforementioned researchers in the *Life at Home in the 21st Century* project (Arnold, 2012) found that in spite of minimal time dining together American families' buying habits strongly reflect an urge to save time. Families stockpiled food, often in huge packages of drinks, soups, snacks, and ice cream from warehouse stores such as Costco and Sam's Club which often required second refrigerators to store. Contrary to the families' belief that these foods saved time, on average they reduced evening meal preparation time by only five minutes, a statistically insignificant savings. In other words, families' anxiety that they had no time was expressed through buying more things and needing more storage (consuming), yet those behaviors did not have the intended consequence of saving time. In another self-defeating cycle, the families turned toward increased consumerism, that is, buying convenience foods as a solution to a problem that is caused by consumerism—that is, the sense of having no time.

Similarly, researchers in 2008 surveyed people who ate at fast-food restaurants and found that 92 percent said it's because the restaurants are quick, 53 percent said they were too busy to cook, and 44 percent said that they did not like to prepare foods for themselves. By contrast, 67 percent of respondents strongly disagreed that eating at fast-food restaurants was a way to socialize with friends and family and 79 percent disagreed that the restaurants had nutritious foods to offer (Rydell et al., 2008). Today, the average American spends only twenty-seven minutes a day on food preparation (Pollan, 2009, p. 3) and Harvard economist and Obama Health Adviser David Cutler found that we eat more when we don't cook the food ourselves. "As the amount of time Americans spend cooking has dropped by about half, the number of meals Americans eat in a day has climbed; since 1977, we've added approximately half a meal to our daily intake" (Pollan, 2009, p. 7).

---

[1] Here, I am speaking primarily of middle- and upper-class Americans, whereas for the working poor "time poverty" is not a myth nor a construction, but a reality that has emerged from wage stagnation and increased cost of living (Mullainathan & Shafir, 2013).

Interestingly, Cutler and his colleagues surveyed cooking patterns across several cultures and found that obesity rates are inversely correlated with the amount of time spent on food preparation (Cutler, Glaeser, & Shapiro, 2003). Although it might seem like more time in the kitchen could yield a higher caloric intake, home-cooked food seems to mediate caloric intake, probably because of the simple fact that cooking at home is unlikely to produce hyperpalatable foods or the increased variety implicated in overeating.

There is nothing inherently wrong with enjoying a variety of tasty and convenient foods—for most of us, life without them would be a dismal form of asceticism. In fact, it is taste, variety, and convenience that ensured the survival of our ancestors. Tastiness signals safe, fresh sources of energy. Variety ensures that we consume a necessary array of micro and macro nutrients. Convenience ensures that we do not expend more energy obtaining food than the calories it provides. So while noting that taste, variety, and convenience have come to make us vulnerable to overeating, it is important not to throw the baby out with the bathwater and conclude that the pleasures of food and eating are inherently problematic.

Mind games

While hyperpalatability, increased variety, and convenience form the foundation of how the food industry convinces us to eat more, there are also countless other powerful techniques in their arsenal, all of which I would broadly chalk up to "mind games." These are very deliberate methods developed through sophisticated and often secret research experiments designed to sow consumer confusion, distort science, manufacture previously unknown needs, and cater to our fantasies of specialness.

Health halos

Recall that a health halo is when a relative nutritional claim such as "low-fat" serves to increase our food intake by distorting perceptions of appropriate serving size and decreasing anticipation of consumer guilt. For example, when eating at restaurants such as Subway, which presents itself as a healthy alternative to other fast food, consumers underestimate the number of calories contained in their main dishes and consequently order higher-calorie side dishes, drinks, and desserts (Chandon & Wansink, 2007). In more psychological terms, we might think of health halos as activating a kind of unconscious rationalization in which we use a "good" behavior to justify a "bad" one. Similarly, research has found that when people think of a three mile walk as a workout instead of a means of transportation they eat more later (Werle, Wansink, & Payne, 2014), presumably because they feel justified after the virtuous behavior of exercise. Such findings suggest that there are complex unconscious forces making moral decisions about consumption in which virtue and pleasure hang in balance. Marketers and advertisers exploit this by using health halos to peddle their products, most absurdly in cases like fat-free gummy bears (Nickerson, 2013).

One of the most insidious uses of health halos is by the supplement industry which has a lengthy history of selling ostensibly healthy products based on weak or bogus claims (Nestle, 2002). Most recently this industry has discovered that it can sell vitamins and supplements in the form of candy, using health halos to create such wolves in sheep's clothing. This started with the chocolate-flavored calcium supplements Viactiv and then quickly developed into a large array of sugar-sweetened gummy vitamins, often for children. Now GNC makes an Omega 3 supplement that is remarkably like a Starburst fruit chew and there are countless gummy vitamins and supplements for adults. Not only are the health benefits claimed by these products scientifically unproven, to the contrary, many of them contain sugar and artificial sweeteners which *do* have a proven record of harmful effects. How the supplement industry is legally permitted to get away with this is the story of Chapter 10.

The sales of many of the luxury junk foods I mentioned in Chapter 4 also rely on health halos, either by invoking an explicit health claim on their label or simply by mentioning a trendy ingredient perceived to be healthy, such as acai berry, green tea, or quinoa. In fact, stores such as Whole Foods Market which sell many of these products use their name and reputation to cast a health halo just by virtue of the product being sold at that store. In other words, the very name "Whole Foods Market" arguably casts a health halo on all of the products it sells, leading consumers to believe that anything they buy there is healthy. To the contrary, Whole Foods Market was recently accused of falsely advertising baked goods such as banana muffins, chocolate chip cookies, and apple pie as "all natural," when the products actually contained synthetic chemical ingredients such as sodium acid pyrophosphate and maltodextrin (Garrison v. Whole Foods Market Inc., 2013).

Yet the marketers of upscale foods continue to exploit health halos to sell more and charge more for their products. For example, in a white paper by the Hartman Group they report, "In a perplexing twist, upmarket consumers are simultaneously driving growth in high-fat-content categories such as olive oil and high-sweetness categories such as honey. The apparent contradiction is part of the complexity of upmarket shifts in food culture. Unprocessed sources of fattiness and sweetness are allowed a backdoor pass." What they are saying is that high fat, high sugar products perceived as "natural" have strong sales in luxury health markets and may be perceived as healthier than comparable fats and sweeteners like sugar or corn oil. While there may in fact be some very good reasons to consume olive oil and honey over sugar and corn oil, the point here is that they have metabolically similar effects which can be obscured by casting them with a marketing health halo. Hartman goes on to advise, "The future is about making trends in food based on desire, play and possibility made possible by unprecedented affluence at the upper end of the market ..... Why not upsell consumers who want to be upsold?" (Hartman Group, 2014). Here we see how marketers use both health halos and the modern hedonism of desire to create the limitless needs of consumer culture, all the while ignoring nutritional wisdom in order to sell more products.

Hyperpersonalization

Marketing foods to special groups such as women, moms, kids, or athletes also serves to make us eat more. Luna Bars and Activia yogurt are two examples of "foods for women" that use the imagery of affluent, slender, mostly white women in yoga poses to suggest that their products have special health benefits different than other yogurts or processed bars. Other industries use similar tricks. For example, in 2001, the pharmaceutical company Eli Lilly was able to secure FDA approval to sell a drug called Serafem for so-called Premenstrual Dysphoric Disorder, a proposed disorder that was highly controversial among scientists and not yet included in psychiatry's diagnostic manual. Commercials for Serafem promised to make you "more like the woman you are" and featured women who appeared highly functional, but slightly cranky, dealing with problems such as having two grocery carts stuck together or misplacing their keys when they had to get to an important business meeting. What was not evident to most women who saw these commercials and went on to take the medication themselves was that Serafem was simply pink Prozac. Serafem was nothing more than fluoxetine (Prozac) which had been recolored and rebranded for a new market. For Eli Lilly, the target audience for this campaign was an untapped market—affluent women with private insurance who were unlikely to buy Prozac because they weren't depressed, but who nevertheless struggled with garden-variety premenstrual irritability and frustration (Koerner, 2002).

Food manufacturers too are constantly looking for ways to develop products that appeal to specific demographic groups. For example, a recent industry white paper reported that with the number of consumers over age 60 expected to double by the year 2050, soft drink manufacturers are beginning to think about the elderly as a new source of sales (Robinson, 2014). The beverage industry is now working to develop more "functional" drinks with "anti-aging" properties that are packaged in ways that are easy to carry and pour for older individuals (Canadean, 2014).

Another such trend in personalized marketing is a phenomenon known as mass customization (Gilmore & Pine, 1997) or what I call the hyperpersonalization movement, in which advertisers appeal to our highly individualized desires and preferences. I first began to notice this trend in Starbucks cafes. As I once waited for a cup of coffee, I heard the barista call out an elaborate drink ready for pickup: "Tall, skinny, decaf white mocha with whip," she hollered. I felt slightly embarrassed for the person who ordered the drink, thinking that she probably didn't expect to have it shouted out for everyone to hear. I gave her a knowing and sympathetic smile, as if to reassure her that I too understood the shame of retrieving an overly complicated drink. It reminded me of a scene in the 1991 movie *L.A. Story*, in which the characters are at a brunch in an upscale restaurant ordering coffee. They go around the table ordering: "I'll have a decaf coffee." "I'll have a decaf espresso." "I'll have a double decaf cappuccino." "Do you have any decaffeinated coffee ice cream?" The scene culminates with Steve Martin's punch line, "I'll have a half double decaffeinated half cap with a twist of lemon" (Martin, 1991). The scene was funny at the time because of its mockery of the demanding, affluent Los Angeles residents who were very different than most Americans in their tastes. I am not sure the scene would be funny to the viewers today because there would be little point of contrast—much of the culture has skewed in this direction.

Around the same time that Starbucks began promoting these hyperpersonalized drinks, Apple came out with the iMac and the iPhone, names which conveyed that you didn't haven't to yield your individuality to a boring and colorless operating system or device. Your friendly and colorful device could be an expression of your identity—an extension of "I." Shortly after Apple introduced the iMac and the iPhone, an avalanche of products with "i," "me," or "my" in their name hit the marketplace. Likewise, standing in a Starbucks today you'll hear a chorus of lengthy hyperpersonalized drinks shouted out from the counter. Recognizing the selling power of hyperpersonalization, Starbucks now advertises "drink how you want it ... " with the Starbucks UK website proudly claiming that there are a total of 87,000 drink combinations that could be ordered at one of their outlets (Starbucks UK, 2014). This degree of indulgence, this constant elevation of the self, gives us the illusion that our desires are actually needs. More importantly, this practice of hyperpersonalization serves to increase overall consumption, otherwise companies such as Starbucks would not allocate huge amounts of labor and money in their catering to these preferences.

Nutritional confusion

The sowing of nutritional confusion is probably the oldest trick in the book used by the food industry. Not only is the creation of nutritional confusion used by the food industry, but also by trusted nutrition organizations that are in fact under the strong financial and political influence of Big Food (Nestle, 2001). The food industry regularly creates and exploits other kinds of nutritional confusion to increase its sales. I've had many patients in my clinical practice say that they encounter so much conflicting nutritional information that they no longer know what they are supposed to eat. For example, one of my patients recently told me that she was ordering breakfast in a cafe and initially planned to have a sausage and egg breakfast sandwich. It was the lowest calorie item on the menu and seemed to have a fair amount of protein which she thought would satisfy her until lunch. She had second thoughts, however, because sausage and other ground meats are often of questionable origin, raising food safety concerns. She then decided to switch her order to a ham and cheese breakfast sandwich which had a slightly higher calorie count, but contained no ground meat. Still waiting for her turn to order, she began to doubt the wisdom of that choice because of the nitrates used in processed meats that have been associated with a higher risk of cancer. She then decided that maybe she should switch to oatmeal, but the oatmeal was very high in carbohydrates and had a high sugar content. Throwing in the towel, she finally ordered a danish because it looked the tastiest. We've all faced similar paralysis with nutritional choices and this confusion is largely promoted or created by the food industry itself. It's a problem of the culture of consumerism in which products must distinguish themselves from others in order to sell, yet the constant advertising meant to distinguish products obscures the truth. The consequent confusion then allows for more marketing opportunities in which businesses can "solve" the problem of confusion by declaring their product above the fray.

The use of the term "natural" on food labels, for example, exploits the health halo phenomenon and appeals to our desire for wholesomeness (National Consumers League, 2012). This term is big business, too. In 2009, the word *natural* was the most frequently used claim on new US food products (Lukovitz, 2009) and in 2014, natural foods constituted a $40 billion per year industry (Negowetti, 2014). Unlike the term "organic" which is highly regulated and has a specific legal definition, the term "natural" is largely unregulated and food manufacturers can use it freely to mean whatever they want (Food and Drug Law Institute, 2014). By using the term "natural" food manufacturers exploit nutritional confusion and exhaustion by offering a product in which we don't have to read the label, count calories, or investigate its provenance because we are assured of its wholesomeness through that one simple term. A recent *Consumer Reports* survey, for example, found that consumers falsely believed that products labeled as *natural* have no artificial ingredients, pesticides, or genetically modified ingredients and were willing to pay more for those foods (Olsen, 2014). As I will further discuss in Chapter 10, the food industry has strongly resisted efforts to regulate the use of the term "natural" on food labels, arguing that it is subjective and would not be possible to define.

These confusion tactics work, as I recently witnessed when visiting a friend who is a health-conscious neuropsychologist and mother of two. She mentioned casually that she doesn't buy any foods with high fructose corn syrup (HFCS) for her kids, but she does buy them Gogurts, chocolate chip granola bars, fig newtons, and fruit roll-ups, all highly sugar-sweetened products. I asked her what she saw as the difference between HFCS and sugar and she replied, "Well, sugar is natural!" I was surprised she held this belief, but I understand why. The sugar industry has long used the perceived "naturalness" of sugar to denigrate artificial sweeteners and even to cannibalize its own market share of products using high fructose corn syrup. Far from natural, though, white table sugar is highly concentrated and refined, and more importantly has the same metabolic effects as HFCS (Rippe & Angelopoulos, 2013). Advertisers and market researchers, however, have jumped on the misperception that sugar is natural and used it to promote the idea that sugar is therefore healthier. Pepsi, for example, recently launched a new campaign extolling "Made with real sugar!"

Honey, too, has similar metabolic effects as sugar, as does turbinado sugar, maple syrup, sugar in the raw, demerara sugar, brown rice syrup, and the countless other kinds of sugar masquerading as natural or healthy (Duffy & Anderson, 1998; White, 2008, 2009). In fact, because the FDA's labeling requirements allow these different sugars to be listed as separate ingredients on package labels, there is an incentive for food manufacturers to use multiple, similar sweeteners in their formulations, creating the illusion that sugar is not the first ingredient. Actually, food scientists' creation of over fifty-six different kinds of sugar (Lustig, 2013) with nonobvious names such as dextran, fruit juice concentrate, treacle, and maltose tricks the average consumer who is simply looking for the word "sugar" at the top a list of ingredients to evaluate how healthy a product is.

Not only does the food industry try to convince us that sugar is natural, but it has gone so far as to suggest that we could die without it. In a recent feeble attempt to counter the emerging research on the ill-effects of sugar, Coca-Cola Vice President and Chief Scientific and Regulatory Officer Dr. Rhona Applebaum sent out a tweet warning that a sugar-free diet "could kill you," citing an article in the *Daily Mail*. Dr. Applebaum did not provide the context of the original article which was that scientists were commenting on the dangers of an extremely low carbohydrate diet comprised of only meat and fat. These scientists specifically stated that it was a diet absent of *naturally* occurring sugars found in milk, nuts, and fruits, and not the added sugars in Coca-Cola products that could be fatal. It is impossible to believe that someone whose title is "Chief Scientific and Regulatory Officer" would genuinely believe that she was tweeting scientifically valid public health information. This was clearly an alarmist manipulation to perpetuate fear mongering and confusion in order to increase profits.

The hydration lie

Similar practices can be seen in what I call the "hydration lie" and it is this campaign that has ushered in the culture of drinks, which I will discuss further in the next chapter. On its website, the American Beverage Association tells us that "drinking fluids is absolutely essential" and that "they are needed to control body temperature and transport oxygen and other essential nutrients to our cells…. We are constantly losing water through breathing, perspiring and through urine. We need to replace these fluids to stay hydrated and healthy" (American Beverage Association, 2014). Industry created the hydration lie along with the accompanying phony "science of hydration," telling us that we must be constantly concerned about dehydration and preempt its effects by "prehydrating." We should prehydrate, they say, not by drinking tap water, but by drinking bottled water, juice, sports drinks, and ready-to-drink teas and soft drinks—in other words, drinks that cost money, come in single-use plastic bottles, and are usually sugar sweetened. If a savvy consumer were to question whether or not it's a good idea to drink a soda to prevent dehydration, the same website goes on to assure them that "water is the predominant ingredient in carbonated soft drinks. Regular soft drinks are made up of 90 percent water and diet soft drinks with zero calories are 99 percent water."

What the real science on hydration says, however, is that there is no need for prehydration (Noakes, 2012b). The human body was designed to get thirsty to prevent dehydration, so drinking *after* you feel thirsty should work as well as it has for the course of human history. Not only that, but the onset and effects of dehydration are far less grave than the beverage industry would have you believe. In fact, one scientist remarked that you'd have to be lost in a desert without water for more than forty-eight hours before suffering the disabling effects of dehydration (Noakes, 2012b). The sports drink industry, however, has created and perpetuated the fear of dehydration (Noakes, 2012a) by creating a staggering number of usually sugar-sweetened sports drinks and beverages, in spite of the very few reported cases of athletes suffering severe dehydration even in long endurance competitions such as marathons (Cohen, 2012).

If we look to a website for a food industry event called Sports Nutrition 2014, it describes the $30 billion sports nutrition market as one that is comprised of products for "sports people from amateurs to pros—and those that buy them for lifestyle and other reasons." The program states that the sports nutrition market holds "seemingly limitless opportunity" and the event promises to answer the question: "Who buys sports nutrition products other than sports people?" Therein lies the limitless opportunity: the marketing of sports nutrition to consumers *other than* sports people by offering a fantasy of athleticism via products which paradoxically undermine fitness and health. Again, we see the relentless cycle of consumption in which we gain weight by overconsuming and then are told that in order to lose weight we need to exercise, buy special food, and drink special drinks, most of which are full of sugar and cost a lot of money.

Distant cousins to these sports drinks are coconut water and other "natural waters," such as maple, birch, barley, cactus, and artichoke waters. These beverages promise the same hydration and electrolyte repletion as traditional sports drinks, but they also bring a health halo of other benefits by virtue of their supposed naturalness. Global sales of coconut water alone now reach $400 million a year (Moss, 2014), and the race is on to find the next natural water blockbuster. Pepsi is gambling on cashew juice as it buys up mass quantities of cashew apples across India. The sudden interest in cashew apples is much to the puzzlement of the farmers, who have historically discarded the fruit after retrieving the nut because it ferments quickly and has a tannic, acrid taste (Strom, 2014). In this particular case, the investment in a new product may have the benefit of reducing food waste (or at least making use of a previously discarded food source), but the larger point is that tremendous resources go into the research and development of prospective blockbuster products, often relying on health halos and nutritional confusion among the general public.

Offering slightly different benefits than sports drinks and natural waters are the energy drinks such as Red Bull and Rock Star, which promise alertness and increased focus. Energy drink sales in the United States are currently at $12.2 dollars per year and are expected to rise to $13.5 dollars in the next two years (IEG, 2012). Many of these drinks offer little more than the benefits of a cup of coffee, but they are sold at a much higher price. The manufacturers are able to get away with this practice by artificially creating a medicinal taste in the formulations, thereby creating a placebo effect in which the consumer feels as though they are receiving some sort of tonic or treatment. In fact, market researchers have found that if they test Red Bull on consumers who don't know it's supposed to be an energy drink, they give it terrible ratings because of its odd taste. Conversely, when consumers test an energy drink with a simple fruity taste and no "medicinal note" they give it very low ratings, presumably because they don't believe it could be an effective energy treatment if it tastes so good (Khatchadourian, 2009). All of these fruity and medicinal flavors are pure invention and are not tied to any real medicine or real fruit. The flavors are chemical illusions created in a laboratory as a way to manufacture desire. The consumer desire for products which promise increased energy is so great that manufacturers have now developed energy toothpaste (Starling, 2014).

Exploiting moms and kids

The food industry has a long history of exploiting mothers and children to increase their sales at the expense of good nutrition and common sense. One of the most troubling and poignant examples of this was how the makers of infant formula convinced mothers, especially poor uneducated ones, to forgo the clearly superior practice of breast feeding in favor of manufactured formula. They did this by convincing health professionals to promote their products and by targeting illiterate women through word of mouth, billboards, and picture books, implying that formula might be superior to breast milk (Nestle, 2002). Such exploitative strategies continue today as Big Food continually targets advertising and marketing to moms, knowing that mothers are most often the nutritional gatekeepers of the household. For example, the food giant Monsanto recently paid "Mommy bloggers" $150 each to attend "an intimate and interactive panel" (Lappé, 2014), which was clearly designed to court a powerful force in social media. Mommy blogs reach a wide audience and hold enormous potential for marketers because the bloggers are viewed as objective and credible sources for nutritional recommendations. When the food industry persuades mommy bloggers to post favorable messages about their products, they reach a huge audience with a message that does not seem like a commercial.

In addition to pandering to moms, there is a lengthy history of marketing junk food directly to kids, which could not occur without the myth that kids should eat special foods that are fun, come with a toy, or be cut into exciting shapes (Mustain, 2014). Children's developmental naiveté makes them vulnerable to consumer messages so much so that research shows that many children cannot distinguish between television programming and paid advertising (Carter, Patterson, Donovan, Ewing, & Roberts, 2011). Increasingly, however, the line between commercials and programming are blurred as corporations pay for product placement in regular television shows, games, and movies, seamlessly blending advertising with entertainment narrative and thereby further obscuring what constitutes an ad. Market researchers also deliberately advertise products to children to create the "nag factor," that is, the potential an advertisement has to get kids to nag their parents to buy them what they want (Linn, 2004). Such ads create a private communication between a corporation and a child, circumventing parents who are unlikely to be watching cartoons or children's programming. Such advertisements are prohibited or restricted in most countries, but the United States has no restrictions on advertisements directed to children of any age (American Academy of Pediatrics, 2006).

When Kraft Foods executive Michael Mudd was asked what he thought was an appropriate age for children to view television ads, he responded that six years was an appropriate age, and that kids at this age are "more mature" and "have more judgment" (ABC News, 2003). It was also Kraft Foods that developed the blockbuster product Lunchables with CEO Bob Eckert stating, "Lunchables aren't about lunch. It's about kids being able to put together what they want to eat, anytime, anywhere" (Moss, 2013). Further promoting children's autonomy in nutritional decision-making, one of the early Lunchables commercials proclaimed, "All day, you gotta do what they say, but lunchtime is all yours." Call me old-fashioned, but in my world no six-year-old has any time that's all theirs, absent of parental supervision or influence.

The devil made me do it (or why we let them)

The existential psychologists I mentioned in Chapter 3 spoke directly to personal responsibility and accountability as the nexus of our psychological well-being. Freedom, they argued, comes with the burden that we must all be accountable for our actions and ourselves. In fact, these existentialists rejected Freud's earlier drive theory in which he argued that behavior is driven by unconscious biological forces, because they viewed it as an overly deterministic model which minimized personal responsibility. Freud's model of the unconscious, in turn, had been strongly influenced by the work of Darwin and was itself a rejection of the repressive Victorian culture in which the self was experienced as an agent of God, rather than as a member of the animal world governed by the dark and primitive forces of sexuality and aggression. Considering the zeitgeist in which each of these models emerged, we can see the phenomenological evolution of the self, shifting from a Victorian self characterized by a deeply religious collective identity, to a more secular and psychological Freudian self, and finally to the highly individualized, bounded, masterful or Empty Self we experience today.

There is no doubt that the food industry stops at nothing in deception and exploitation to sell products, but placing all of the blame for overeating on it obscures our collusion, perhaps absolving our consciences for bad decision-making. Yet positioning ourselves as hapless victims of industry is dehumanizing and ultimately undermines our sense of agency. Understanding some of the complex, unconscious mechanisms which mediate our collusion in nutritional deception is central to combatting it, and it is with this in mind that the second half of this chapter examines how our psychological defenses allow us to be led down the path of seduction.

Health halos as denial and rationalization

Health halos are more than just the explicit nutritional claims made by manufacturers, but also ways that our imaginations unconsciously imbue foods with healthy properties, allowing us to conveniently deny their unhealthy properties. Such denial and self-deception allow us to anoint foods with properties in order to assuage our own guilt and justify our indulgences. In other words, health halos are both cognitive distortions and psychological defenses.

A few years ago, for example, my husband and I were on vacation and wandered into a bakery looking for a treat. We asked the young woman behind the counter what she recommended. She said that the cinnamon rolls and chocolate croissants were the most popular items, but that if we were looking for something healthy then we might want the carrot cupcakes because they had carrots and raisins in them. Sadly, adding a few ounces of carrots and raisins won't turn a frosted confection of sugar, flour, butter, and sweetened cream cheese into something healthy. Much like Allison uses juicing to psychologically "undo" the ill-effects of fast food, it is tempting to take one healthy ingredient and use it to tell ourselves that it makes the rest of the item healthy.

Along similar lines, a friend recently sent me an email asking if I had a good cupcake recipe, "preferably for the healthy kind." I was puzzled by her request and it surprised me that there is any notion of a healthy cupcake floating around. I sent her my favorite cupcake recipe and teasingly said, "for a healthier version, omit sugar, butter, and flour." The joke, if you are not a baker, is that omitting the butter, sugar, and flour leaves only eggs, vanilla, and baking soda, which wouldn't make much of a cupcake. We know from the low-fat experiment of the 1990s that trying to make "healthier" cookies and cupcakes, such as the Snackwell corporation tried to do, simply led to adding more sugar and increased overall consumption because people were unsatisfied with the "healthy" version of these treats. In short, when we try to tell ourselves that there are healthy indulgences such as cupcakes, we are simply tricking ourselves with denial in order to eat more.

Hyperpersonalization and narcissism

Psychologists Csikszentmihalyi and Rochberg-Halton argued that consumer objects exert two dynamic forces: differentiation, in which objects separate the owner and emphasize individuality from others, vs. similarity, in which objects "symbolically express the integration of the owner with his or her social context" (1981, p. 38). Given that possessions are often perceived as part of the extended self, one form of the expression of individuality and uniqueness is through the selection and use of products and brands (Belk, 1988). In fact, postmodernists such as Jean Baudrillard (1970, p. 45) argued that establishing difference or distinction is the *only* objective of consumer choice, a phenomenon which consumer psychologists refer to as simply "need for uniqueness" (Tian & McKenzie, 2001). I would extend this idea of a "need for uniqueness" to include food preferences and special diets, such that the desire to have our foods express the complexities of our identities is likely responsible for many of the specialized products that populate grocery store shelves.

While some diets such as vegetarianism or veganism clearly express important identity politics, other special diets seem to be striving for a sense of uniqueness. Gluten-free products, for example, which currently dominate store shelves have had an unexpected explosion in popularity given that very few people have celiac disease or gluten intolerance. Many people, quite soundly, are moving their diets away from refined grains, but many people don't realize that gluten-free products often substitute starches from tapioca, rice, or corn that have similar metabolic effects as gluten (Gulli, 2013). Yet the top reason consumers cite for purchasing gluten-free products is that they perceive them to be healthier (Marcason, 2011), even though there is no published experimental evidence to support health claims for gluten-free eating for the general population (Gaesser & Angadi, 2012). Likewise, many perceived food allergies and intolerances may simply be expressions of specialness, of me-ness, giving us new ways of setting ourselves apart from others. While it is true that there has been an enormous increase in food allergies in the past thirty years (or at least the ability to detect them) (Sicherer, 2011), there is also some evidence that many of these perceived food allergies are imagined (Chang, Burke, & Glass, 2010). The luxury food stores are most likely to be the purveyors of these specialized foods. This could simply be a function of their more affluent shoppers having the nutritional knowledge and the financial means to know about and purchase these products, but I suspect that these dietary preferences also reflect a sense of privilege and entitlement that is more pronounced in the upper classes. The more important point, though, is that the food industry uses allergies, intolerances, and special diets to sell more, often jumping on trends and creating health halos with nutritional claims, even going so far as to market gluten-free water (Sisson, 2013).

Scapegoating Big Food

Gratifying what Freud called the pleasure principle comes at heavy price. When we indulge in our pleasure-seeking desires, the ego and its repertoire of psychological defenses is left with a bill of guilt and shame. When we indulge in junk food, who better to blame than marketers and advertisers whom we know to be evil? Advertisers are the villain we love to hate—a scapegoat on which to displace or redirect the disappointment and self-loathing we experience when we engage in self-defeating behavior. While it is easy to think about those in Big Food and the persuasion industry as nefarious manipulators, it is probably also true that we construct or project a distorted and villainous image of these players to better make them a suitable target of externalization on which we can squarely place the blame for all things bad. As we saw with Big Tobacco, there are in fact many industry titans, advertisers, and marketers who knowingly elevate profits at the expense of public health, but it is also important to recognize that some of these figures are very much caught up in their own magic.

Cultural critic Raymond Williams argues that advertising is an attempt made by "magic" to associate consumption with human desires to which it has no real reference (2009). It must not be assumed, Williams wrote, "that magicians—in this case, advertising agents—disbelieve their own magic. They may have a limited professional cynicism about it, from knowing how some of the tricks are done. But fundamentally they are involved, with the rest of society, in the confusion to which the magical gestures are a response…the conversion of numerous objects into sources of sexual or pre-sexual satisfaction is evidently not only a process in the minds of advertisers, but also a deep and general confusion in which much energy is locked" (Williams, 2009, p. 23). In other words, the limitless desire created by marketing and advertising is a kind of magic in which the magicians themselves fall for the illusion.

More importantly, though, is the way that consumers construct an image of these magicians, projecting sinister qualities onto them as a way of designing a repository for blame. When we place blame wholly on the magicians for tricking us, however, we ultimately degrade ourselves by discounting free will.

We then feel as though we are powerlessly swept along in a tide of behavior over which we have no control. Psychologists refer to this attributional style as an external locus of control, that is, the belief that external factors are responsible for our behavior, whereas an internal locus of control refers to a sense that we can control events affecting us (Rotter, 1966). The question of "nutritional locus of control" is at the heart of regulatory debates over food marketing, taxing, and labeling because the central question is always who is responsible for overeating?

Although I have argued here that we collude with the food industry in overeating, the reality is that little collusion is required because the food industry has such a powerful arsenal of ingredients. Sugar, in particular, is the ingredient implicated in almost all hyperpalatable and ultra-processed foods and is increasingly viewed by many scientists as a drug of addiction (Avena, Rada, & Hoebel, 2008; Gearhardt, Roberts, & Ashe, 2013). In fact, sugar is arguably the central link between overeating and the culture of consumerism, as we shall see in the next chapter.

6

Sugar and Sweet

Sugar has alternatively been called evil, toxic, deadly, pure, and divine. Nowhere else do we see the psychology of overeating converge with the culture of consumerism quite so clearly as with the consumption and production of sugar, in which the inborn biological taste for sweet has driven the most remarkable upward production curve of any food in the history of the world market (Mintz, 1985, p. xxi). Because of its unique history and overwhelming presence in the world's food supply, we can use the story of sugar to examine the culture of consumerism, the development of hyperpalatable food, the neuroendocrinology of overeating, the mechanisms of food addiction, and the regulatory failures that promote the consumption of the global industrial diet.

Harken back to the funnel diagram from Chapter 3, depicted again in Figure 6.1. The funnel shows how the Western doctrine of consumer capitalism and its exploitation of labor and resources exerts downward force onto excessive spending, overeating, and personal ruin at the individual level.

In the next two chapters, we will see how the massive economic force of the sugar trade has led to excessive consumption of sugar, ever-increasing production of more sugar-sweetened products, and eventually to personal ruin in the form of depression, obesity, diabetes, fatty liver disease, cancer, and even Alzheimer's.

The sugar trade

Never before in human history did humans have regular access to sugar as we do today, and certainly never in the high concentrations now consumed. Historically, sugar was available only through fruit and occasionally honey. Not only that, the fruit available to early humans was far less sweet than

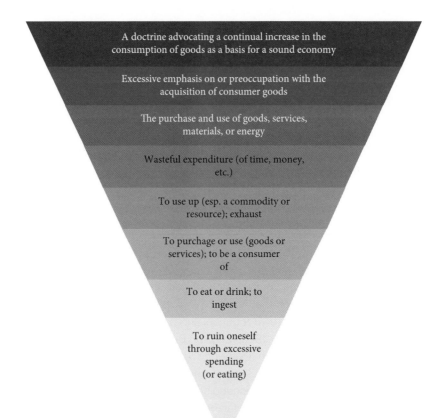

FIGURE 6.1 *Funnel of consumption.*

the highly cultivated fruits of today which have been deliberately bred for their high concentrations of fructose (Robinson, 2013). Not only was the sugar content of those undomesticated fruits much lower, but consumption of fruit came with a hefty dose of fiber that slowed gastric absorption of the sugar, a phenomenon largely lost today as most ultra-processed foods are separated from their fiber as part of the refining process. Even raw sugarcane, if you've never seen it, is a highly fibrous stalk that hardly resembles the refined white sugar we find on our tables today.

There are numerous excellent political and historical analyses of the West's sugar trade (Abbott, 2008; Macinnis, 2002; Mintz, 1985), but briefly there are a few key facts which are important to the psychology of sugar consumption: After an early heyday of Arab cultivation in the Fertile Crescent, sugarcane was brought to the New World by Christopher Columbus in his second voyage in 1493. Shortly after its cultivation on the island of Santo Domingo, the first enslaved Africans were imported to work on the plantations and by 1516 refined sugar was being shipped back to Europe. From 1650 onward, sugar began to shift from a luxury item into a commonplace part of the European diet, particularly in England where its growth by 1900 supplied nearly one-fifth of the calories in the English diet (Mintz, 1985). Notably, England's sugar plantations in the Caribbean were based on slave labor whereas its other industries back home were based on voluntary labor, therefore placing sugar production in the colonial system of forced, race-based labor since its very inception.

As anthropologist Sidney Mintz put it, "A single source of satisfaction—sucrose extracted from the sugar cane—for what appears to be a widespread, perhaps even universal, human liking for sweetness became established in European taste preferences at a time when European power, military might, and economic initiative were transforming the world" (1985, p. xxv). Thus the taste for sugar, as cultivated by and traded in the West, emerged from and depended on labor exploitation, superiority, conquest, and expansion, or what Gabriel and Lang call *consumerism as an economic ideology*, in which deregulation and the pursuit of higher living standards drive transnational corporations and global capitalism (Gabriel & Lang, 2006, p. 9).

According to numerous scholars and journalists, conditions of near-slavery exist virtually unchanged today in the form of indentured servitude on the sugar plantations in the Dominican Republic (Camejo & Wilentz, 1990; Simmons, 2010; Stokes, 2012). Ninety percent of the cane workers on these plantations are Haitian immigrants who live in squalid huts, are unable to leave the plantations, and are forced to buy meager provisions from the company store at inflated prices (Martínez, 1995). According to US diplomatic cables obtained by WikiLeaks (2007), the sugar companies typically pay the equivalent of approximately $3 US for every ton of cut sugarcane. Very strong workers can cut two tons of cane in a day ($6), but many older workers who continue to toil in the fields for lack of any other income often fall short of one ton in a day and are paid less than the legal minimum wage, set at $2.50 (US) per day for cane workers by the Dominican labor code. The same diplomatic cable goes on to report:

Many of the workers in this sector are involved in the production of commodities that are exported to the United States.... These workers are predominately Haitian or of Haitian descent, both the undocumented ones and those with work permits. The most commonly reported violations include hiring non-Dominicans in violation of the law; denying written work contracts to employees who request them; paying salaries that are below the legal minimum; employing children in violation of the law; making salary deductions that are not authorized under the law; denying employees the monetary benefits to which they are legally entitled; failing to submit social security deductions to the relevant government offices; shorting workers in the assessment of their production; discriminating against workers based on national origin and gender; and preventing employees from unionizing.

The owners of one of the largest sugar companies Flo-Sun are the Cuban-American Fanjul brothers. The Florida-based Fanjul brothers donate generously to Republican and Democratic lawmakers alike and have close ties to many elected officials, including direct telephone access to the Oval Office according to some reports (Starr, 1998). The Florida Independent reported that Flo-Sun spent $695,000 in 2010 alone in lobbying the US House, Senate, and Department of Agriculture, and since 2005 has spent a total of $3.65 million lobbying the federal government (Daly, 2011). On the occasion when US trade and diplomatic interests are at odds with the Fanjuls, as occurred with the Dominican Republic-Central America-United States Free Trade Agreement, they have reportedly resorted to bribery of Dominican officials to protect their interests (LaForgia & Playford, 2012). Similar lobbying efforts extend to all of Big Sugar, with the *Washington Post* reporting that in a five-year period the sugar industry spent $49 million on federal campaign donations and lobbying (Wallsten & Hamburger, 2013). This lobbying and fund-raising not only serves to maintain subsidies and trade protections for sugar production, but also protects the unregulated sale and marketing of sugary products by opposing legislation on package labeling, marketing to children, and placement of sugar-sweetened products in hospitals and schools.

The biochemistry of sugar

The preference for sweet in humans and in many other animals is stronger and more prevalent than the preference for any other taste (Pfaffmann, 1977). Not only does it just taste good, research has also shown that sweets can alleviate depression, premenstrual symptoms, and mediate stress (Gibson, 2006; Oliver, Wardle, & Gibson, 2000). Although the liking for sweet varies across cultures and is mediated by many factors, the positive hedonic response to sweet is universal and is considered an evolutionary adaptation that encourages suckling (Liem & Mennella, 2002). Sweetness signals that food is safe and good to eat and discourages the consumption of spoiled or poisonous foods, which by contrast are often signaled by a foul odor or bitter taste (Bartoshuk, 1991; Bartoshuk, Duffy, & Miller, 1994). The taste for sweet among humans is present not only at birth (Jerome, 1977; Ramirez, 1990; Steiner, 1977), but often in utero due to exposure to the maternal diet (Maone, Mattes, Bernbaum, & Beauchamp, 1990; Mennella & Beauchamp, 1998). Receptors for the taste of sweet are found not just on the tongue, but throughout the mouth, gut, and pancreas (Margolskee et al., 2007; Sclafani, 2007). Sugar has pain-reducing or analgesic effects in children (Pepino & Mennella, 2005; Stevens, Yamada, & Ohlsson, 2004) and its ability to activate the endogenous opioid system may be related to its addictive properties (Segato, Castro-Souza, Segato, Morato, & Coimbra, 1997), which I will discuss further in the next chapter.

The two major sugar crops are sugarcane and sugar beets, although sugar and syrups can also be produced from tree saps, sugar palm, and increasingly from cereals, such as corn or maize (Popkin & Nielsen, 2003). High fructose corn syrup, for example, was developed as the sugar industry sought better and cheaper ways to increase production, using the US corn subsidy to do so. HFCS is comprised of glucose and fructose, is sweeter than table sugar, and more cheaply made, so less is needed to achieve the same sweetness. However, after recent documentaries such as *King Corn* revealed disturbing facts about corn production, many consumers became suspicious of the artificiality of HFCS which had the unfortunate consequence of making table sugar look good by comparison.

Not only do we have an innate biological liking for sugar, but most of us develop powerful associations to sweets during childhood, during which the taste of sweet becomes developmentally entwined with treats for good behavior, birthday celebrations, and holidays. We might think about these associations from a behaviorist perspective in which classical and operant conditioning both serve to increase our liking for sweet. Classical or Pavlovian conditioning involves the pairing of two stimuli, in which an organism associates the two stimuli in a learned response, such as Pavlov's dogs did with a ringing bell and food. For many of us, the taste of sweet becomes associated with love and celebration during childhood and we therefore learn to associate pleasure and nurturance with the taste for sweet. Operant conditioning, by contrast, can either increase or decrease the frequency of a behavior through positive or negative reinforcement. The hedonic reward for consuming sweets then reinforces the behavior and because many parents, grandparents, and schools provide sweet treats for children as a reward for good behavior, that reinforces the seeking of sweets as a reward.

Another way to explain our association to sweets is through a psychoanalytic lens, in which we might view the taste for sweet as activating a regressed and playful fantasy of childhood. The recent enormous popularity of cupcakes, for example, speaks to the power of these colorful, whimsical confections in our imagination. Of course cupcakes are no different in taste or ingredients than a slice of cake, but a slice of cake is frankly boring in comparison to the sensual and playful imagery of a cupcake. Notably, many of the popular cupcake shops and cookbooks use retro designs and imagery, nostalgically invoking the 1950s Betty Crocker homemaker. Similarly, the sugar industry has historically exploited such nurturing maternal fantasies with advertisements featuring moms serving piping hot pies and towering cakes. We don't *actually* need to have had a nurturing mom who made delicious cakes to invoke this regressive nostalgia either. Often the idealized imagery of mothers and families seen on television and in advertising creates powerful nostalgic fantasies for experiences we never actually had (Coontz, 1992)—in other words, they create a longing for experiences we wish we'd had.

Arguably no other story captures the regressive, captivating power of sugar than the book *Charlie and the Chocolate Factory* and its film *Willy Wonka and the Chocolate Factory* (Dahl, 1967, 1971), in which young Charlie Bucket escapes his dismal, impoverished life by entering the technicolor psychedelic fantasy world of Willy Wonka. The film transports the viewer into a fantastical version of childhood safe from the prying eyes of adults, in which candy can be eaten for every meal and rivers are made out of chocolate. Interestingly, the film evokes the colonial past and present of sugar production with its premise that the extraordinary confections created by the white overlord Willy Wonka are produced by the labor of Oompa Loompas, the small men and women of color who toil day and night in the factory to create candy for English children.

The sweetening of the world's diet

In what Barry Popkin calls the "sweetening of the world's diet," the consumption of sugar has been increasing globally since World War II as per capita income has risen and as the proportion of the population residing in urban areas has increased (Popkin & Nielsen, 2003). The global sweetener market is currently estimated to be around 190 million tons of white sugar equivalent and the annual value of the world trade of sugar exceeds 24 billion dollars or around 60 million tons (Credit Suisse Research Institute, 2013). Caloric sweeteners, defined as all caloric carbohydrate sweeteners except naturally occurring sugars, now play a very large role in the US diet (Cavadini, Siega-Riz, & Popkin, 2000; Harnack, Stang, & Story, 1999; Nielsen, Siega-Riz, & Popkin, 2002), with over 600,000 items in the American food supply, or 80 percent containing added sugars (Lustig, 2013). The American Heart Association recommends that individuals consume no more than half of their daily discretionary calories in added sugar (Johnson et al., 2009); however, most Americans consume two to four times that, or 335 calories every day (Harris, 2012). NHANES data shows that Americans on average now eat 16 percent of their total calories from added sugars, defined by the USDA as sugars and syrups that are added to foods during processing or preparation. Foods high in added sugars include soda, energy/sports drinks, fruitades, fruit punch, grain-based desserts, sugar-sweetened fruit drinks, dairy-based desserts, and candy (USDA, 2000). Added sugars include white sugar, brown sugar, raw sugar, corn syrup, corn-syrup solids, high fructose corn syrup, malt syrup, maple syrup, pancake syrup, fructose sweetener, liquid fructose, honey, molasses, anhydrous dextrose, and crystal dextrose. Added sugars do not include naturally occurring sugars such as lactose in milk or fructose in fruits and these naturally occurring sugars do not cause significant health problems.

Sugar toxicity

In 1972, English nutritionist John Yudkin presciently published a book entitled *Sweet, White, and Deadly*, in which he argued that sugar was dangerous to human health. Now something of a cult classic among sugar researchers, his book was the first to advance the notion that sugar was poison. Yudkin's work was largely discredited by the sugar industry at the time of its publication and fell into obscurity, but his work has recently been rediscovered and validated as scientists have been making alarming discoveries about sugar which are consistent with Yudkin's early claims. Sugar consumption is associated with numerous chronic diseases such as cardiovascular disease (CVD) (DiNicolantonio & Lucan, 2014), obesity, high blood pressure, and stroke (Lichtenstein et al., 2006). Moreover, high intake of added sugars can decrease the intake of nutrient-rich foods (Institute of Medicine, 2005).

In addition to its clear role in overweight and obesity, sugar is now implicated as a causal or influential factor in many other diseases, including cancer, polycystic ovarian syndrome (PCOS), and Alzheimer's disease, in addition to the cluster of disorders which constitute metabolic syndrome: type 2 diabetes, hypertension, lipid problems, cardiovascular disease, and non-alcoholic fatty liver disease (de la Monte & Wands, 2005; Lustig, 2010; Park et al., 2001; Stanhope & Havel, 2008, 2009, 2010; Steen et al., 2005). Epidemiological studies demonstrate an association between obesity and cancer (Donohoe, Doyle, & Reynolds, 2011; Renehan, Tyson, Egger, Heller, & Zwahlen, 2008; World Cancer Research Fund/American Institute for Cancer Research, 2007), but increasingly there is evidence that it is not just obesity, but the consumption of sugar which may contribute to the growth of certain types of cancer cells, particularly those with insulin receptors (Belfiore & Malaguarnera, 2011; Boyd, 2003; Frasca et al., 2008). In other words, consumption of sugar is an independent primary risk factor that causes disease unrelated to excess calories, overweight, or obesity (Hu & Malik, 2010; Malik & Hu, 2012; Malik, Popkin, Bray, Després, & Hu, 2010a).

Not only is evidence mounting that links sugar consumption with cancer, but sugar is increasingly implicated in other diseases. Brown University researcher Dr. Suzanne de la Monte has called Alzheimer's disease, non-alcoholic fatty liver disease, polycystic ovarian syndrome, and type 2 diabetes as parallel conditions of insulin resistance, likely resulting from changes in the Western diet, namely ultra-processed foods (de la Monte, Re, Longato, & Tong, 2012). Calling Alzheimer's disease "type 3 diabetes," de la Monte writes, "(G)rowing evidence supports the concept that AD is fundamentally a metabolic disease with substantial and progressive derangements in brain glucose utilization and responsiveness to insulin and insulin-like growth factor [IGF] stimulation" (p. 53). This is nascent research and in time the working hypothesis that sugar causes PCOS and Alzheimer's disease might be ruled out. The scientific method requires years of replicating controlled trials to build the evidentiary strength necessary to make an absolute claim about causality. Needless to say, the health consequences of sugar consumption are devastating and increasingly there is recognition that it is not just an individual health problem, but a public health crisis taking an enormous financial toll. In one recent report, Credit Suisse estimated that the consumption of sugar worldwide costs the global health care system $470 billion annually, representing over 10 percent of all health care costs, and could rise to $700 billion by 2020 (Credit Suisse Research Institute, 2013).

As if all this weren't bad enough, research is also increasingly pointing to the addictive nature of sugar. Neuroscientists and animal behaviorists have been studying sugar's addictive potential and have found that in some studies laboratory rats prefer sugar over cocaine and even heroin (Ahmed, 2012; Lenoir, Serre, Cantin, & Ahmed, 2007). Such findings suggest that even consumption of small amounts of sugar can make us vulnerable to powerful cravings for more, a result that has been replicated with the artificial sweetener sucralose (Splenda) (Grimm, 2012). Addiction behavior in response to sugar and sweetness is well established in rat models, but has not been replicated in human studies (Benton, 2010), a topic which we will return to in the next chapter on food and addictive behavior.

The culture of drinks

The sweetening of the world's diet that has taken place over the past forty years has shifted such that today the increased consumption of sweets is now taking place mostly in beverages (Duffey et al., 2011; Duffey & Popkin, 2008; Malik et al., 2010b; Ng, Ni Mhurchu, Jebb, & Popkin, 2012), ushering in what

I call the "culture of drinks" resulting in the beverage industry's generation of over $42 billion annually (Beverage Digest, 2014). Sugar-sweetened beverages (SSBs) account for more than half of the increase in added caloric sweeteners in the past several decades and consumption of SSBs represents 10–15 percent of total energy needs across age ranges (Bray, Nielsen, & Popkin, 2004; Nielsen & Popkin, 2004; Popkin, 2010; Popkin & Nielsen, 2003), with extremely high consumption among children. Recent estimates put the consumption of added sugars at 15.9 percent (60 g/d) of energy in the diets of children aged 2–5 years old and 18.6 percent (90 g/d) of energy among children aged 6–11 years old. Most of this sugar was provided by energy-containing beverages (Drewnowski, Mennella, Johnson, & Bellisle, 2012; Popkin & Nielsen, 2003).

One of the reasons that the consumption of sugar-sweetened beverages is so concerning is that when carbohydrates such as sugar are consumed in liquid form it can cause passive calorie overconsumption (Ebbeling, Willett, & Ludwig, 2012), producing less satiety than when the calories are consumed in solid form. We then overcompensate for this deficit in satiety by increasing energy intake at subsequent meals (DiMeglio & Mattes, 2000; Harnack et al., 1999; Mattes, 1996; Mourao, Bressan, Campbell, & Mattes, 2007; Wang, Ludwig, Sonneville, & Gortmaker, 2009). In other words, drinking sweetened beverages makes us eat more (Pan & Hu, 2011) and causes weight gain (Malik, Schulze, & Hu, 2006).[1] Moreover, the consumption of high fructose corn syrup and sucrose that is typically found in SSBs has a uniquely adverse effect on health that alters metabolism and increases risk for obesity, type 2 diabetes, and cardiovascular disease. In the most recent review of the research on the effects of sugar-sweetened beverages, Malik and Hu wrote, "The prevailing mechanisms linking SSB intake to weight gain are low satiety of liquid calories and incomplete compensatory reduction in energy intake at subsequent meals, leading to an increase in total energy intake. SSBs also induce independent metabolic effects through their contribution to a high dietary glycemic load, leading to inflammation, insulin resistance, and impaired B cell function. In addition, regular consumption of SSBs is associated with high blood pressure and accumulation of visceral adipose tissue and dyslipidemia through increased hepatic de novo lipogenesis" (Malik & Hu, 2011, p. 1161). In other words, the staggering increase in consumption of juice, energy drinks, sports drinks, flavored milks, and sodas is linked to rising rates of obesity and many other health problems in the United States and worldwide (Bermudez & Gao, 2010; Malik et al., 2006).

---

[1]The few researchers who dispute the relationship between SSBs and obesity have been shown to have ties to the beverage industry (Allison, 2007; Center for Science in the Public Interest, 2007; Harris & Patrick, 2011).

As the culture of drinks has emerged, sugar has also become the vehicle for caffeine in the form of energy drinks and coffee beverages. When I look out over my classroom, I am greeted by a sea of plastic Starbucks cups filled with pink and green frothy concoctions topped with whipped cream. Starbucks, perhaps more than anyone else has cracked the code on selling sugar in the form of coffee drinks, and now so-called "Ready to Drink Tea and Coffee" bottled beverages is the leading category in consumer packaged goods, with sports drinks and energy drinks as the second and third categories (IRI, 2010). Because Starbucks' sales were historically concentrated in the morning when people want coffee, they had to experiment with a number of ways to increase afternoon sales, eventually leading to the development and trademark of the wildly successful Frappuccino which helped them transition from selling coffee to selling sugar (Koehn, 2001).

Artificial sweeteners

Artificial sweeteners originated in the late 1800s, but did not become widespread until the expansion of food science and post–World War II consumerism. Unlike other growing industries, the food industry could not enjoy the limitless desire of consumer culture because of the finite number of calories an individual can consume daily. The solution was artificial sweetener. Artificial sweeteners promised limitless consumption with no consequences (de la Pena, 2010). Much like the use of plastic credit cards and digital transactions provide the illusion of easy purchases distanced from financial consequences, consuming sweets that "don't count" represents the ultimate consumer fulfillment: endless desire and constant gratification. Bulimics too, seek to limitlessly consume while avoiding or mitigating the ill-effects of overeating. In *Empty Pleasures: The Story of Artificial Sweeteners from Saccharine to Splenda*, historian Carolyn de la Pena argues that the consumption of artificial sweeteners constitutes a form of socially acceptable bulimia, in which we can consume what we desire, but strip the desired foods of their negative consequences (p. 6). It is yet another example of the persistent abdication of financial and nutritional reckoning that has led to the culture-wide accounting crisis discussed in Chapter 4.

Of course, the sugar industry views the artificial sweetener industry as a market threat and has a lengthy history of funding research on the negative health effects of artificial sweeteners, filing lawsuits against its manufacturers, and creating websites such as TheTruthAboutSplenda.com (de la Pena, 2010). Undeterred by these efforts, the quest for the holy grail of artificial sweeteners continues by food scientists. So great is the potential profit of a palatable noncaloric sweetener that food and drink makers invest heavily into the discovery of new possibilities. David Thomas, Executive Vice President of Research and Development at Dr. Pepper Snapple who leads a seventy-member research team that includes scientists, engineers, and certified flavorists, says, "We're spending more on sweetener technology than we ever have …. We have Ph.D.-level people fully focused on sweetener technology" (Robinson-Jacobs, 2014). Meanwhile, his competitors at PepsiCo have boosted global spending on research and development, which includes increasing research on sweeteners by 27 percent to $665 million since 2011.

The use of artificial sweeteners, also known as high-intensity sweeteners or low-calorie sweeteners, has been slowly increasing in the United States (Sylvetsky, Welsh, Brown, & Vos, 2012) and are now preferentially consumed by individuals with higher incomes and higher education levels (Credit Suisse Research Institute, 2013). Far from allowing us the pleasures of sugar without the ill-effects, however, consumption of these sweeteners is a deal with the devil. Both rat and human studies have shown that such sweeteners may actually increase caloric intake from other sources (Swithers, Baker, & Davidson, 2009; Swithers & Davidson, 2008), and like sugar they are linked to diabetes, metabolic syndrome, and cardiovascular disease (Swithers, 2013, 2014; Tellez et al., 2013). Researchers have also found that consumption of artificial sweeteners caused glucose intolerance and functional alterations to intestinal microbiota, suggesting increased susceptibility to metabolic abnormalities and disease (Suez et al., 2014).

With the use of artificial sweeteners we see another of the many cycles of consumption, in which the attempt to solve the problems of one type of consumption (sugar) leads us only to another form of consumption (artificial sweeteners). This is nothing more than robbing Peter to pay Paul. As I argue throughout this book, the solution to overconsumption is never another type of consumption, as marketers and advertisers would have you believe, but is simply consuming less.

When my clinical patients ask me what would be the one single thing they could do to lose weight, I unhesitatingly answer: "Give up refined sugar." That recommendation is always immediately and categorically rejected as both impossible and undesirable. The number of patients I've worked with over the years who've done it is exactly zero. Anecdotally speaking, I've been successful in helping patients cope with the loss of a loved one, manage crippling anxiety, emerge from a suicidal depression, and safely leave abusive relationships. Never, though, have I successfully helped someone give up added or refined sugar. That is largely, of course, because no one has wanted to. For most Americans, giving up added sugar would involve a massive upheaval in lifestyle and would require immense behavioral change, perhaps on par with giving up tobacco, alcohol, or caffeine. Instead, what most people want is to lose weight and stop overeating while maintaining themselves in the culture of consumerism and the global industrial diet, in other words, having their cake and eating too. Certainly some people can do that successfully, but for many of us the neurochemical and metabolic effects of sugar take us hostage in a way that make it very difficult to eat a partial diet of ultra-processed foods and effectively regulate that consumption—the reasons for which I will further explain in the next chapter. After giving up added sugar altogether, the second best strategy for weight loss is giving up sweet drinks (Chen et al., 2009). Most nutritionists and endocrinologists I know say that the first and often only thing they do in working with clinical patients is to get them off sugar sweetened and artificially sweetened drinks.

The bittersweet truth

When I was a little girl, my dad got two old rickety field horses for me and my sister and he named them Coffee and Sugar. Which one do you think I wanted? Let me tell you, no six-year-old girl wants a horse named Coffee. There is nothing appealing about that bitter grown-up drink. I can also assure you that the coffee we had in rural Oklahoma in the 1970s was not the stuff anyone reading this book is drinking today. I begged, pleaded, and cajoled my sister to trade horses with me—I even tried to get her to keep the same horse, just trade names. No dice. Of course today I would love to have a horse named Coffee and would hate to have a horse named Sugar.

The reason that Coffee and Sugar were such great names for a pair is because the bitter taste of coffee is an acquired taste and one that is usually acquired by pairing it with the more desirable stimulus of sugar (Baeyens, Eelen, Van den Bergh, & Crombez, 1990; Fanselow & Birk, 1982). In fact, the more often we consume a bitter liquid paired with sugar, the more our preference for it increases (Zellner, Rozin, Aron, & Kulish, 1983). This is one of the other challenges in giving up sugar. Not only do desserts and sweets taste so good, but with many foods and drinks sugar offsets bitter compounds that are unpalatable to some people.

For example, two of my patients, Lisa and Riley, both overweight by at least 60–80 pounds are struggling with their weight and trying to reduce. Both coincidentally report starting their day with a Starbucks chai latte which contains 42 grams of sugar and 250 calories (Starbucks UK, 2014). Understandably, Lisa and Riley want caffeine to help them wake up; however, when we discussed the possibility of switching over to coffee or plain black tea so that they could have caffeine without sugar or artificial sweetener, both said that coffee and plain black tea were too bitter for them to drink unsweetened. Because of their self-reported sensitivity to bitter tastes,

I suspected that they each might be supertasters. *Supertasters* refers to the subset of the people, most commonly women (Bartoshuk et al., 1994), who perceive the two related compounds of phenylthiocarbamide (PTC) and 6-n-propylthiouracil (PROP) as extremely bitter (Bartoshuk, 1991). PTC and PROP occur naturally in caffeine, beer, grapefruit juice, and dark green vegetables such as brussels sprouts. Consuming caffeine which is naturally bitter without the accompanying taste of sweet is a particular challenge for the supertaster. I had Lisa and Riley each conduct a simple, inexpensive test for supertasting that involves placing a paper PTC strip on the tongue and both of them indeed turned out to be supertasters. Those results are worrisome given that recent research has shown a higher incidence rate of metabolic syndrome among individuals who are both supertasters and have a high liking for sweets (Turner-McGrievy, Tate, Moore, & Popkin, 2013).

At a certain point, Lisa and Riley will almost certainly have to give up the taste of sweet in order to get to a healthy weight and lower their risk for related health problems; however, that may prove very difficult because of the emotional comfort that sweets provide them. Another similarity between these two young women is that they are both very smart, shy, and isolated. Neither of them have many social relationships nor much experience with romantic relationships. Both of them feel that their weight keeps them from taking more social risks or developing romances because of their body self-consciousness. However, the very behavior that is causing their overweight (sugar consumption) also happens to be one of the few small pleasures they have. As a compassionate psychologist, it's difficult for me to suggest they give up the daily pleasures of chai, ice cream, or chocolate in order to achieve the long-term gain of improved confidence, health, and possible relationships. Many clinical psychologists working with patients with weight struggles face the same challenge. For a person who is depressed, anxious, or isolated, indulgent foods are one of the few gratifying moments of their day, yet these foods are ultimately self-defeating and keep them trapped in depression, isolation, and anxiety. That may sound like a lot like alcoholism or drug addiction; however, food addiction is not recognized as a diagnosis. The movement to recognize food as an addictive substance has recently generated a large and compelling body of research, but one that is hotly contested. This debate over so-called "food addiction" is the subject of the next chapter.

7

Hyperpalatable Foods, Hormones, and Addiction

One morning my patient Allison came stumbling tearfully into my office, collapsed into a chair, and asked me if I had any gum. Sobbing, she said that she was hungover and miserable. The night before had begun well enough at a happy hour with friends. She'd had a couple of glasses of wine and some light appetizers. She was pleased with her impulse control and level of consumption, reporting that because she had to drive home she had carefully watched her alcohol intake and found it easy to eat only what she had planned in advance. After she got home, though, she opened a bottle of wine and sat on her patio, drinking the entire bottle while smoking almost a full pack of cigarettes. At that point, she walked to a nearby fast-food restaurant and ordered a large soda, chicken nuggets, egg rolls, and a brownie. The next morning she felt bloated, hoarse, dehydrated, and achy. As we talked I helped her to understand what happened as a cascade of hormonal chaos. These impulse control failures were activated by alcohol consumption and the hangover was the withdrawal effects of alcohol, cigarettes, sugar, and hyperpalatable food.

Allison often experiences negative cognitive, behavioral, and physiological consequences as a result of overeating, yet she continues to overeat. Like addicts of other substances, she passes her days aware of how overeating causes many of the problems in her life, returning to the source of the problem for comfort from the intense distress it causes. The American Psychiatric Association (2013) defines substance dependence as a cluster of cognitive, behavioral, and physiological symptoms indicating that the individual continues using the substance despite significant substance-related problems, including:

- taking the substance in larger amounts or over a longer period than was originally intended.

- expressing a persistent desire to cut down or regulate substance use and report multiple unsuccessful efforts to decrease or discontinue use.

- spending a great deal of time obtaining the substance, using the substance, or recovering from its effects.

- experiencing craving for the substance, as manifested by an intense desire or urge for the drug that may occur at any time but is more likely when in an environment where the drug previously was obtained or used.

- continuing substance use despite having persistent or recurrent social or interpersonal problems caused or exacerbated by the effects of the substance.

- continuing substance use despite knowledge of having a persistent or recurrent physical or psychological problem that is likely to have been caused or exacerbated by the substance.

- experiencing tolerance as signaled by requiring a markedly increased dose of the substance to achieve the desired effect or a markedly reduced effect when the usual dose is consumed.

- experiencing withdrawal as a syndrome that occurs when blood or tissue concentrations of a substance decline in an individual who had maintained prolonged heavy use of the substance.

Although food is not recognized as an addictive substance, consider the following: Allison expresses a persistent desire to cut down or regulate overeating and reports multiple unsuccessful efforts to do so. She spends a great deal of time shopping for food and going to restaurants (obtaining the substance), and then later feels physically and emotionally bad from overeating (recovering from its effects). She describes intense desire for foods (craving), especially for sweets and fried food. Even though she blames her romantic failures and depression on overeating and being overweight (persistent or recurrent social or interpersonal problems), she has not been able to change her eating habits. Finally, she reports increasing the amount of hyperpalatable food she eats over time (tolerance) and feeling lousy after overeating (withdrawal). In other words, Allison meets many of the diagnostic criteria for addiction, yet there is currently no recognized disorder for food addiction.

To better understand how Allison loses control and feels powerless against these cravings and impulses requires a basic understanding of metabolism, neurochemistry, and the science of addiction. This chapter examines the appetite-regulating hormones which control hunger and satiety; the neurotransmitters which regulate hedonic reward; and the emerging science of food addiction as they each relate to the culture of consumerism and the global industrial diet.

Appetite-regulating hormones

That neuroendocrinology has anything to do with the culture of consumerism might not be immediately apparent, but the two could not be more closely related. The neurochemical and hormonal dysregulation implicated in overeating is a direct result of food science, marketing, increased consumerism, and the global industrial diet. Specifically, the ultra-processed foods which dominate the global food landscape aren't just high in calories—they have powerful neurochemical effects which hijack the body's finely tuned self-regulatory mechanisms.

Glucose, insulin, and glycemic index

Providing energy is glucose's primary role in the body. After a meal, blood glucose rises and liver cells link excess glucose molecules into long chains of glycogen, the short-term storage form of glucose. The liver can then later convert this glycogen back into glucose as needed by the body. After meeting its immediate energy needs and filling up glycogen stores, the body converts any excess glucose into fat. The pancreas responds to rising blood glucose by secreting insulin into the blood, and the amount of insulin released corresponds to the amount of glucose consumed. Historically, nearly all foods high in glucose or fructose were delivered with high fiber thereby slowing down gastric absorption of sugar. Today, however, industrial foods and beverages like cookies and fruit juice are processed by removing the fiber, making them more fattening since the body is unable to use the highly concentrated load of fructose for immediate energy needs and therefore stores the rapidly absorbed excess energy as fat.

The speed of glucose absorption is referred to as glycemic response, that is, how quickly the glucose is absorbed, how high blood glucose rises, and how quickly it returns to normal. The related glycemic index (GI) developed by Dr. David Jenkins (1981) is a ranking of foods on a scale from 0 to 100 according to the extent to which they raise blood sugar levels after eating. Sweets, high-carbohydrate fast food, and refined breads elicit a high glycemic response because they are rapidly digested and absorbed causing spikes in blood glucose with levels falling to below baseline shortly after digestion, causing increased hunger (Lennerz et al., 2013). By contrast, low glycemic foods such as legumes, dairy, meats, and nuts slow digestion and absorption, producing gradual rises in blood sugar and insulin levels. Low GI foods therefore maintain satiety and allow the body more time to process glucose, allowing it to be burned as energy rather than stored as body fat (Chiu et al., 2011).

Ghrelin and leptin

Besides insulin, ghrelin and leptin are two other primary appetite-regulating hormones which work together to create homeostasis between appetite and body weight. Sometimes called the hunger hormone, ghrelin is a short-acting hormone produced in the stomach which sends appetite-stimulating signals to the hypothalamus when the stomach is empty (Dickson et al., 2011). Circulating ghrelin levels are the highest right before a meal and the lowest right after.

Leptin, discovered in 1994 and sometimes called the satiety hormone (Zhang et al., 1994), is a long-acting hormone produced by fat cells or adipose tissue and effectively reports one's aggregate fat mass to the brain. Increases in body fat result in increases in leptin, signaling the brain to inhibit hunger and increase energy expenditures in order to restore homeostasis in body fat. In other words, weight gain increases leptin which *should* signal the brain to decrease food intake and result in weight loss; however, it is clear that in overweight and obese individuals leptin is not effectively sending the message to reduce caloric intake to correct for increased fat mass. Why? Research shows that overweight and obese individuals have high levels of leptin, but their brains cannot read it—they are leptin-resistant (Caro, Sinha, Kolaczynski, Zhang, & Considine, 1996). Consequently, they wind up with high body fat stores while continuing to be hungry, in effect stuck with a broken thermostat of appetite/body weight regulation. Imagine that you set your home thermostat to 70 degrees in the winter time, but the thermometer which reads the ambient temperature was broken. The heat would continue to run well after the house was warmed to 70 degrees. You would be living in an oven, but your thermostat would register the temperature of a tundra.

What causes this leptin resistance? An early hypothesis was that obese individuals might have a congenital or genetic defect in leptin receptors which caused obesity by failing to regulate appetite. Laboratory studies showed, however, that very few obese individuals had such a genetic defect (Considine, Considine, Williams, Hyde, & Caro, 1996; Farooqi & O'Rahilly, 2005). In the vast majority of obese individuals, the quantity and quality of leptin receptors appeared to be normal (Considine & Caro, 1997; Considine et al., 1996). More recent studies have shown that there are likely a number of mechanisms involved in leptin resistance (Myers, Cowley, & Münzberg, 2008), but relevant to the scope of this book are the findings that many factors are environmental and behavioral, namely overfeeding and the consumption of a high fructose, high carbohydrate diet (Havel, Townsend, Chaump, & Teff, 1999; Kolaczynski, Ohannesian, Considine, Marco, & Caro, 1996; Wang et al., 2001). In other words, leptin resistance is partially the result of diet, specifically high carbohydrate, energy dense diets like the current Western diet.

If leptin resistance is a result of diet, it would seem that a modification in diet would correct leptin resistance and restore levels to normal. In other words, a shift away from a high sugar, high carbohydrate diet ought to result in weight loss, decreased leptin levels, and increased leptin sensitivity. Unfortunately, it's not that simple. Although weight loss does in fact result in decreased leptin concentrations, the loss also provokes a physiologic response which defends the obese levels of adiposity. That is, consumption of obesogenic foods results in long term, perhaps permanent changes in the neural systems which modulate energy balance and fiercely protect adiposity or fatness (Myers, Leibel, Seeley, & Schwartz, 2010). This once adaptive tendency of the brain to protect fat and defend against weight loss makes the development and production of hyperpalatable foods all the more insidious, as the resultant leptin increase and leptin resistance create a path of no return from obesity. This is why it is so difficult to lose weight and keep it off—the brain strongly resists a simple restoration to pre-overweight levels of leptin and leptin sensitivity.

Are all calories created equal?

The science of appetite-regulating hormones has clarified a related debate in nutritional studies, which is the question of whether all calories were created equal. The common wisdom among dietitians and dieters had long been that in order to maintain weight one must expend the same number of calories consumed. The two corollaries are that a calorie surplus leads to weight gain and a calorie deficit leads to weight loss. Until recently, a scant few scientists challenged this "calories in/calories out" model (Taubes, 2007), also commonly referred to as the thermodynamic model because the first law of thermodynamics states that a form of energy may change, but the total is always conserved. The thinking was that any deficiency in calorie intake would result in the burning of stored fat or weight loss; and conversely, any surplus of calories would result in fat storage or weight gain. The discoveries of leptin and ghrelin, however, have shown that certain foods activate metabolism in ways that affect satiety and fat storage *irrespective of overall calorie balance*.

Specifically, the increased insulin produced by eating high glycemic and high carbohydrate foods causes energy to be stored as fat, leaving the individual hungry because ghrelin is not suppressed. Furthermore, as one begins to routinely overeat and gain weight, leptin resistance sets in, such that the brain does not register the excess fat and does not adjust appetite or energy expenditure. To be clear, it's not that the thermodynamic model is invalid—it's that the mathematical simplicity of calories in minus calories out does not capture the body's complex system of homeostasis. The analogy I often use with patients to describe the metabolism of a high glycemic diet is that their gross paycheck might total $1,000, but they only get $600 for immediate use and the other $400 is withheld. Those behind-the-scenes withholdings in their paycheck are equivalent to how the liver processes sugar and stores it as fat when eating high glycemic foods. The $600 represents energy available for immediate use and the $400 represents calories stored as fat. Eating low glycemic foods in moderation allows access to all of the "earnings" or calories with none of it stored as fat because the brain's homeostatic mechanisms are protected. In other words, all $1,000 is available to use without withholdings.[1]

The neurochemistry of reward

Increasingly, scientists are studying food as a potentially addictive substance because of the two related mechanisms of food reward (its reinforcing and motivational effects) and hedonic value (its palatability and pleasure-giving properties). While the terms "palatability" and "reward" are often used interchangeably, they are in fact different processes which often occur in tandem. Kent Berridge (1995) identified the motivational effect of food as "liking" and the hedonic aspect of food as "wanting." This distinction between liking and wanting is important because of the diminishing pleasure that we sometimes receive from strongly desired behaviors and substances. In other words, we can badly want something or crave it and then when we get the desired substance find that we don't like it as much as expected, that is, it does not provide the expected reward, as often occurs with drug addiction. In simpler terms, we can want something that we don't really like.

---

[1]Some researchers have challenged this model of de novo lipogenesis and instead argue that dietary carbohydrate is not converted to fat, but instead causes the oxidation of dietary fat which is the pathway to increased fat storage (Hall, 2012; Hellerstein, 1999, 2001).

Note that these neurological experiences of liking and wanting correspond to the consumer ethic discussed in Chapter 2, in which the modern hedonism of desire rests on the daydreams of novel products. Just as wanting often supersedes liking with substances of abuse, so too we see this elsewhere in consumer culture. Contrary to the fulfillment consumers imagine, they instead find themselves disappointed that the actual consumption of products does not satisfy the desire. Describing desire as more powerful than reward, sociologist Zygmunt Bauman wrote, "The traditional relationship between needs and their satisfaction will be reversed: the promise and hope of satisfaction will precede the need and will be always greater than the extant need ..." (1998, p. 25). This ethic of consumer desire then corresponds to the neurological substrates of liking and wanting because consumer culture depends on hedonic desire in order for unnecessary goods and experiences to be attractive. In other words, "desire does not desire satisfaction. To the contrary, desire desires desire" (Taylor & Saarinen, 1994, p. 11).

You see how this is all coming together now. The finely designed foods that activate bliss point are nearly always foods that undermine leptin so they necessarily lead to overeating not only because they taste so good, but because we never feel full on them. Over time, the resulting leptin-resistant condition makes our brains think we are starving so we keep eating. To put it another way, it is the diet of global consumer capitalism that is causing widespread leptin resistance and consequently overeating, overweight, and obesity. Eating foods high in sugar, fat, and salt inevitably makes us eat more foods high in sugar, fat, and salt or desire desires desire. Again we see that the funnel of consumer culture in which the doctrine advocating continued increases in the consumption of goods leads to overconsumption of food and drink and eventual self-ruin through excessive spending and eating.

Food and addiction

It might seem evident that food can be addictive based on the rhetoric in popular culture. The twelve-step program Overeaters Anonymous, for example, has long promoted the idea that food is addictive and has used the AA model of treatment for "food addicts." Scientifically, however, there was not conclusive evidence that food is addictive until quite recently (Avena et al., 2008; Blumenthal & Gold, 2010; Corwin & Grigson, 2009; Volkow, Wang, Fowler, & Telang, 2008). One reason was simply that unlike drugs such as cocaine, nicotine, or alcohol, we need food to survive.

Based on studies of the neurological response to hyperpalatable foods in both rats and humans, many researchers are now arguing that the ultra-processed foods of the global industrial diet are more similar to drugs of abuse than to the natural energy resources we historically consumed (Gearhardt, Davis, Kuschner, & Brownell, 2011a). Specifically, these manufactured foods have been altered in a manner similar to addictive drugs, providing elevated potency of ingredients and rapid absorption into the bloodstream. In a disturbing parallel to how street drugs of abuse are refined and manufactured, Michael Moss (2013) found that:

> .... One of the most compelling, and unsettling, aspects of the role of salt, sugar, and fat in processed foods is the way the industry, in an effort to boost their power, has sought to alter their physical shape and structure. Scientists at Nestlé are currently fiddling with the distribution and shape of fat globules to affect their absorption rate and, as it's known in the industry, their "mouthfeel." At Cargill, the world's leading supplier of salt, scientists are altering the physical shape of salt, pulverizing it into a fine powder to hit the taste buds faster and harder, improving what the company calls its "flavor burst." Sugar is being altered in myriad ways as well. The sweetest component of simple sugar, fructose, has been crystallized into an additive that boosts the allure of foods. Scientists have also created enhancers that amplify the sweetness of sugar to two hundred times its natural strength.

Needless to say, such chemical alterations are the hallmark of drug production. The natural coca leaf, for example, is only a mild stimulant (Hanna & Hornick, 1977), but when highly refined into cocaine or crack, it delivers an exponentially stronger hedonic reward and is far more addictive (Verebey & Gold, 1988). Similarly, marijuana used to provide a mild high, but has now been cultivated into a highly potent hallucinogenic compound often delivered through concentrated oils and now "edibles" (ElSohly et al., 2000; Wang, Simone, & Palmer, 2014b). Further supporting the notion that highly refined foods such as sugar create more addictive potential are studies with rats, in which researchers have found that the reward value of sweet liquids is greater than that of intravenous cocaine (Ahmed, 2012), and in some cases heroin (Lenoir, Cantin, Serre, & Ahmed, 2008).

In addition to the parallels between the refinement and production of addictive drugs and hyperpalatable foods is an emerging neuroscience on the effects of hyperpalatable foods on the brain. Similar to other drugs of abuse, high fat, high sugar diets are associated with changes in the opiate and dopaminergic pathways of the brain in both rats and humans (Hajnal, Smith, & Norgren, 2004; Kleiner et al., 2004; Mason & Higley, 2012). The hormone ghrelin, for example, is implicated in regulating reward perception in the cholinergic–dopaminergic pathways in the brain and their interactions with the ventral tegmental area of the brain, an area that is involved in sexual desire and addiction (Dickson et al., 2011; Le Moal & Simon, 1991). Not surprisingly, Naltrexone, a drug used to treat alcohol dependence by blocking opioid receptors and diminishing reward, has been shown to reduce the consumption of high sugar, high fat foods in binge eaters, just as it reduces alcohol consumption in alcohol-dependent individuals (Drewnowski, Krahn, Demitrack, Nairn, & Gosnell, 1995).

There is additional supporting evidence that like other substance abusers, food addicts have similar personality characteristics and use food to regulate mood. Specifically, impulsivity is associated with the addictive consumption of food, and individuals who report acting more rashly when experiencing urgent emotions endorse more symptoms of addictive eating (Murphy, Stojek, & MacKillop, 2014). Other studies have shown that many self-identified food addicts use food to self-regulate in order to escape a negative mood state (Ifland et al., 2009) and that high-fat sweets in particular are frequently used to regulate emotions (Canetti, Bachar, & Berry, 2002; Cooper, Frone, Russell, & Mudar, 1995). Moreover, the combination of increased liking for carbohydrates in the context of decreased mood effects parallels how other drugs of abuse are craved and used as mood regulators (Corsica & Spring, 2008).

A common clinical dilemma in working with people who overeat as a means of providing themselves comfort is that in order to help them reduce that behavior, they must have some other means of comfort to replace food. In my experience this can be incredibly difficult. I have a patient, Bethany, who came to me recently for help with fertility problems. A 42-year-old single woman who has never been in a serious relationship, Bethany decided she wanted to have a baby on her own. Working with a fertility clinic and an anonymous sperm donor, she attempted eight intrauterine inseminations which failed, and then moved on to the more expensive and intrusive procedure of in vitro fertilization. After four failed in vitro fertilization attempts and over $60,000 spent on these procedures, she decided to seek psychological help deciding whether or not she should move onto the next level of intervention, which is in vitro fertilization (IVF) using a donor egg.

I was surprised at Bethany's first visit to my office to see that she was morbidly obese. I have worked with a number of women dealing with fertility problems and being significantly overweight greatly diminishes their chances of conception. Because fertility precipitously declines for women over the age of 35, it's important for women in this age group to do everything possible to maximize the chances of fertilization. Not only that, but in the case of in vitro fertilization, the woman must go under general anesthesia for the egg retrieval. Many doctors will not perform elective procedures that require general anesthesia on people who are morbidly obese because of the increased risk of complications. In Bethany's case, she had actually lost seventy pounds in order to do the IVF procedures, but she recently gained that weight back, now weighing just over 300 pounds.

Right away Bethany said she wanted help with nutrition and eating. As I began to learn about her eating habits we discussed some initial steps she could take just to start *thinking* about food differently. When I am working with patients who want to change their eating habits, I often do not start with specific behavioral recommendations, but rather with conversations about their relationship to food and their "food thinking." I learned that Bethany liked cooking, but did not like cooking for one. She also told me that she needed to eat every couple of hours or else she was overwhelmed by ravenous, unpleasant hunger. After breakfast of a bagel and cream cheese, she often ate one or two energy bars throughout the morning and then a reasonably healthy lunch which she would bring with her to work. She reported that she had to eat dinner by 5:00 p.m. or she would again become overwhelmed by a desperate feeling of hunger. For dinner she said that she knew she should cook something or pick up healthy deli food, but that she really enjoyed takeout. A neighborhood restaurant made fried potstickers that she loved, so she usually got that along with their spicy fried chicken wings. She often finished the evening with a pint of ice cream and/or packaged chips or other snack food.

When I first brought up some small behavioral changes that Bethany might consider, I sensed that she was resistant. We talked about her starting to track her food online or in a written journal without attempting to make any changes at first—just to get in the habit of tracking. When she came back to my office the next week, she began the session by sheepishly reporting that she had just started the tracking the night before. I had the feeling that I was a teacher or monitor checking up on whether she had done her homework and I also had the sense that she wasn't being entirely honest. This counter-transference feeling signaled to me that we were suddenly at odds with each other in the arena of food and not in the kind of therapeutic alliance that could exact any meaningful change.

I gave more thought to Bethany's situation, considering her isolation, her perceived failure at never having a romantic relationship, and the real likelihood that she might never have a child. Adding to that, the experience of being morbidly obese is a profoundly isolating one, as many obese individuals describe the stigma they experience as a series of micro-insults which accumulate daily. One former patient of mine who was morbidly obese referred to herself as a "fat leper" as a way to convey the social treatment she perceived by others. As I tried to imagine Bethany's lived experience I was overwhelmed by a profound sense of loss, loneliness, and hopelessness. How on earth could she give up her nightly fried food when it was the only thing she had to look forward to? Back when she had been able to imagine the pleasure of being a mother Bethany was able to give up comfort food, but as that possibility diminished she came to have no other affective, existential, or neurological pleasure other than food. It was her whole world.

Paradoxically, Bethany's weight is likely keeping her from many of things she wants: a relationship, a baby, a richer social life, and a better job; yet she is unable to give up her only comfort. The leap of faith required to change her eating habits is too great, such that when she imagines her life without the companion of hyperpalatable comfort food it seems bleak and impoverished. When I consider Bethany's impossible situation, it makes me incredibly angry at the food industry. Bethany is a casualty of their success, just as the many people who died from lung cancer were casualties of the tobacco industry and just as drug addicts are casualties of the dealers and manufacturers of drugs. Although it is not clear that she suffers from an addiction, it is clear that her use of food for self-soothing has undermined her psychological and social well-being. She has been dehumanized and socially discarded because of her fatness, just as the street addict has been relegated to invisibleness and non-personhood.

Food addiction and the DSM

Because there has not been conclusive evidence that food is addictive until very recently, the American Psychiatric Association has never recognized food addiction as a substance disorder, yet many food researchers are now calling for such recognition. Much of the research on food now shows that it has these addictive effects. For example, rats fed a diet of hyperpalatable foods show the behavioral signs of withdrawal, tolerance, and continued use despite negative consequences (Vanderschuren & Everitt, 2004), and individuals who endorse many symptoms of food addiction experience more food-related cravings and demonstrate more intense neural activation when consuming highly palatable foods (Gearhardt, Corbin, & Brownell, 2009; Gearhardt et al., 2011d). Other studies have shown an inverse relationship between BMI and illicit drug use (Blüml et al., 2012), a lower risk for substance use disorders in obese individuals (Simon et al., 2006), and lower rates of nicotine use (Blendy et al., 2005) and marijuana abuse (Warren, Frost-Pineda, & Gold, 2005), suggesting that overeating attenuates the use of other drugs possibly because the food itself functions as a drug. Not surprisingly, then, in what is increasingly referred to as "addiction transfer" (Blum et al., 2011), food can become the new drug of choice as a result of alcohol or drug abstinence, often leading to weight gain among recovering addicts (Gold, Frost-Pineda, & Jacobs, 2003). Conversely, a small but significant portion of patients who undergo bariatric surgery for weight loss show an increased risk for substance abuse (Conason et al., 2013). All of this research supports that food, or certain kinds of food, can be just as addictive as other substances of abuse.

Although food addiction does not appear in the *DSM* section on substance use, a different section of the manual on feeding and eating disorders states the following: "Some individuals with disorders described in this chapter report eating-related symptoms resembling those typically endorsed by individuals with substance-use disorders, such as strong craving and patterns of compulsive use. The resemblance may reflect the involvement of the same neural systems, including those implicated in regulatory self-control and reward in both groups of disorders. However, the relative contributions of shared and distinct factors in the development and perpetuation of eating and substance use disorder remain insufficiently understood" (*DSM-5*, p. 329). This passage suggests that subsequent editions of the *DSM* may eventually recognize food as addictive, and many scientists are explicitly calling on the American Psychiatric Association to do so given the very strong emerging research (Volkow, Wang, Tomasi, & Baler, 2013). Arguing for the recognition of food addiction, researcher Ashley Gearhardt and her colleagues summarized these similarities between hyperpalatable foods and addictive drugs (Gearhardt et al., 2011a). They note that like other addictive drugs, hyperpalatable foods:

1 activate dopamine and opioid neural circuitry

2 trigger artificially elevated levels of reward

3 are absorbed rapidly into the bloodstream

4 alter neurobiological systems

5 cause compensatory mechanisms that result in tolerance

6 are combined with additives to enhance rewarding properties

7 elicit cue-triggered cravings

8 are consumed in spite of negative consequences

9 are consumed in spite of a desire to cut down

10 impact disadvantaged groups to a disproportionate degree

11 cause high public health costs

12 result in long-term alterations from exposure in utero

The recognition of food addiction as a formal diagnostic category has considerable public policy implications. Tobacco, alcohol, and other addictive drugs are all recognized as substances of abuse in the *DSM* and are subject to regulation as a matter of public health. If hyperpalatable foods were also recognized as dangerous addictive substances, then lawmakers would have much firmer ground to stand on in efforts to tax, regulate, and label such foods.

More recently, however, other researchers have called "food addiction" a misnomer and instead have proposed that "eating addiction" is a more valid scientific construct (Hebebrand et al., 2014). They argue that the term "food addiction" places blame on the food industry for producing addictive foods and that labeling foods as such implies that they contain an inherently addictive property—something that has not been conclusively proven in human models. They suggest that the term "eating addiction" is more accurate because it places emphasis on the behavior rather than substance. Other so-called behavioral addictions include gambling and are recognized in the *Diagnostic and Statistical Manual* (American Psychiatric Association, 2013). The debate over eating addiction vs. food addiction may seem like a subtle semantic distinction, but the implications are significant given the differences in regulation for casinos (i.e., for the behavioral addiction of gambling) vs. tobacco (i.e., for the substance addiction to nicotine). In the coming years, additional research will illuminate which of the two constructs is the more accurate and valid.

Returning to the culture of consumerism and the market as religion, we can now see how the global industrial diet and its elaborately engineered foods create a snowballing cycle of consumerism, in which we need more to be satisfied. Failing to see the neuroendocrinological effects of these foods, namely how they undermine satiety and increase fat storage, is to miss a fundamental link between the individual's consumption of food and the culture which promotes consuming more. The emerging science of food addiction which shows that the refinement of hyperpalatable foods is much like the refinement of highly potent, rapidly absorbed drugs such as cocaine and heroin suggests that the makers of industrial foods may not be unlike any other drug dealer, who creates dangerous irresistible products which compromise public health. Establishing food addiction or eating addiction as a diagnostic category is therefore one of the most important steps toward increased awareness and/or regulation of these products. Yet, changes to psychiatry's diagnostic manual are complicated in part because of the influence of Big Pharma. In fact, Big Food and Big Pharma are two powerful bedfellows of consumer culture, as we shall see in the final chapters.

8

Binge Eating Disorder, the *DSM*, and Consumer Culture

The *Diagnostic and Statistical Manual* (American Psychiatric Association, 2013), now in its fifth edition, has been the standard reference text in the mental health field for the past sixty years. Published by the American Psychiatric Association, it catalogs all mental disorders and is used by psychologists, nurses, social workers, and virtually all mental health and medical professionals in the United States, as well as in many other parts of the world. The manual is also used as the basis for undergraduate abnormal psychology classes, training in graduate psychology and psychiatry programs, clinical treatment decisions, and health insurance billing. In addition to this widespread clinical use, the manual's criteria have been adopted by an extraordinary number of federal organizations and laws such as the National Institute of Mental Health, the Americans with Disabilities Act, the Veterans Administration, prison systems, and education agencies. In short, the ways in which the *DSM* describes and categorizes mental disorders have far-reaching effects on regulatory efforts, research, and treatment of many health conditions and behaviors, including overeating, overweight, obesity, and addiction.

Eating disorders and the *DSM*

The previous edition of the diagnostic manual, known as *DSM-IV*, was used for nearly twenty years until the long-awaited *DSM 5* was finally published amid some controversy in 2013. In the earlier *DSM-IV*, the APA had recognized two distinct eating disorders: Anorexia Nervosa and Bulimia Nervosa. Anorexia Nervosa is characterized by significant underweight (85 percent or less than healthy body weight) and has two diagnostic subtypes: restricting type and bingeing/purging type. Restricting type refers to individuals who engage in severe food or caloric restriction, whereas bingeing/purging type refers to those who engage in episodes of extreme overeating followed by compensatory behaviors such as purging, laxative use, or excessive exercise. Bulimia Nervosa is characterized by binge eating episodes, followed by compensatory behaviors in individuals who are not underweight.[1]

In other words, there was no diagnosis for binge eating without purging or compensatory behavior; however, a significant literature had emerged on binge eating without purging. Because of the increased scientific recognition of binge eating without purging, which was perhaps in turn due to a population-wide increase of overeating, the *DSM 5* Task Force was charged with determining whether people who binge eat without compensatory behaviors were "disordered" in the same or similar way as those diagnosed with Bulimia or Anorexia. After reviewing the research, the task force concluded that the evidence supported a third diagnostic category, and thus Binge Eating Disorder (BED) was codified in 2013.

The *DSM* now defines Binge Eating Disorder as follows (American Psychiatric Association, 2013):

A Recurrent episodes of binge eating. An episode of binge eating is characterized by both of the following:

1 Eating, in a discrete period of time (e.g., within any two-hour period), an amount of food that is definitely larger than what most people would eat in a similar period of time under similar circumstances.

2 A sense of lack of control over eating during the episode (e.g., a feeling that one cannot stop eating or control what or how much one is eating).

B The binge-eating episodes are associated with three (or more) of the following:

1 Eating much more rapidly than normal

2 Eating until feeling uncomfortably full

3 Eating large amounts of food when not feeling physically hungry

---

[1] A common misunderstanding of these two diagnoses is that only bulimia involves bingeing and purging, whereas, in fact, either disorder can involve bingeing and purging. The key to the differential diagnosis is body weight, not behavior.

> **4** Eating alone because of feeling embarrassed by how much one is eating
>
> **5** Feeling disgusted with oneself, depressed, or very guilty afterward
>
> **C** Marked distress regarding binge eating is present.
>
> **D** The binge eating occurs, on average, at least once a week for three months.

One obvious question is whether or not Binge Eating Disorder is simply food addiction or eating addiction? If so, would that not be more appropriately categorized as a substance disorder or behavioral addiction, as discussed in the previous chapter? The early research suggests that despite many similarities, BED represents a unique condition (Gearhardt, White, & Potenza, 2011c) involving episodic overeating, whereas food/eating addiction involves chronic overconsumption. Moreover, like the other eating disorders, BED may emerge from eating-related cognitive distortions and body image concerns, which is not necessarily true for disorders of addiction which emerge from physiological dependence. Such questions of diagnostic validity and nosology will be worked out in time, but the more important questions for the purpose of this book are: (a) what is the relationship between Binge Eating Disorder and consumer culture, and (b) what might be the unintended consequences of this new diagnosis?

Medicalizing normal

While the American Psychiatric Association views itself as a scientific body that *describes* psychopathology, in so doing, it also *generates* psychopathology by presenting a symptom repertoire to individuals. Once any new diagnosis is codified it extends a new symptom repertoire to the members of that culture, in some ways creating more diagnoses by offering a recognized means to express distress. In other words, adding BED to the *DSM* may well create more binge eaters by presenting a culturally recognized syndrome. Former *DSM-IV* Task Force Chair and now outspoken critic of *DSM 5*, Allen Frances wrote in his book *Saving Normal* (2013):

> I meet the criteria for binge eating disorder and have for almost as long as I can remember. It started in my early teenage years. Stealth trips to my mother's overly stocked pantry and bulging refrigerator leading to

solitary nighttime pig-outs of epic proportions. In college, I wrestled at 177 pounds but after the match would begin a two-day binge that would bring me up to a Monday weight of 191—and would then have to starve and dehydrate to get back to 177 by the next Saturday. I have always been the scourge of buffet lines and all-you-can-eat restaurants. Never have I gone for more than a week without a monster binge. The only way I can stay a svelte twenty-five pounds overweight is to avoid all breakfasts and lunches and by exercising several hours a day. Am I just a run-of-the-mill glutton with terrible eating habits and lousy self-control or am I a DSM-5 mental patient with binge eating disorder? (Frances, 2013)

Frances argues that BED is a low-threshold diagnosis, meaning that it does not require extremes of behavior to qualify for inclusion and consequently sweeps too many people into its reaches. This speaks to one of the inherent problems with authoring any diagnostic manual, which is the challenge of diagnoses appearing or disappearing as the book is revised based on new scientific information. For example, I have a patient who had never been diagnosed with any disorder prior to May 2013. Although she experienced what she referred to as "body issues," she did not meet criteria for any eating disorder. By her report, she went to a bakery about once a week and binged on two or three large cinnamon rolls, feeling guilty and regretful afterwards. She stated that after one of these episodes it wasn't too difficult for her to adjust her food intake over the next day or two so that over the long run she never put on weight. Certainly I can't defend this as a healthy practice, but is it a mental disorder? She had a slender frame, but nothing close to the 15 percent underweight required for a diagnosis of Anorexia Nervosa, nor did she engage in any of the pathological compensatory behaviors described by the *DSM*. These overindulgences caused her some distress, but did not interfere with her daily activities, nor did they cause weight gain since she corrected for them through self-regulation. In my view, the biggest problem with this behavior was the huge quantities of sugar she consumed, but overconsumption of sugar is not currently a psychiatric illness. However, when she went to bed on May 17, 2013, she had no diagnosis, and when she woke up on May 18 she qualified for Binge Eating Disorder.

Certainly, almost any time a new diagnosis is added to the *DSM* or broadened in its scope there are people it "catches" in its net for whom the diagnosis is appropriate. For example, many years ago, there were a set of children struggling with autism-like symptoms who did not fully meet the criteria for Autism Disorder. The *DSM* Task Force responded to this by creating the Asperger's Disorder diagnosis. Suddenly a group of children who didn't previously qualify for any diagnosis now had one. This recognition of Asperger's Disorder allowed researchers to test treatments and interventions, provided schools with additional resources for special education, and provided treatment coverage for people who were suffering. After several years on the books, however, Asperger's Disorder became wildly overdiagnosed resulting in overmedication, overtreatment, and placed far too much demand on schools to provide special services to children (Mayes, Calhoun, & Crites, 2001; Rosenberg, Daniels, Law, Law, & Kaufmann, 2009). The diagnosis became so trendy that the term "aspy" became fashionable as an adjective to describe personality characteristics such as introversion, shyness, and social awkwardness—hardly the makings of a neurodevelopmental disorder.

Responding to this rampant overdiagnosis, the *DSM 5* Task Force did away with the Asperger's diagnosis and significantly limited the scope of the reconfigured Autism Spectrum Disorder. Such revisions and corrections are part and parcel of any system of classification—even the planets in the solar system are organized and described differently than they were thirty years ago. Problems arise, however, when prisons, schools, and health insurance companies tie eligibility and coverage for services to *DSM* diagnoses because that places tremendous legal and social responsibility on an imperfect system of classification. The *DSM* simply does not have the psychometric rigor necessary to vest it with the authority to determine so many educational, legal, political, and medical decisions.

These problems of overdiagnosis and underdiagnosis are what statisticians refer to as Type I and Type II errors. In statistical terms, a Type I error is the incorrect rejection of a true null hypothesis, that is, a false positive. By contrast, a Type II error is the failure to reject a false null hypothesis, or a false negative. What this means diagnostically is that when the *DSM* adds or expands diagnoses, as it did with the addition of Asperger's Disorder, it will inevitably create false positive diagnoses, whereas when it eliminates a diagnosis or limits its diagnostic criteria, it will result in Type II errors or false negatives—people who ought to have the diagnosis no longer qualify. That there are such diagnostic mistakes because of imperfect taxonomy is not a reason to throw the baby out with the bathwater. It is impossible to avoid errors in any taxonomic system and the makers of the *DSM* are charged with the unenviable task of balancing the two kind of errors. In the current climate of consumerism, however, there is a bias toward erring on the side of false positives which has the effect of increasing consumption and profitability through inappropriate diagnoses and unnecessary treatments (Frances, 2013; Moynihan & Cassels, 2005; Welch, Schwartz, & Woloshin, 2011).

Such overdiagnosis and overtreatment is not just a problem in psychiatry—it has become a serious and well-documented problem throughout the American medical system (Brownlee, 2007; Welch et al., 2011). The development of a health care system that is primarily a for-profit enterprise creates a system in which physicians must compete for market share or patients, and they are rewarded with higher profits when they sell more of their product, namely tests, screenings, pills, and treatments. Moreover, physicians must often recoup investments in costly equipment which results in even more unnecessary diagnoses and treatments. This drive for profitability is the foundation of the US health care system, and it courts the Type I error, or false positive diagnosis. By contrast, erring toward Type II errors or watchful waiting and conservative treatment decisions would reduce spending and consumption, therefore restricting any economy based on consumer spending. In other words, the funnel of consumer culture in which a sound economy is based on continual increases in consumption leads not only to overeating, but also to overtreatment and overmedicating as part of the spending economy.

Returning to the diagnosis of Binge Eating Disorder, while it is certainly true that chronic binge eating is unhealthful, the reality is that *occasional* binge eating is characteristic of virtually every species. Likely stemming from our evolutionary past, bingeing when a food source was available was adaptive for most of human history and became enshrined in many cultural rituals. It is risky to define a disorder based on symptoms that at times are nothing more than part of the human condition, although many *DSM* diagnoses are just that. This phenomenon is what Allen Frances refers to as "medicalizing normal" and he argues that the *DSM* medicalizes normal in many cases, as seen in diagnoses for AD/HD, social anxiety, and depression. Most recently, for example, the *DSM* eliminated what was known as the "bereavement exclusion" for the diagnosis of Major Depressive Disorder (MDD). In previous editions of the *DSM*, one was excluded from a diagnosis of MDD if they had experienced the loss of a loved one within the past two months. The logic was that within that time frame any symptoms of depression were simply an expression of normal grief, and not a disorder. With *DSM 5*, however, the criteria changed and those grieving the loss of a loved one were no longer excluded from the diagnosis, serving to pathologize normal sadness and encouraging clinicians to medicate those experiencing grief, thereby increasing aggregate consumption of medications and treatments.

Just as we distinguish between depression vs. bereavement, perhaps we should also distinguish between those who suffer from extreme binge eating and those who occasionally binge eat or simply overeat. Surely, there are many who will benefit from treatment of Binge Eating Disorder, but what about the people who will be incorrectly diagnosed with BED, that is, the new false positives? It is these people at the mild end of the continuum of behavior, such as my patient who binged on cinnamon rolls, who will be most vulnerable to marketing by the pharmaceutical industry. Why?

Because the line between binge eating and overeating is blurry, because of the social desirability of being thin, and because of the appeal of taking a pill to solve a complex and challenging behavioral problem, mild binge eating is an ideal condition for treatment by what's known as "lifestyle drugs." Lifestyle drugs refer to treatments for non-painful or non-life-threatening conditions, such as erectile dysfunction, baldness, or inattention which are aggressively marketed by pharmaceutical companies, often through direct-to consumer (DTC) advertising. In 1997, the United States became one of two countries to allow pharmaceutical companies to advertise their products directly to consumers through television commercials and magazine advertisements (Ventola, 2011). Prior to that time, the only way to find out about branded medication was through a physician. Now the refrain, "Ask your doctor…" is present in any number of advertisements for drugs that treat depression, social anxiety disorder, adult ADD, and erectile dysfunction. In spite of evidence that many of these drugs are no more effective than placebos, and often less so, the pharmaceutical industry continues to aggressively market them, demonstrating that desire for profits outweighs concern for personal well-being or any concern for the effects of unnecessary and excessive medication.

We've already seen how the food and supplement industry manufacture desire among the affluent and healthy by creating products for longevity, youth, energy, and better fitness. Just like energy bars, sports drinks, and supplements, many lifestyle drugs offer the promise of becoming the uber-capitalist, in which unlimited choice, youth, freedom, and productivity are there for the taking. For example, many drugs previously prescribed for conditions like AD/HD and narcolepsy are now widely used off-label as "neuroenhancers" by high functioning individuals wanting to increase productivity (Repantis, Schlattmann, Laisney, & Heuser, 2010). While the drug companies are not technically allowed to market these medications for such use, it is clear they profit heavily from it. Other drugs for conditions like baldness, vaginal dryness, erectile dysfunction, or hormone replacement promise us vitality, beauty, and virility. Advertisements for these conditions exploit our deepest existential terrors about mortality, aging, and isolation. These drugs not only offer the possibility of a "better you," but they promise our unconsciouses that perhaps we can forestall loneliness, aging, or death.

The creation of the lifestyle drug market has long been the dream of pharmaceutical executives as a means to expand their market from the sick to the healthy. In fact, Merck's former chief executive Henry Gadsen once told *Fortune* magazine that he wanted Merck to be more like the chewing gum manufacturer Wrigley's (Moynihan & Cassels, 2005, p. ix). To that end, Big Pharma has been on a decades-long campaign to brand and sell not just treatments, but disorders as well. The class of drugs known as SSRIs (serotonin specific reuptake inhibitors or selective serotonin reuptake inhibitors), for example, are the most widely prescribed lifestyle drugs for psychiatric conditions including anxiety disorders, eating disorders, addictions, subclinical depression, and even menopause. Initially approved and prescribed for depression, these drugs such as Prozac, Zoloft, and Paxil have had very mixed results in efficacy studies with many clinical trials failing to show significant treatment differences against placebos in either mild, moderate, or severely depressed individuals (Kirsch, 2010). In fact, the widely accepted "chemical imbalance" theory of depression, which is hypothesized to be insufficient levels of serotonin, has never been conclusively proven. In meta-analyses which evaluate dozens of published and unpublished clinical trials, the findings suggest that SSRIs and related drugs may be nothing more than glorified placebos. But they sure do sell.

Adding a new low-threshold diagnosis such as Binge Eating Disorder captures millions more people as potential users of prescription medication. Early research estimates that 3 percent of the US population would qualify for Binge Eating Disorder at some point in their lifetime, and another 7 percent of the population would be considered subthreshold, meaning that they engage in binge-eating episodes, but do not meet full criteria for the diagnosis (Hudson, Hiripi, Pope, & Kessler, 2007). That's 30 million people in the threshold or subthreshold range of BED are now in the crosshairs of possible medication, particularly since an individual needn't meet full diagnostic criteria for any illness to be prescribed a medication, as doctors very often prescribe drugs either off-label or for subthreshold cases (Stafford, 2008). Note that many of these commonly prescribed medications such as Prozac, Ritalin, and Adderall can cause very serious side effects including weight fluctuations, psychosis, suicidality, and addiction. There are now enormous numbers of people at risk for these side effects, including the millions of children on stimulant medication alone, with a troubling 10,000 of those children still only toddlers (Visser et al., 2014).

Disease mongering and consumer culture

In the culture of consumerism, diagnoses themselves become powerful currency in that the very existence of a diagnosis manufactures needs by creating new consumer demand. In other words, the broadening or adding of diagnoses to the *DSM* and the ensuing overtreatment are simply another means of increasing overall consumption in the form of treatments, books, pills, and diets. The manufacturing of disease is an odd twist on the manufacturing of desire because who would desire a disease? Yet Big Pharma's marketing, advertising, and "disease awareness" campaigns, often referred to as disease mongering, generate huge profits by convincing people they have illnesses that need prescription treatment. The American Psychiatric Association is partly culpable, or at least unintentionally complicit in Big Pharma's disease mongering because the addition or expansion of any new diagnosis opens the door for more prescriptions and increased profitability. To be sure, psychiatry and psychopharmacology have great solutions and treatments for the moderate to severely mentally ill; however, the trend since 1997 has been to capture the mild end of the diagnostic continuum for the purpose of marketing and selling pills and other treatments. One in five adults now takes at least one psychiatric drug such as an antidepressant, antipsychotic, or anti-anxiety medication (Wang, 2011) and the use of psychiatric medications among adults grew 22 percent from 2001 to 2010 (Medco, 2011). This is largely accomplished through the lax regulation that allows advertising directly to consumers with commercials which often do not even mention a specific condition, but merely promise a carefree life of running along the beach, jumping through dandelions, or lip-synching to fun music while cooking dinner. In other words, they hold up a beautiful life and suggest that we could have such a life if only we had the advertised disorder and its treatment. Comedian Chris Rock (2005) poignantly captures this in one of his standup routines:

> Every night on TV you see a weird-ass drug commercial trying to get you hooked on some legal shit. And they just keep naming symptoms till they get one that you fucking got. It's like: are you sad? Are you lonely? Do you got athlete's foot? Are you hot? Are you cold? Whatchyou got? You want this pill motherfucker? You got to take this pill! They don't even tell you what the pill does. You see a lady on a horse or a man in a tub. And they just keep naming symptoms. Are you depressed? Are you lonely? Do your teeth hurt? What the fuck? I saw a commercial the other day that said, "Do you go to bed at night and wake up in the morning?" Oh shit, they got one! I got that! I'm sick, I need that pill!

Binge eating as the crystallization of cultural psychopathology

The *DSM* is often referred to as psychiatry's Bible, and much like the Christian Bible its adherents often evangelize its message far and wide, failing to recognize the text as a cultural and historical artifact. Like any artifact, the *DSM* is locally and epochally valid, but it is not universal or ahistorical. The *DSM* is an important but flawed book that is caught in a disciplinary identity crisis, as psychiatry and psychology have simply never offered the validity of the natural sciences. In their efforts to bolster its validity, the makers of the *DSM* have advanced a biomedical model of behavior which conceives brain and mind as organisms to be understood scientifically or medically.

By contrast, phenomenologists think about the "lived body" or our subjective experience of ourselves and how behavior is an expression of ourselves and the culture. That is not to say that the psychological suffering described in the pages of the *DSM* is not valid or real, nor does it mean that there may not be biological bases to the diagnoses—it is simply to say that the phenomenology and expression of those illnesses is shaped by time, place, and culture. The classification of binge eating as a psychiatric disorder, however, has the effect of reinforcing the idea that overeating is a failure of the self—a consequence of a broken brain or a lapse in willpower. This way of thinking about overeating places the locus of behavior entirely on the bounded individual, decontextualized from surrounding cultural and economic forces.

Manipulation and control of the body, especially the female body, can be seen across history and across cultures in practices such as foot binding and corseting. In the 1980s, Susan Bordo argued that Anorexia Nervosa was a disorder which crystallized the psychopathology of our culture. She wrote that anorexia "appears less as the extreme expression of a character structure than as a remarkably overdetermined symptom of some of the multifaceted and heterogeneous distresses of our age. Just as anorexia functions in a variety of ways in the psychic economy of the anorexic individual, so a variety of cultural currents or streams converge in anorexia, find their perfect, precise expression in it" (Bordo, 1986, p. 226). In similar logic, we might think of BED as a new crystallization of cultural psychopathology in that it expresses the cultural problem of overeating and overconsumption via individual disorder. Any time a culture has extreme values or practices there will be individuals in that culture who "house" or express those extremes in what appear to be individual pathology, but simultaneously serve as proxies for all of us.

These proxy disorders are sometimes referred to as "culture bound syndromes" or "idioms of distress," which are illness metaphors accompanied by a set of recognized behaviors, symptoms, and language which communicate sickness. In South Asia, for example, Dhat is a culture-bound syndrome characterized by the fear of loss of semen. It is a "disorder" which likely expresses anxiety about virility or shame about sexual impulses and masturbation. Likewise in Japan, the disorder Taijin Kyofusho is a type of agoraphobic social anxiety characterized by fears of offending others with one's body odor or poor hygiene, reflecting perhaps the high value the Japanese place on order and cleanliness. All cultures have such tacit symptom repertoires offered to its people as a means of expressing distress—an internalized "menu" from which we unconsciously choose symptom sets as ways to express the difficulties of living. We might, for example, think about the "human Barbie," a woman who has cosmetically and surgically altered herself to appear uncannily like a Barbie doll (LaFerla, 2013), as someone who has crystallized both the cultural glorification of slender Nordic beauty and the acceptance of surgical procedures to alter one's appearance. She serves as a proxy for complex cultural phenomena, but at an individual level she might be diagnosed with Body Dysmorphic Disorder, thus demonstrating how the *DSM* serves as both manual and artifact of a given place and time.

Thinking about *DSM* disorders as culture-bound syndromes does not rule out the possible biological or neurological causes of mental illnesses, but it *redistributes* the locus of origin onto the culture, and not just onto or within the individual. In other words, a disorder might well originate in neurochemical or neuroanatomical pathology, but be activated or exacerbated by cultural pathology. Often it is difficult to see the cultural pathology that influences individual diagnoses because we reside in a blind spot which keeps us from seeing how individuals can serve as diagnostic proxies for the culture.

Americans are particularly vulnerable to serving as such diagnostic proxies for three reasons: first, the discipline of psychology has historically been overly focused on the individual as its unit of study, often ignoring contexts such as race, class, gender, region, and ethnicity in the construction of the self. Second, the Western self is so highly individualized that it experiences itself as ahistorical, bounded, and contained from an interconnected, collective ecosystem. Third, the prevailing biological/chemical imbalance model guides our thinking toward the individual and the brain as the units of diagnosis and treatment. All of these forces converge in a way that cause us to experience cultural ills interiorly rather than thinking of diagnoses as expressions of something outside of ourselves.

In the case of BED, the cultural pathology is overconsumption, and more specifically the overeating of foods that are toxic or simply too much for the body. An illusion is created by the *DSM*, however, that overeating is a disease of the individual. Psychiatry and psychology enhance that illusion through the powerful message that pushes people to blame themselves for overeating and to seek solutions at the individual level through diets, pills, and surgery. Treating overeating this way serves to let the food industry and policy makers off the hook because psychiatry's disease paradigm absolves them of responsibility. Much like the tobacco industry did, the highly profitable food industry places all accountability and locus of control on the individual, the effects of which are reinforced by the highly profitable industries of psychiatry and Big Pharma. Speaking to this, Allen Frances wrote,

> BED is being offered as psychiatry's answer to the obesity epidemic (which is rapidly overtaking smoking as our most deadly public health threat). Unfortunately psychiatry has no answers here—no cure for binge eating or for obesity. But even more to the point, BED distracts attention from what could provide a real cure for the obesity epidemic. We need a dramatic change in public policy. Our society is getting way too fat not because of an epidemic of this newly devised mental disorder, but rather through the ever present and always tempting availability of cheap, delicious, convenient, caloric, and horribly unhealthy fast food, snacks, and sodas.... Mental disorder is not causing the obesity epidemic. And treating a fake mental disorder can't fix it. It won't help to label as psychiatrically sick the victims of our dumb public policies; it's far better to change the policies.... Phony psychiatric labels won't help. Making BED focuses attention on the wrong culprit; it is not the individual who is sick, it is the public policy. (Frances, 2013, p. 183)

At the individual level, treatment for overeating cannot simply be going on a diet or taking prescription medication, but must involve a rejection or rethinking of the food landscape and consumer culture. I can assure you that from a clinical perspective this is a Herculean task. Even patients who come to me highly motivated to change are daunted by the dramatic paradigm shift involved in rethinking all of their food choices and critically reevaluating their relationship to consumer culture.

Hoarding: Another disorder of consumption?

Another disorder which was newly added to *DSM 5* is Hoarding Disorder, characterized by persistent difficulty discarding or parting with possessions regardless of their actual value. Hoarding is a result of a strong perceived need to save the items and a response to acute distress associated with discarding them. It usually results in the accumulation of a large number of possessions that congest and clutter active living, such that their intended use is substantially compromised (American Psychiatric Association, 2013). Although they are not categorized together nor are they thought to be etiologically related, Binge Eating Disorder and Hoarding Disorder both represent excesses of consumption, such that it is unsurprising that they were added to the *DSM* at the same time. Both disorders involve a frenzy of acquisition and consumption used to stimulate or calm the self through food or consumer goods. Simply put, they are both expressions of a culture grappling with the excesses of prosperity and abundance.

Often not a part of the mainstream dialogue in psychology is how our possessions, or what archaeologists call material culture, affect our well-being. The desire for stuff, the attachment to stuff, the burden of caring for and storing stuff, and the difficulties of getting rid of stuff have an enormous psychological impact on us. Recall that the UCLA researchers who studied contemporary American families found that the large number of possessions including toys, clothing, and food cluttered active living spaces and created stressful household bottlenecks. The people they studied were not diagnosed with Hoarding Disorder, nor did they exhibit the extreme breakdown in functioning required for that diagnosis; however, they and their households suffered from the ill-effects of buying and acquiring too much stuff (Arnold, 2012). Similarly, a striking photo-ethnography *Material World: A Global Family Portrait* features the work of sixteen photographers who traveled to thirty nations to document typical families' material possessions. The families were photographed outside of their homes with the entire contents of the home staged alongside them. As you might imagine, there is tremendous variability in the quantity and quality of possessions across cultures. Notably, many of the families in developing countries are surrounded by a scant few possessions, often simply food preparation tools such as mortars and pestles, whereas other families, typically those in North America and Western Europe, are surrounded by a staggering number of possessions. These families often posed with expansive collections of items like Beanie Babies, bringing into relief the way that culture and materialism mediate our identities.

I once worked with a patient who frequently went shopping and bought heaps of clothing, which she would fondle and try on at home, but then would always return to the store. She viewed this behavior as a clever strategy to control her spending—that is, she could have the high of buying new things without the damage to her pocketbook. It was an effective trick which satisfied an impulse without any obvious negative consequences. It struck me, however, that this was essentially "shopping bulimia"—a type of bingeing behavior meant to create the feeling of consumption and satiety, followed by purging or undoing meant to expunge the overconsumption. Unlike the compensatory behaviors in bulimia, however, there was no physical harm in returning the unused merchandise to a store, and many stores have adopted lax return policies because their market research proves that this increases sales.

This buying and returning of clothes parallels the bingeing and purging of Bulimia Nervosa, just as another recent phenomenon known as "shopping hauls" parallels Binge Eating Disorder. Similar to unboxing videos, shopping haul videos document buying sprees of cheap clothing usually by young women that are then posted to the internet. Watching several of these videos one can see a manic glee in the presentation of clothing, shoes, and handbags—a triumph of acquisition. Unlike binge eating, which is often done in secret and followed by shame and guilt, clothing hauls are something to take pride in and are publicized. Both kinds of "episodes" are very similar—they involve an episode of overconsumption, usually of cheap and potentially toxic goods in which volume is valued over quality.

Accounting for why people consume material objects, earlier theorists offered the following explanations: (a) acquisition is a way of assuaging anxiety, (b) acquisition represents a desire for security and status by having more than one's neighbors, (c) acquisitive tendencies result when self-assertive tendencies are weak, and (d) the desire for an object rarely represents a desire for the object itself, but rather is a symbolic triangulation between the object, the person desiring it, and a hoped-for effect on another person (Pearce, 1936). Binge Eating Disorder and Hoarding Disorder might be what Kottler termed "disorders of acquisitive desire" (1999). "Like substance abuse and eating disorders, problems of acquisitive desire represent a multifaceted cluster of enduring cognitive, behavioral, and social factors that are linked with other symptoms, such as anxiety, depression, and impulsivity." Acquisitive desire does not refer to a single *DSM* disorder, but rather an underlying construct that involves an intense desire to acquire, possess, or hoard objects.

Note that Hoarding Disorder and Binge Eating Disorder have very different etiologies, courses, treatments, and outcomes. The similarities I draw between them have to do with the cultural and economic context in which they flourish, as well as the underlying drives of desire and acquisition. Consider as a parallel the two diseases cholera and malaria. These are two very different diseases, but certain climatic conditions must be met for each to thrive and spread. The same is true for bingeing and hoarding: the economic and cultural conditions of prosperity and consumerism must be met for the disorders to thrive, but as they play out at the individual level they have distinct neural substrates, cognitive processes, and hormonal mechanisms.

Through the codification of Binge Eating Disorder we can see the forces of numerous embedded cycles of consumption, depicted in Figure 8.1. First, food companies develop and market hyperpalatable foods which are engineered to be irresistible. Individuals eat and overeat the food, leading to overweight, obesity, and psychological distress. The APA codifies this behavior as an illness and includes it in its highly profitable book the *DSM*, offering the pharmaceutical companies a new market share. Desperate individuals then try to replace the consumption of food with the consumption of medication and treatment, often to no avail because they remain surrounded by the

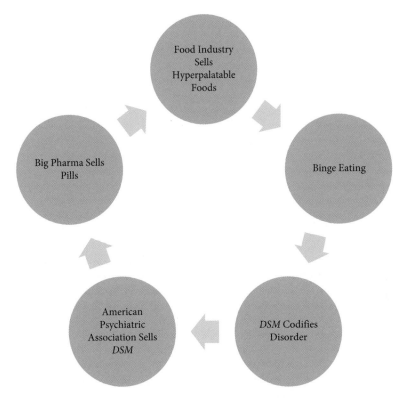

FIGURE 8.1 *Embedded cycles of consumerism.*

irresistible hyperpalatable food. In other words, both the disease and the cure are simply different forms of overconsuming which trap us in a cycle that does not address the underlying cultural and economic ill.

Note that the two industries responsible for these cycles of consumption are Big Food and Big Pharma, both regulated by the Food and Drug Administration. As we shall see in the next chapters, the FDA's regulatory decisions are at the heart of consumer culture and mediate the tension between consumerism *as a moral doctrine* and a *social ideology*, in which individual choice and freedom are often at odds with the protection of the psychological and physical health.

9

The Bedfellows of Consumer Culture: Big Food and Big Pharma

As two of the biggest global industries of consumer culture, Big Food and Big Pharma run similar operations and use many of the same tactics to manufacture consumer desire. In many cases, the pills of Western medicine are incredibly similar to the branded, ultra-processed foods of the global industrial diet. Not only do the two industries use many of the same techniques to market their products and generate demand, but they also enjoy a symbiotic relationship in which they supply each other with demand. For example, many medications are used to treat the effects of overeating, overweight, and obesity, but such use may actually perpetuate overeating in the promise to undo or counteract overconsumption. Although Western medicine is no doubt a triumph of innovation and science, the *business* of medicine is a different story than the *science* of medicine, and pharmaceutical companies are beholden to shareholders to constantly increase profits, just as the food companies are.

Expanding markets in food and drugs

The expansion of market share is a good point of origin at which to examine Big Food and Big Pharma's twin roles in consumer culture and the manufacture of desire. In order to constantly increase profits, both industries must constantly develop new products and expand into new markets. As we've already seen, the food companies do this through the relentless development of new products, flavors, and packages using irresistible, hyperpalatable ingredients. The drug companies too are constantly developing new products through the research and development of new medications, but also through expanding their market share for existing drugs.

Me-too drugs

Much to the surprise of many Americans, pharmaceutical companies need not prove that a new drug is any more effective than a drug already on the market, and in fact, a new drug can actually be worse than a drug already on the market. Pursuant to the Kefauver-Harris Drug Amendment (1962), drug makers have the burden of proof to merely show that a new drug is more effective than nothing. Consequently, pharmaceutical companies are able to introduce copycat drugs known as "me-too drugs" to compete with competitors' nearly identical drugs already on the market. In other words, GlaxcoKlineSmith can sell Paxil to compete with the nearly identical Prozac sold by Eli Lilly, just as Pepsi might release a new soda to compete with Coke or Taco Bell might release a new value meal to compete with MacDonald's. In fact, 77 percent of the new drugs approved by the FDA between 1998 and 2002 were such me-too drugs, classified by the FDA as no more effective than existing drugs treating the same condition (Angell, 2005).

Not only are the comparative efficacy standards low for the approval of new drugs, but they need only show these modest effects in an astonishing two drug trials, irrespective of how many other trials have failed to show results (Khan, Leventhal, Khan, & Brown, 2002; Kirsch, Moore, Scoboria, & Nicholls, 2002; Kirsch & Sapirstein, 1998). In other words, the FDA does not review the entire body of research on a new drug application, but only the studies selected by the drug manufacturer. By repeating clinical trials over and over, often using nefarious methodologies such as placebo washout and data suppression to inflate results (Kirsch, 2010), drug companies can easily eek out the requisite two studies to give the appearance of efficacy. Prozac, for example, has failed to outperform placebos in numerous controlled studies, yet is still one of the most widely prescribed antidepressants, and GlaxcoKlineSmith's highly profitable drug Paxil is simply a copycat of the not-so-effective Prozac.

Some economists have rightly noted that me-too drugs can lower prices by introducing competition into the marketplace (Hollis, 2004); however, me-too drugs are often accompanied by aggressive disease-mongering campaigns which convince people to "ask their doctor" for unnecessary medications, ultimately leading to increased expenditures and health care costs which does not yield market efficiency. In other cases, drug manufacturers have brought high-priced me-too drugs to market to compete with one of their own drugs nearing patent expiration. The British company AstraZeneca, for example, did this when the patent for their blockbuster drug Prilosec was nearing the end of its life, thereby cannibalizing its own market share with its new drug Nexium. Nexium was no more effective than Prilosec, nor the low-priced generic versions of Prilosec which were about to hit pharmacy shelves, but the lax evidentiary standards for efficacy allowed it to come to market anyway.

The success of these me-too drugs depends on a marketplace large enough to accommodate several similar competing drugs often prescribed for lifelong conditions such as high cholesterol or high blood pressure— conditions which are increasingly the result of or strongly correlated to overeating, overweight, and obesity. Such conditions create a large and steady market demand because sufferers must take the treating medication daily for years or even decades (Angell, 2005). Note the similarities to the food and beverage industry, in which very similar products compete for lifelong brand loyalty in a vast marketplace created through the manufacture of desire. Unlike real taste differences between competing foods and beverages, however, me-too drugs are unlikely to result in any difference in treatment effects. Because the drugs are nearly identical, often only chemical mirror images of each other known as left and right isomers (Glasgow, 2001), consumer preferences for one me-too drug over another are likely due to the name, color, or advertisements for the pill. Hardly a triumph of innovation— that is simply a triumph of sophistry.

Phony foundations and grassroots groups

Another way in which both the food and drug industries have expanded market share is by creating misleading foundations and phony grassroots groups to trick consumers. Such entities are designed to create an illusion of a nonprofit group promoting public health and wellness, but in fact are simply corporations in disguise. In 1998, for example, when the FDA approved the drug Paxil for Social Anxiety Disorder (SAD), the sales challenge for its manufacturer GlaxcoKlineSmith was that few people had ever heard of the disorder. As documented by Brendan Koerner (2002), soon after the FDA approval of Paxil for SAD several "grassroots" organizations sprang up, including the Social Anxiety Disorder Coalition and Freedom From Fear. This "disease awareness campaign" did not mention Paxil nor GlaxcoKlineSmith, but instead featured posters, radio, and TV ads featuring everyday people with the slogan "Imagine Being Allergic to People." This campaign was the handiwork of a PR firm hired by GlaxcoKlineSmith to market Social Anxiety Disorder itself. Since then, there have been countless "disease awareness campaigns" which follow the same pattern of creating mock grassroots groups populated by sufferers of an obscure and often low-threshold condition. Calling the phone number or visiting the website for the group invariably counsels people to ask their doctor about a specific medication. This marketing of the disease instead of the cure is tremendously efficient for drug makers because it does not involve the enormous labor and expense of developing a new drug. Instead, it takes an existing drug and locates new markets and indications for its use.

Similarly, the food industry has created a number of foundations and councils designed to appear as nonprofit groups devoted to public health. The International Food Information Council, for example, has a website in English and Spanish which is "dedicated to the mission of effectively communicating science-based information on health, nutrition and food safety for the public good" (2014). Funded by companies such as Cargill (no relation), Dr. Pepper Snapple, Kraft, and Monsanto, the council makes patently false claims on its website, such as "the causes of diabetes continue to be a mystery." Similarly, Coca-Cola has created the Beverage Institute for Health & Wellness (BIHW) as part of its "ongoing commitment to use evidence-based science to advance knowledge and understanding of beverages, beverage ingredients, and the important role that active healthy lifestyles play in supporting health and wellbeing" (2014). This website too makes numerous misleading claims, such as "studies show that under some circumstances, intake of sugars can boost performance on cognitive tasks." Creating a veneer of scientific credibility, they provide four academic references at the bottom of that page, yet none of those studies has anything to do with human cognition or performance on cognitive tasks. In other words, the average consumer would have no way to properly evaluate these claims because great effort has been to made to create an illusion of a nonprofit consumer education resource supported by published science.

Pharmerging markets

The newest cash cow for both the food and pharmaceutical industries is the emerging global market in which the appetites of new middle-class consumers in places like China and India are slaked with pent-up desire. First to respond to these new markets was the fast-food industry which expanded rapidly during the intense globalization of commerce in the 1990s. Now food manufacturers increasingly see these expanding markets as destinations for sodas, chips, and other ultra-processed foods. For example, in the first quarter of 2014, Coca-Cola saw an increase in global sales marked by a 12 percent sales increase in China and a 6 percent increase in India (Warner-Cohen, 2014). Pepsi, now shifting toward sales of healthier snacks in developed markets, is investing heavily in China and India for sales of sodas and traditional snack products (Forbes, 2013). In other words, after these foods and beverages have done significant public health damage in developed economies, consumer demand in those places shifts toward healthier products to stem the tide of obesity and related illnesses. The food manufacturers then respond to this demand by creating new "healthy" options and in turn export their cheaper unhealthy products to developing economies.

Not surprisingly, many of the same locations targeted by the food industry have also been identified as so-called "pharmerging markets." Pharmaceutical consulting company IMS Health first coined this term in identifying seven countries whose drug markets were expanding at twice the world average: China, Brazil, Russia, India, Mexico, Turkey, and South Korea. Initially predicted to account for 20 percent of sales growth in 2009, these seven countries far surpassed that, accounting for 29 percent of growth instead (Campbell & Chui, 2010). IMS Health advises drug manufacturers eyeing pharmerging markets to choose "the right portfolio to ensure alignment with the high growth opportunities and local customer needs" and to consider that "disease profiles, treatment paradigms and diagnostic rates in the pharmerging markets are … unique and no one country can be defined as a single market…. Adaptability and customization are key" (Campbell & Chui, 2010, p. 7). In another IMS report, they describe pharmerging markets as "virgin forests" with drug company executives "licking their chops" (Hill & Chui, 2009). While certainly it is true that bringing medications to new markets can promote public health and reduce human suffering, the crude language of devouring and deflowering used in this report can hardly be interpreted as humanitarian in tone.

In order for many of these medications to be profitable internationally, the disease too must often be exported in order to create demand for the cure. In *Crazy Like Us: The Globalization of the American Psyche*, Ethan Watters argues that mental health disorders in particular are spreading across cultures "with the speed of contagious diseases" and replacing indigenous forms of illness in their wake. For example, he chronicles how Japan's cultural understanding of depression has recently undergone a profound shift, much like how fast food changed their culinary landscape. This "Americanization" of mental illness is simply a new variation on disease mongering in which cultural understandings and expressions of psychiatric illnesses are altered through media messages and marketing. Taken together, all of these techniques allow food and drug companies to expand their consumer base often through deceptive practices and misinformation, and in most cases, the average consumer is powerless against these efforts.

Conflicts of interest

Another parallel way in which the food and pharmaceutical industries advance their interests is through rampant conflicts of interest which increase their sales and obscure scientific evidence unfavorable to their products. Such conflicts of interest are most often characterized by handsome speaker fees to physicians and nutrition researchers, as well as partnerships between corporate alliances and professional organizations that dispense advice about nutrition and medications to the public. Also widespread is the practice of supporting scientists with industry grants for research, resulting in a great many peer-reviewed journal articles on overweight or obesity which are indirectly funded by fast-food makers or soda giants. Not surprisingly, this nutrition research is rivaled by an equal number of articles on medication efficacy funded by drug companies.

Researchers with industry funding are now often obligated to disclose those conflicts which is clearly an improvement over the past when such ties were often secret. Disclosure by itself, however, does not neutralize the conflict of interest, nor does it necessarily enable readers of research to better evaluate the validity of the results. Not only that, but these disclosures often appear as only footnotes or fine print in journal articles. They are generally not included with the abstract which is sometimes the only portion that a nonspecialist or nonsubscriber to an academic journal might read. More importantly, anything in print, especially in an academic journal, has a way of taking on the valence of truth even when qualified by a fine print disclosure indicating that the results might be influenced by industry ties.

A related problem is that researchers do not always properly disclose their conflicts of interest. I found one instance, for example, where nutrition researchers failed to disclose a conflict of interest in the publication of a journal article on sugar-sweetened beverages and obesity, yet a local newspaper subsequently revealed that one of the authors held stock in the MacDonald's company (Allison, 2007). The journal later published an erratum disclosing the conflict of interest, but that erratum still does not appear when one downloads the article. It is only accessible by navigating to a later issue of the journal and viewing the "Erratum" section, which refers to mistakes or omissions in previous issues. In other words, you would only see the disclosure if you meticulously read every issue including the Erratum section, but not if you simply arrived at the article through PubMed or another scientific database. This is puzzling, since unlike print issues, it is simple to correct a digital journal article so that future readers will see the corrected information and many journals do just that.

Even when professional organizations require their members to disclose financial conflicts of interests, this information is not always available to the public. For example, the American Society for Nutrition, known for its many ties to the food industry (Nestle, 2001), requires its board of directors to complete and submit an attestation disclosing conflicts of interest. Yet when I wrote to the association requesting these attestations, they would not release them. I was told by the Governance and Marketing Coordinator that they "only collect conflict of interest attestations for internal use and generally do not share the disclosures with the public" (V. Bloom, personal communication, August 27, 2014). Nor is it possible to use the Freedom of Information Act, a tool often used to expose corruption and conflicts of interest, to force release of this information because it is a private organization.

The pharmaceutical industry too is accused of widespread institutional corruption, which undermines objectivity and integrity. Legal scholar Marc Rodwin argues that although we expect drug firms to develop products to improve public health, to the contrary, they often undermine public health by developing highly profitable products with minor value, all the while ignoring more valuable, but less profitable innovations (2012). We are currently facing just such a market failure in the development of antibiotics, such that only five new antibiotics were approved by the FDA from 2003 through 2007 and only four new classes of antibiotics have been launched in the past forty years (Cooper & Shlaes, 2011). The antibiotics currently on the market are increasingly impotent against antimicrobial-resistant superbugs, posing a daunting global health risk (Pollack, 2010). While public health depends on effective antibiotics, there is little incentive for drug makers to invest in new ones because of their low profitability, namely because antibiotics are low-cost medications that people usually only take for a few days at most. Because the market cannot solve this problem, the US and other governments are considering financial incentives such as tax breaks, subsidies of clinical trials, and patent extensions to spur the development of vitally needed antibiotics. Meanwhile, the drug companies promote their profitable, but often nonessential drugs through financial incentives to physicians and the encouragement of inappropriate or off-label prescribing to further increase profits (Rodwin, 2012).

A related problem is that a great deal of medical and nutritional research has been relocated from the halls of academe into the offices of corporate entities selling the very products that they are supposedly investigating. These companies conducting private and often secret research do not have the same obligations to report unfavorable results or conflicts of interest that university scientists do, at least in theory. Such conflicts of interest, along with the distortion and commodification of scientific information, ultimately have the effect of undermining real science. The scientific method practiced in its pure form is a beautiful thing. The evidentiary strength offered by ethically conducted placebo-controlled, double-blind trials is enormously valuable both for the truth and for public health. Sadly, though, the commodification of food and medicine undermines the work of our best scientists with integrity who refuse industry sponsorship and funding.

Overeating and new markets

Ultimately, overeating creates new markets in two ways: (1) because the more serious casualties of overeating suffer severe health consequences which convert them into consumers of expensive health care; and (2) because nearly everyone struggling with overeating becomes a potential consumer for diets, diet foods, personal trainers, dietitians, commercial weight loss products, books, exercise videos, and gym memberships. The food industry itself is one of the biggest beneficiaries of overweight and obesity because of the enormous market for new foods which promise weight loss and better health. Brands such as Skinny Cow, FiberOne, WhoKnew, Glutino, PopChips, and Skinny Girl Cocktails are all highly profitable brands responding to consumers' desperate attempts to avoid the ill-effects of overeating. Many food companies are now also in the weight loss business through their subsidiaries. Nestlé, for example, reaps huge profits in its sales of the Jenny Craig weight-loss program. Because many diets, especially fad diets, cause an initial rapid loss of water weight, they create an illusion of efficacy and serve as a positive reinforcer for chasing the next fad diet or product. The simplest diet of eating less food is lost in the fray, perhaps *because* it is obvious and free, and therefore an unsatisfactory "product" in the culture of consumerism in which high-dollar promises have more psychological currency than low-cost common sense.

Allison, for example, is not interested in any diet or weight loss plan that doesn't cost money. In fact, the more expensive and the more gimmicky the plan, the more she believes it will be effective. Allison nearly always believes that spending money will help her reduce consumption, failing to see the paradox therein. As an unwitting acolyte of the *Market as religion*, she strongly believes that value can be adequately signaled by price (Dobell, 1995) and thus the more she spends, the more effective the weight loss plan will be. In similar logic, she recently decided to spend $5,000 on a dating service called It's Just Lunch, instead of choosing one of the many lower cost or free dating websites. She believed that the high price tag indicated exclusivity, yet there was no way to evaluate that because there is no way to view or assess the entire pool of available men using the service. Much like fancy weight loss retreats and spas promises quick results in a luxury setting, It's Just Lunch capitalizes on the affluent consumer's need for uniqueness and desire for exclusivity, without necessarily delivering a superior product. Ultimately, many diet and dating companies are selling a fantasy of social class and preying on fears related to beauty, weight, desirability, and loneliness. The fundamental problem with looking for solutions in the form of pills, diets, special foods, psychologists, and dietitians is the belief that the market can solve problems that it causes. This is not to say that there aren't some very qualified professionals, services, or well-written books to help people with overeating. The challenge is that in a frenetic marketplace in which useless services by underqualified professionals are bought and sold, it is difficult for the average person to meaningfully distinguish among all of the choices.

Self-medication through food and drugs

The parallels between food and psychiatric drugs are not just on the production side, but on the consumption side as well. Both placebos and health halos are similar in that they temporarily make us feel better, but ultimately undermine psychological and physical well-being. Consuming Activia yogurt, for example, makes us feel like we are eating something healthy without us realizing the high added sugar content, just as taking Prozac for subclinical depression might improve our mood through a placebo effect, but can then cause troubling side effects and undermine our sense of agency in self-improvement. Consumption of these chimeras can often involve fantasy, longing, and distortion in which we feel like we are doing something healthy, but the science points otherwise.

Consuming pills and food represents complex wish fulfillment, desire, and identity, mediating both who we are and who we want to become. If we think about increased consumption as a defense mechanism used to respond to feelings of alienation, malaise, and loss of community, then it follows that both pills and food would serve as a means of self-medication. In other words, addressing these existential ills with products of consumer culture amounts to treating the disease with the same pathogen that infected us in the first place. The current configuration of the self as empty, however, points us toward these pseudo solutions because we experience distress interiorly as a problem of the individual. This experience is reinforced by the prevailing biological and neurochemical model promoted by psychiatry, which locates disorder and distress inside the self or the brain. Paradoxically, however, dysphoria is often very likely a result of consumer culture in which needs and desires are constantly created, but never met through the products intended to offer relief.

The relationship between Big Pharma and Big Food, in which one form of consumption is used to treat the ills of another rather than the more direct solution of reducing overall consumption, is another example of the triumph of consumerism *as moral ideology* over consumerism *as advocacy*. Behind this triumph are a great many powerful industries, including Big Food, Big Pharma, and Big Tobacco, all in cahoots in their undermining of public health for shareholder profits. The increased health care costs from overeating, overweight, and obesity create more sick people every day, representing more customers for Big Pharma and its treatments for diabetes, high blood pressure, coronary heart disease, and metabolic syndrome. Such so-called "downstream" solutions to overeating generate new profits, whereas "upstream" solutions, such as taxing sweetened beverages or improving nutrition labels, stand to reduce overconsumption and prevent widespread public health problems (Dorfman & Wallack, 2007). In other words, downstream solutions locate illness and behavioral change in the individual which serves to increase aggregate consumption, whereas upstream solutions locate pathology within consumer culture, serving to decrease aggregate consumption. This tension between upstream and downstream solutions is at the heart of debates over government regulation, a fraught topic to which we will finally turn.

10

The Regulation of Well-Being: FDA and the Nanny State

Allison purchases countless nutritional supplements in the form of pills, drinks, bars, gummies, powdered shakes, and elixirs. When she talks about these products she describes them as able to speed up her metabolism, burn fat, increase muscle mass, suppress appetite, increase energy, improve skin, and even increase pheromone production (in spite of the fact that scientists have never proven that humans even have pheromones (Wysocki & Preti, 2004)). These purchases are consistent with industry trends in the past several years in which there has been a sharp increase in the sale of such "nutraceuticals" (Brower, 1998). This increase is in part due to the lax supplement laws which allow manufacturers to bring these products to market far more easily than pharmaceutical drugs, and with labels and health claims which are not subject to the stricter laws governing food. It seems that the more expensive these products are, the more likely Allison is to buy them, probably because the price tag enhances their placebo effect. Allison is not a particularly savvy consumer, nor does she shoulder any responsibility for investigating labels or health claims. Still, she is not exactly a hapless victim either, as she may enjoy the deception of these products offering the fantasy of change through magic. These products tell beautiful lies, but lies they are. Although Allison may be complicit in the deception, my fundamental sense of fairness tells me that she is being tricked and exploited by a powerful opponent. When I've told her about the lax laws which allow the sale of such snake oil, she doesn't believe me. She simply does not think it is possible that such products could be for sale if their benefits are unproven. She repeatedly counters my claims by asking, "How could that be legal?"

Similarly, university students in my classes have expressed disbelief when I've shown them the efficacy data on pharmaceutical drugs, also asking the question, "How could that be legal?"

Front and center in the determination of which food and drugs are legal and what claims they may make is the US Food and Drug Administration, along with the other agencies charged with protecting consumer interests. The FDA has historically enjoyed a reputation as a powerful and rigorous protective agency, with numerous public surveys over the past half-century showing that Americans consider it one of the most popular and well-respected agencies, giving it a 70–80 percent approval rating, far higher than other measures of confidence in the federal government (Carpenter, 2014, p. 12). Yet in spite of the widespread consumer trust in the FDA, the regulation of nutrition and public health is hotly contested, with such efforts often characterized as unwelcome government paternalism or nanny state politics. Opponents of regulatory efforts often cry foul, citing that increased regulation would amount to a nanny state or socialism. In the unthinkable, we could even wind up like Sweden.

In the preface of the tenth edition of *Food Politics*, Marion Nestle chronicles some of the harsh criticisms the first edition of the book received, casting her as America's "foremost nanny" and accusing her of dismissing personal responsibility for nutrition. Reviewers on Amazon posted comments such as: "Nestle forgot a not-so-little thing called WILL POWER!", and "One of the foremost food nannies in this country has produced a book that heaps the blame for obesity, diabetes, and heart disease on food producers, marketing executives, and even school principals. Everyone, it seems, is responsible for those love handles except for the very people who are carrying them around," and finally, "Individuals incapable of thinking for themselves will truly appreciate…Food Politics. [Hasn't the author] ever heard of personal responsibility, exercise, and appropriate dieting?"(Nestle, 2002). Such outrage reflects the strong political feelings over free will vs. the nanny state, leading us back to the tensions among the different forms of consumerism which introduced this book (Gabriel & Lang, 2006). We recall those definitions of consumerism here:

1 consumerism as *a moral doctrine*—consumer choice and acquisition are the vehicles for individual freedom, happiness, and power for developed countries.

2 consumerism as *a political ideology*—in contrast to the nanny state and its paternalism, the modern state protects transnational

corporations and the consumerist ideology exalts choice and freedom for the consumer to acquire glamorous and stylish goods.

3   consumerism as *an economic ideology for global development*—in contrast to the austerity of communism, consumerism is seen as the driver of free trade and the nurturing of new consumers is seen as the key to developing economies.

4   consumerism as *a social ideology*—establishes class distinctions such that material commodities fix the social position and prestige of their owners.

5   consumerism as *a social movement*—consumer rights are characterized by advocacy for the protection of value and quality for the consumer often through regulation.

The tension among these, namely the tension between consumerism as *a political ideology* and consumerism as *a social movement*, is at the nexus of these regulatory debates. Arguably, many of the most devastating public problems in the United States have been tied in some way to regulatory failure: mass shootings, tobacco, obesity, diabetes, subprime mortgages, and widespread student loan defaults, just to name a few.

The regulatory agencies: A brief primer

While the complex and byzantine scheme of federal food regulation is far outside my purview as a clinical psychologist, individual well-being is very much within my purview. Numerous federal regulatory agencies are charged with protecting our well-being, but for the most part I restrict my focus to a discussion and evaluation of the FDA, as it has the most oversight over food labeling and exclusive oversight over pharmaceutical drugs. One of the questions at the heart of this chapter, and one I've tried to answer for myself for many years, is whether the FDA is hero or villain in its regulation of food and drugs? Some have suggested that the FDA is a lax or even corrupt agency (Burros, 2007; Evans, Smith, & Willen, 2005; Klein, 2005), but this may be nothing more than scapegoating as the FDA has only as much power as Congress gives it and is also subject to review by the judicial branch through litigation against it.

The FDA originated with the 1906 Pure Food and Drug Act, a law which prohibited interstate commerce of adulterated and misbranded food and drugs. Theodore Roosevelt signed the act in 1906 as a means to "civilize capitalism." Roosevelt was an enthusiastic supporter of American enterprise and innovation, but was concerned by the ruthlessness and self-interest he saw in the marketplace (Hilts, 2004). Initially staffed by chemists and inspectors with the mandate to intervene against industry on behalf of the consumer, the FDA as we now know it was formed in 1930. Now housed within the Department of Health and Human Services, the agency has been increasingly vested with authority over food, dietary supplements, and beverages by the passages of the Federal Food, Drug, and Cosmetic Act of 1938 (FDCA), the Nutrition Labeling Enforcement Act of 1990 (NLEA), the Public Health Security and Bioterrorism Preparedness and Response Act (BTA), and the Food Safety Modernization Act (FSMA), among other laws. Today the purview of the FDA has grown to oversee the products of 95,000 businesses, or about one quarter of the US economy, estimated to be at over $1 trillion worth of goods a year (Hilts, 2004, p. xiv).

Along with the FDA, the US Department of Agriculture (USDA) also monitors food safety, although its purview includes only meat, poultry, and egg products, about 20 percent of the food supply, while the other 80 percent falls under the purview of the FDA. The USDA has several other mandates as well, some of them arguably at odds with each other. For example, its Center for Nutrition Policy and Promotion works to improve the health and well-being of Americans by developing and promoting dietary guidance that links scientific research to the nutrition needs of consumers, whereas its Agricultural Marketing Service works to strengthen and expand markets for American agricultural products (Schlosser, 2004).

While the oversight of food safety is shared by the FDA and USDA, the oversight of food labeling and advertising is shared by the Federal Trade Commission (FTC), the FDA, and the USDA. Since 1954, the FTC and the FDA have operated under a Memorandum of Understanding, under which the FTC has assumed primary responsibility for food advertising, while the FDA has taken primary responsibility for food labeling (FTC, 1994). Pursuant to the Nutrition and Labeling Education Act (NLEA) of 1990, the FDA was also mandated to regulate health claims on food packaging, standardize nutrient content claims, and require that more detailed nutritional information be included on the product labels of foods and nutritional supplements (Shank, 1992), resulting in the Nutrition Facts label now required on most packaged foods.

Table 10.1 summarizes the regulatory purview of the FTC, FDA, and USDA, respectively. This is by no means an exhaustive list of each agency's

TABLE 10.1 Regulatory purview of FDA, USDA, and FTC

Agency	FDA	USDA	FTC
Label and inspect meat, poultry, and processed eggs (20 percent of US food supply)		X	
Promote agricultural industry interests		X	
Teach nutrition to public		X	
Create Food Pyramid/My Plate		X	
Label and inspect fresh fruits and vegetables, dairy, baked products, and seafood (80 percent of US food supply)	X		
Protect public health by providing consumers with "accurate, science-based information" about food	X		
Strengthen and expand markets for American agricultural products		X	
Monitor nutrient content and health claims on most food labels	X		
Create and oversee mandatory Nutrition Facts label	X		
Monitor and report on the advertising of food to children			X
Investigate complaints of misbranded food	X		
Evaluate safety of pharmaceutical drugs (pre-market)	X		
Evaluate safety of supplements (pre-market)			
Evaluate efficacy of pharmaceutical drugs (pre-market)	X		
Evaluate efficacy of supplements (pre-market)			
Oversee recall of unsafe foods	X	X	
Oversee recall of unsafe supplements (post-market)	X		
Oversee advertising claims for dietary supplements and weight loss products			X
Monitor and develop effective enforcement strategies for new advertising techniques and media, such as word-of-mouth marketing			X
Oversee labeling and sales of tobacco (not e-cigarettes)			X
Review and evaluation of a food's "health claim" (pre-market)	X		

charge, but is meant to serve as a simplified listing of agency responsibilities relevant to the topics of this book.

Supplements and pharmaceutical drugs

During most of its history, the reach and authority of the FDA has been continually expanded by Congress; however, in a recent reversal Congress took steps to deregulate or restrict the FDA's authority, most notably in the oversight of nutritional supplements. From 1938 to 1990, the FDA had regulatory authority over nutritional supplements, and starting in 1990 the agency increasingly issued more recalls and warnings to supplement manufacturers. In a backlash to the increased oversight, the supplement industry launched a formidable lobbying effort with Congress which resulted in the passage of the Dietary Supplement Health and Education Act of 1994 (DSHEA). Allowing profitability to trump consumer protection, Congress recognized that "the nutritional supplement industry [was] an integral part of the economy of the United States" (Dietary Supplement Health and Education Act, 1994) and stripped the FDA of most of its authority to regulate these products.

Now pursuant to DSHEA, neither the safety nor the efficacy of dietary supplements need be proven before such products come to market, nor does the FDA prescreen any supplements prior to their sale (Barrett, 2007; Cohen, 2000; Kaczka, 1999). This is in sharp contrast to the previous regulatory oversight of supplements, as well as to the historic and ongoing oversight of pharmaceutical drugs, in which pre-market approval by the FDA is required. Instead, supplement manufacturers are now charged with self-policing product safety before bringing them to market. Not only is there no pre-market burden of proof for supplement product safety, but the FDA can only restrict the sales of a supplement *after* it has come to market by proving that it is unsafe and has caused harm to consumers (Barrett, 2007).

The passage of DSHEA then represented a sea change in regulatory authority in which the new law shifted the legal and scientific burden of proof from industry to the regulatory agency, thereby privileging consumerism as *a political ideology* over consumerism as *a social movement*. Ultimately, this created a marketplace which encourages indiscriminate consumption of unproven and often sugar-laden supplements in the form of beverages, bars, powders, gummies, and pills. This unnecessary and potentially harmful market joins the prescription drug marketplace which is saturated with unnecessary and potentially harmful copycat and lifestyle drugs. Not only do these markets imperil public safety, but they further contribute to overconsumption by reinforcing the belief that eating, drinking, and taking pills solves problems.

The fox guarding the henhouse

In another significant conflict of interest, the FDA is now partly funded by the drug companies themselves due to the passage of the Prescription Drug User Fee Act (PDUFA) in 1992 (FDA, 2005). In an effort to speed up the lengthy process of drug approval, Congress allowed the FDA to collect a substantial application fee from drug manufacturers at the time a new drug application is submitted for approval. To be fair, it is not uncommon for an organization or agency to assess a user fee to cover the expenses and resources involved in processing applications. Colleges and universities, for example, require application fees and the Department of State requires fees to process passport applications. These are reasonable means for cash-strapped agencies to recoup operating expenses which are generated by users and applicants. These other examples, however, do not involve regulatory agencies collecting fees to cover the cost of evaluating the very products they regulate. The result is that no other federal regulatory agency derives such a large proportion of its operating budget from the very industry it is charged with overseeing (Senak, 2005).

Not only does the FDA now derive a significant portion of its budget from the drug companies themselves, but the passage of PDUFA also resulted in the reassignment of much of the agency's staff from the Office of Drug Safety to work on new drug approvals because strict new timelines were mandated (Avorn, 2007). Jerry Avorn, a physician and critic of PDUFA, describes one FDA scientist who was "often criticized for being too concerned about drug-risk data and was told by his supervisor to remember that the agency's client was the pharmaceutical industry. 'That's odd,' [the scientist] replied, 'I thought our clients were the people of the United States'" (Avorn, 2007). Shifting the FDA's sense of accountability from the citizenry to private industry, the Prescription Drug User Fee Act has then had the dual effects of diminishing the safety oversight of existing drugs, as well as introducing financial conflicts of interests to the approval process.

Health and nutrient claims

As discussed in Chapter 6, the food industry has countless tricks they use to sell more of their products. Because their profits are so closely tied to the visual appeal and nutritional perceptions of packages, they devote enormous time and money to designing these packages and creating the clever claims which adorn them. Here we revisit the topic of food labeling as it relates to FDA oversight.

On its website, the FDA promises that it "has your back" by requiring labels on packaged food products to not be false or misleading in any way. It further declares that the agency "monitors food products to ensure that the labels are truthful and not misleading" (FDA, 2014). What is not at all obvious to the average consumer, however, is that from a legal perspective there are actually numerous types of health and nutrition claims on food packages, each subject to a different set of rules and standard of proof. Some nutrition claims are tightly regulated by the FDA and require preapproval for use, whereas others require no authorization or preapproval. Not only that, but the FDA does not specify the level of scientific support needed to prevent false or misleading information (Negowetti, 2014). Not surprisingly, then, research has shown that consumers cannot distinguish among the different types of claims and are willing to purchase products based on inaccurate perceptions of healthy ingredients (Silverglade & Heller, 2010).

Recall that nutrition claims on food packaging often lead to overeating through the creation of health halos. In fact, there has paradoxically been a tremendous increase in the number of claims made on food labels as rates of obesity have increased in the United States, likely because consumers who want to lose weight are seeking healthier foods (Urala & Lähteenmäki, 2007). It is this desire to simultaneously consume more and consume less that makes such nutrition claims highly profitable. One such area of confusion is with products labeled *natural*. As previously discussed, the term "natural" is largely unregulated and food manufacturers can use it freely to mean whatever they want (Food and Drug Law Institute, 2014). Consumer research has found that consumers mistakenly believe that products labeled as *natural* have no artificial ingredients, pesticides, or genetically modified ingredients and are willing to pay more for those foods (Batte, Hooker, Haab, & Beaverson, 2007; Thompson, 1998).

Several federal agencies including the Government Accountability Office (GAO) and the FTC have noted that under current FDA guidelines it is difficult for consumers to evaluate health claims, and many legal experts are now calling on the FDA to reexamine its guidelines for health claims in light of this confusion (Government Accountability Office, 2011). Despite this, the FDA has repeatedly deferred action on defining the term "natural," citing "resource limitations and other agency priorities" (FDA, 1993), as well as arguing that the term is subjective and would not be possible to define (FDA, 2012). Defining the term "natural" would in fact be difficult, yet is that not the very hallmark of the law: defining and operationalizing difficult concepts? How else could our society function if we did not define elusive concepts? How, for example, do we define the difference between a minor and an adult, a felony and a misdemeanor, murder or manslaughter? All laws and regulations deal with terms that are difficult to define. Why would the term "natural" be any different?

Not only are current claims of *natural* misleading, but failure to regulate the term has the effect of harming the companies that work hard to develop and bring to market genuinely natural products. Instead, companies using nefarious practices to compete in the marketplace falsely use the term "natural," when in fact they have not put in the hard work and innovation necessary to compete and win through honest consumer demand. Here we can further see that the issue of food regulation is not always as simple as consumer protection vs. free market because in this case, increased regulation of the term "natural" would not only protect the consumer, but would also reward companies that develop and bring foods to market that actually are natural.

Nutrition Facts label

In 2014, the FDA proposed the first major set of revisions to the Nutrition Facts label since its introduction twenty years ago. One of the many proposed changes was that added sugars be disclosed on the new label. Because added sugars and highly concentrated fructose are so unhealthy, it is crucial that labels distinguish these from naturally occurring sugars, something that is not currently done.[1] At one time, the USDA reported the added sugar contents of foods on their Nutrient Data Laboratory website, but in 2012 they simply gave up due to "constant changes in formulations for commercial, multi-ingredient foods" and because added sugars "must be extrapolated or supplied by food companies, many of which are not willing to make public such proprietary information" (USDA, 2014). Because added sugars are introduced during processing and refinement, mandatory disclosure would numerically reveal the degree to which a food's palatability has been engineered. In other words, it would serve as a kind of "hyperpalatability quotient" for many foods. Quantifying and reporting added sugars stands, then, not only to give us nutritional information, but to give us philosophical and psychological information, in that it can function as a metric for the manufactured desires of consumer culture. The higher the added sugar, the more likely the product is a chimera of consumer culture and the more capable it is of hijacking finely tuned neurological mechanisms.

Yet the added sugars proposal has been controversial and has generated many comments from both the scientific community and the general public. The Union of Concerned Scientists organized a statement in support of listing added sugars signed by 280 scientists, physicians, public health officials, and

---

[1]As this book went to press, the FDA released sweeping changes to the Nutrition Facts Label, including the addition of added sugars.

many leading food scholars (Union of Concerned Scientists, 2014). By contrast, the American Society for Nutrition opposed the proposal. According to its mission statement, the American Society for Nutrition "promotes excellence in nutrition research and practice, seeks to improve public health and clinical practice worldwide; provides reliable nutrition information to those who need it, and advocates for nutrition research and its application to development and implementation of policies and practices related to nutrition" (American Society for Nutrition, 2014a). Quoting from the ASN's letter (2014b) to the Food and Drug Administration, their stated rationale for the opposition to the added sugars proposal was that:

- There are no analytical methods to distinguish between naturally occurring sugars and those added to foods or beverages,…. and therefore manufacturers may encounter difficulties in accurately declaring the amount of added sugar in a final product.

- The inclusion of added sugars on the label may confuse consumers and create the perception that naturally occurring sugars are somehow more beneficial because they are "natural" and do not have health effects similar to added sugars.

- There is no supporting evidence that indicates that the inclusion of added sugars on the food label will translate into the American public reducing caloric intake from added or total sugars or total energy intake, therefore leading to a reduction in chronic disease risk and weight management.

- Adequate consumer testing to determine consumer understanding of terms including total sugars, added sugars, and sugars, and how this information is translated by consumers should be conducted prior to any determination to change the food label, not after. Consumer studies to determine how and if declaration of added sugars impacts healthful eating are highly important and should be conducted as well.

Let's take a look at these arguments one by one: First, the suggestion that manufacturers may not be able to accurately declare the amount of added sugar in a product is absurd. Given the sophisticated laboratory tests that food manufacturers conduct to determine consumer preferences for sugar, salt, and fat, they know exactly how much sugar goes into every product. If they didn't know how much sugar was in a product how would they know how much sugar to order? These foods are manufactured in highly mechanized laboratories and factories in which everything is carefully measured and calibrated down to the milligram. Even any home cook could tell you how much sugar they added to a recipe by simply using a measuring cup.

The second claim, that the inclusion of added sugars on the label may confuse consumers, had a single footnote citing a supplement of the *Journal of the Federation of American Societies for Experimental Biology* (Bertino, Liska, Spence, Sanders, & Egan, 2014). I was not able to access the full text of the study and contacted *FASEB* to find out why. They told me that the journal supplement is nothing more than a collection of abstracts from the proceedings of the 2014 Experimental Biology Conference, and more importantly that the abstracts do not represent peer-reviewed work. When I went to the conference schedule itself, the citation was for a poster session first-authored by someone named Veronica Egan with an affiliation of Via Vi, LLC in Portage, MI. The Via Vi company has no online presence and a search of Veronica Egan on LinkedIn states that she is a market researcher at the Kellogg Company, as are the other four authors of the presentation. The abstract reports that the authors conducted an online survey of 1,000 consumers, but provides no other information about the methodology, how the sample was selected, or what questions were asked. Describing the methodology of any research study is the hallmark of scientific rigor because such detailed descriptions allow other researchers to evaluate and replicate the study, adding evidentiary strength. In other words, the American Society for Nutrition, an organization which promises "excellence in nutrition research" supported a claim in a letter to the US Food and Drug Administration with the citation of a *single* poster session which did not undergo peer review and was authored by five Kellogg employees.

The third claim, that there is no evidence that the inclusion of added sugars on the food label will translate into the American public reducing caloric intake, is not entirely true either. For one, it is very difficult in research simulations known as analogue studies to accurately predict what people will do in a real-world setting. We do know, however, that disclosing and publicizing nutritional information such as calorie counts has an effect on some consumers (Block & Roberto, 2014; Gregory, Rahkovsky, & Anekwe, 2014; Wei & Miao, 2013). There is also the possibility that while such information may not have the immediate effect of reducing caloric intake, over time, combined with other public health measures, it could cause behavioral change. Even if the disclosure of added sugars does not cause behavioral change, however, is there not in fact merit to simply disclosing the truth on the basis that people have a right to know what is in their food? There is clearly a similar moral and legal basis for truth in lending disclosures, so why would there not be for food labeling?

Another major challenge is the placement of the Nutrition Facts label, as well as the placement of other claims and symbols on packages. In a recent article arguing for more comprehensive food labeling, former FDA Commissioner David Kessler reports that the food industry has historically claimed the front of package for its promotion, with regulated labeling confined to the side or back of food packages (2014). Not only have food manufacturers claimed the front of packages for product promotion, but they have developed their own visual schemes and iconography, such as hearts, stars, and checkmarks, promising the healthfulness of the products within, often misleading consumers. Kessler argues there is no good reason or legal basis that this convention should be accepted.

In 2011, the Institute of Medicine (IOM) released a report on front-of-package labeling, calling on the FDA to allow only four items on the front of packages: calories, saturated/trans fat, sodium, and sugars. They further recommend a point system that would include either checkmarks or stars indicating the overall healthiness of the product. Research has shown that front-of-package labels impact nutritional decisions, with one recent study showing that a front-of-package label with a visual representation for added sugars curbed consumer preferences for sweet and led to more negative attitudes about sugar-sweetened products (Adams, Hart, Gilmer, Lloyd-Richardson, & Burton, 2014).

Not surprisingly, there is a direct parallel in the labeling of pharmaceutical drugs in which research has shown that drug labels confuse consumers about the benefits and risks associated with pharmaceutical products, as well as the efficacy of such products (Schwartz & Woloshin, 2011; Schwartz, Woloshin, & Welch, 2009; Woloshin & Schwartz, 2011). In 2014, the Institute of Medicine convened a workshop with the Food and Drug Administration on how best to communicate the benefits and risks of pharmaceuticals. Two panelists at the workshop, Drs. Steven Woloshin and Lisa Schwartz, have long advocated for a drug facts box which would show how the drug compares to a placebo. To date, however, Big Food and Big Pharma have largely prevailed in maintaining their right to create labels designed to sell products and have avoided disclosure of ingredients, additives, risks, or efficacy.

In 2013, the FDA promised that it would soon "propose guidance for the industry regarding nutrition labeling on the front of food packages, and plans to work collaboratively with the food industry to design and implement innovative approaches to front-of-package labeling that can help consumers choose healthy diets" (FDA, 2013). While that is clearly a step in the right direction, the "collaborative" approach suggests that the full force of the FDA's authority would not back compliance. As we shall see in the next section, such collaborative approaches allowing for self-policing by industry tend to be ineffective wishful thinking.

Many of these labeling efforts intended to protect consumers are laudatory; however, they miss a crucial point. Foods in packages are the products of consumer culture and with the exception of few foods such as legumes, nuts, and canned or frozen fruits and vegetables most packaged foods will never be as healthy as the whole foods that do not require packages. The efforts to better label foods, while certainly necessary for public health, inadvertently promote the faulty thinking that some ultra-processed foods are as nutritious as minimally processed or whole foods. In other words, they operate within the paradigm of consumer culture, perpetuating the "eat more" and "consume more" message, just through a different type of marketing message. Pro-health marketing is marketing nonetheless, and it reinforces our trust and reliance on labels, slogans, and advertising. With that said, of course we still should work to improve labels because packaged foods aren't going anywhere, but it is important to realize that even a label describing a food as "healthy" is somewhat misleading because food is "healthy" *only in relation to other* packaged foods.

The unintended consequences of lax labeling

In addition to increased nutritional confusion among consumers, another serious consequence of lax food labeling has been increased litigation as consumers have looked to the courts to step in where the FDA has failed. I am no legal expert, but it seems to me that if the FDA were an effective regulatory agency, no one would have to file a lawsuit over an ice cream sandwich. Consider the following excerpts from Belli et al. vs. Nestle USA (2014):

> In the present case, Plaintiff was injured by the Defendant's illegal sale of its misbranded Eskimo Pie. Plaintiff paid money to purchase illegal products that were worthless and could not be legally sold or possessed.
>
> Plaintiff would not have purchased Defendant's Eskimo Pie had she known that the product was illegal and could not be lawfully possessed.
>
> Plaintiff was deceived into purchasing Eskimo Pie in substantial part because of these label statements and because of these statements believed that Eskimo Pie was healthier than other similar products and/or healthier than Eskimo Pie without the statement.

It's absurd and tragic to consider the money and time involved in a lawsuit over an Eskimo Pie, yet there has been a surge of such class-action lawsuits claiming deceptive labeling and advertising, including suits against Naked Juice, Fruit Roll-Ups, Bear Naked Granola, and Wesson Oil. In 2004, the Center for Science in the Public Interest created its litigation department "when consumer protection at the federal level by the FDA, FTC, and USDA was at a shameful low point, to fill the void left by the inactive government agencies by using state and federal courts to help correct corporate misbehavior" (Center for Science in the Public Interest, 2014b). Such litigation, while arguably necessary as an act of desperation, is a costly and piecemeal approach to effective food regulation. Not only that, but many judges have referred such cases back to the FDA, recognizing that the authority and enforcement of food labeling has been vested to it by Congress (Watson, 2014).

Self-policing by the food industry

One of the most controversial topics in regulation is the issue of self-regulation or self-policing by the food industry. In my view, asking the food industry to police itself is like asking the devil what the temperature is in Hell. Here I am speaking of the multinational food and beverage corporations with huge and concentrated market power, generally referred to as Big Food (PLoS, 2102) and not of the many admirable smaller companies who have committed themselves to social responsibility and a set of pro-social corporate ethics (Ethisphere, 2015). Big Food has gone to great effort to show that they are "sitting at the table" with health organizations to tackle public health problems and have repeatedly argued that they are capable of producing healthy products and providing accurate nutritional information to consumers. The appearance that Big Food is "sitting at the table" with public health advocates and nutrition scientists is nothing more than a public relations illusion. In 2011, for example, shortly after the IOM issued its hard-hitting report on front-of-package labeling, the Grocery Manufacturers Association (GMA) and the Food Marketing Institute (FMI) announced their "Facts Up Front" campaign. Much in the same way that a naughty child will offer a set of voluntary behavioral guidelines to avoid punishment, Facts Up Front was nothing more than industry trying to call off the dogs of regulation. Not only that, but the GMA and FMI who proposed Facts Up Front used many deceptive practices to create an appealing and heartfelt image for the campaign, such as registering the domain name factsupfront. org (instead of.com) to create the illusion of a nonprofit organization behind the labeling effort.

The idea that these food companies might join public health advocates to fight obesity is like Lex Luthor joining forces with Superman to fight the even more villainous Ming whose evil-doing puts the entire planet in peril. But *Superman* is a comic book designed to appeal to our sense justice, fairness, and goodness. Wouldn't it be nice if food companies could just develop delicious products *and* have heartfelt concern for our health? Most of them don't, though. Much in the same way that kidnapping victims suffer from brainwashing by their captors known as Stockholm Syndrome, we too are held in a powerful psychological grip by the food companies. We are captive. In what psychoanalysts call "identification with the aggressor" (Freud, 1967) people in weak positions overwhelmed by an inescapable threat often unconsciously collude with their aggressor in "tenuous agreements" in order to reduce anxiety (Frankel, 2002). In other words, they mitigate their sense of powerlessness by convincing themselves that their more powerful adversary deserves compassion, or isn't as bad as they seem. So too, acceptance of Big Food's benevolent imagery and messages of public health functions psychologically as a means to allow us to feel as though they are on our side, rather than undermining our health and increasing our mortality.

One of the main reasons we cannot reasonably expect Big Food to voluntarily stop making unhealthy products is because they have invested tremendous time, money, and labor in the research and development of their delicious products. From the company's perspective, they simply cannot afford to lose return on that investment. Not only that, but for any one food company or even an alliance of several to discontinue the sale of hyperpalatable foods would amount to unilateral disarmament in which a market opening would be left for any other company to fill, thereby taking away the hard-earned profits of the company who took the moral high road.

In his book *Salt, Sugar, Fat: How the Food Giants Hooked Us*, Michael Moss describes a meeting of industry insiders in which some of the captains of industry made an early case for stemming the tide of obesity by ratcheting down their formulations. Stephen Sanger, then CEO of General Mills, vehemently opposed any self-imposed regulation by the food companies themselves. He reportedly said that consumers bought what they liked, and they liked what tasted good, irrespective of nutrition. "'Don't talk to me about nutrition,' he said, taking on the voice of a typical consumer. 'Talk to me about taste, and if this stuff tastes better, don't run around trying to sell stuff that doesn't taste good.' To change course would jeopardize the sanctity of the recipes that had made his products so successful" (Moss, 2013). In other words, Sanger abdicated any moral position and instead deferred to the market as the arbiter of this problem. His position, repeated by many other food industry titans, elevates consumerism as an *economic ideology*, a *political ideology*, and a *moral doctrine* in which free trade, unbounded choices, and free will all triumph over consumerism *as a social movement*, in which the rights and health of the average citizen could be protected.

While some industry efforts at self-regulation may yield modest success, there are numerous failures suggesting that we cannot rely on such efforts. For example, the tobacco industry's campaign to prevent youth smoking was not only a thinly veiled attempt to deflect legislative action, but research showed that this program may have actually encouraged young people to smoke more (Wakefield et al., 2006). Yet the campaign generated the appearance of social responsibility and goodwill even though it caused more harm than good (Landman, Ling, & Glantz, 2002; Wakefield et al., 2006). In another such example, recall that DSHEA charged the supplement industry with policing itself when it stripped the FDA of authority to prescreen supplements. This experiment has clearly failed as evidenced by the numerous troubling reports of supplements which contain dangerous contaminants and ingredients not listed on the labels (Offit & Erush, 2013). In fact, dietary supplements now account for nearly 20 percent of drug-related liver injuries in hospitals (Navarro et al., 2014). Because DSHEA gave pre-market policing authority to the supplement industry, the FDA is now legally powerless to stop these sales until enough people have become ill or have died.

Some researchers argue that self-policing would be possible if rigorous standards such as transparency and predefined scientific benchmarks were defined and adopted (Sharma, Teret, & Brownell, 2010). Many others, however, argue that the data show that self-policing by industry cannot be effective. For example, The Lancet NCD Action Group stands against public-private partnerships in the regulation of alcohol or hyperpalatable foods, arguing that there is little evidence that self-regulatory approaches are effective. They recommend that "public regulation and market intervention are the only evidence-based mechanisms to prevent harm caused by the unhealthy commodity industries" (Moodie et al., 2013). Other public health advocates such as Michael Jacobson, Executive Director of the Center for Science in the Public Interest, argue that successful labeling efforts like the Nutrition Facts label are a success only "because the FDA, and not the food industry, decides what's on the label and what the label looks like" (Center for Science in the Public Interest, 2014a).

The FDA: The final verdict

While perhaps deeply flawed, the FDA provides an extraordinary service to the citizens of the United States (and also to the businesses of the United States). Even the most vocal opponents of regulation would agree that some regulation is good and that the US regulatory system provides some of the safest conditions for medicine and food in the world. That we can publish criticisms such as this one and use laws such as the Freedom of Information Act to demand transparency are freedoms that should not go unnoted. Still, there is no getting around the many failures of the FDA in the regulation of food, drugs, and supplements.

Taking aim at these failures, the satirical website The Onion recently posted a phony headline stating, "FDA Recommends At Least 3 Servings of Foods With Word 'Fruit' On Box" (The Onion, 2014). The mock article "quotes" the FDA commissioner as saying, "Though we have in the past advised eating a minimum of three pieces of actual fruit per day, it is now acceptable to eat any food labeled with the word 'fruit,' including variations such as 'fruity,' 'fruit-a-licious,' or 'fruit-blasted', including sweetened cereals or gummies shaped like fruit." And they conclude with, "The FDA's new recommendations are expected to be followed up by other guidelines under which anything successfully chewed and swallowed can now be considered a vegetable." It is not clear if The Onion is suggesting that the FDA is corrupt or impotent, but it brings into relief the agency's failure.

Regulatory capture or regulatory defeat?

Central to understanding these failures is the question of whether or not the FDA is the victim of "regulatory capture"? Regulatory capture refers to a form of political corruption in which a regulatory agency charged with acting in the public interest is "captured" and begins to advance the commercial interests of big business or special interest groups (Stigler, 1971). The culture of consumerism exerts force toward regulatory capture because it elevates production, consumption, prosperity, and freedom above consumer protection. Yet it is not clear that regulatory capture is the explanation for the FDA's failures. The leading expert on regulatory capture, Harvard historian Daniel Carpenter argues instead that business-friendly measures by the FDA have historically arrived more at the behest of scientific organizations, consumer activists, and patient groups rather than industry itself (Carpenter, 2014, p. 10). Such influence is not, strictly speaking, regulatory capture because it is not the result of commercial interests or corruption.

If the FDA has not succumbed to regulatory capture as Carpenter maintains, then perhaps it has succumbed to something more like regulatory defeat? David Kessler— who is not only former commissioner of the FDA, but a well-respected physician, lawyer, and winner of the Public Welfare Medal from the National Academy of Sciences—defends the agency's integrity and characterizes it as a David against the Goliath of big business. In *A Question of Intent* (2001), Kessler describes how for years tobacco companies virtually incapacitated the FDA through Congressional lobbying and powerful lawyers, but the agency ultimately triumphed. Citing an enormous purview, a small budget, and powerful influence by the food industry, Kessler argues that the FDA simply does not have the resources nor the legal authority to combat or compete with the food industry.

Supporting the notion of regulatory defeat, are the countless examples we've seen in which federal agencies seem to have just given up in the face of Big Food or Big Pharma. Recall, for example, that it was the FDA itself that advocated for the 1992 passage of the Prescription Drug User Fee Act (PDUFA) which allowed it to collect application fees from drug manufacturers for approval. While the act was a clever strategy to bring in more funding and effectively funnel profits from Big Pharma into regulation, at the same time it was an act of resignation, in that the FDA could not secure sufficient appropriations from Congress to hire the staff necessary to oversee a lengthy backlog of drugs awaiting approval. PDUFA then effectively privatized the cost of regulation, ultimately ceding governmental control of citizen protection. Alternatively, a tax on pharmaceutical companies could have funded the FDA, and would have had the advantage of removing the agency from fund-raising from the companies it oversees.

Another example of regulatory defeat is the USDA's discontinuation of reporting the added sugar content of foods on their Nutrient Data Laboratory website. Recall that the USDA gave up this reporting due to "constant changes in formulations for commercial, multi-ingredient foods" and because added sugars "must be extrapolated or supplied by food companies, many of which are not willing to make public such proprietary information" (USDA, 2014). In other words, it was too hard and the agency couldn't force companies into compliance. Note that these "constant changes in formulation" were probably done by food companies for the very purpose of avoiding detection in their use of unhealthy ingredients. In fact, the continual development of new kinds of sugar with indecipherable names is arguably done only so that food companies can avoid listing sugar as the first ingredient on a package. It is unlikely that using seven different types of sugar in a breakfast cereal would add anything by way of taste or texture that could not be accomplished with white table sugar or brown sugar. Perhaps a trained chef would argue for the importance of using different types of sugar in a single recipe, but it's hard to believe that the target market for most breakfast cereals (kids) would appreciate the nuanced caramelization and flavor profile achieved through multiple sugars. In other words, these are all complex and expensive efforts coming at enormous production costs, done by food companies in order to foil regulatory oversight.

Not only must the FDA allocate tremendous resources to the study and evaluation of food content and labels, but it must also capture the consumer's eye with its own Nutrition Facts label, meaning that it must compete with high-dollar Madison Avenue advertisers and graphic designers. The images, names, slogans, symbols, logos, and licensed characters which constitute the $1 trillion package design industry (Horovitz, 2011) are used to build, reinforce, and convey brand identity to consumers. Because even small changes in package design can have a huge impact on sales, food manufacturers are not about to cede any precious package space to the FDA without a fight. Even if the FDA were to gain increased control of package space, it is difficult to see how the agency could compete with the high-priced sophisticated graphic design of colors, typography, images, and messages that attract consumer attention. Walk into any federal agency and you're likely to see something akin to an Orwellian mural in which defeated workers toil away under fluorescent lights in dumpy offices, whereas the professionals and scientists who work in the private sector often have fancy, cozy offices with amenities like gyms, catered lunches, and even ping pong tables.

This inability to financially compete with private industry is likely responsible for the recent defeat of the front-of-package labeling advocated by the IOM in favor of the industry-advocated Facts Up Front label. After the GMA and FMI launched a $50 million campaign to promote Facts Up Front (Bottemiller Evich & Parti, 2014), FDA Deputy Commissioner for Foods Michael Taylor capitulated, stating that Facts Up Front "may contribute to FDA's public health goals" and that the agency would "exercise enforcement discretion for certain aspects of the theme" (Scott-Thomas, 2012). While it is nice to see cooperation among industry and government, this shift by the FDA likely represents resignation more than anything else. In a more clear statement of defeat, Taylor argued that even when the FDA proves that a claim is misleading, clever marketers easily come up with another compelling claim right away. "Going after them one-by-one with the legal and resource restraints we work under is a little like playing Whac-a-Mole, with one hand tied behind your back" (Taylor, 2010). We can see this, too, in the regulation of the term "natural." Even if the FDA had the resources and willingness to regulate the term, the reality is that once food manufacturers are restricted in their use of that term, they will simply seize upon another unregulated term like "pure" or "wholesome" instead. It's a cat and mouse game in which ultimately the FDA cannot regulate every word in the dictionary. Of course, that still doesn't mean they shouldn't try. To wholly give into Big Food because regulation is hard and terms are difficult to define would be catastrophic.

Limitations on authority and enforcement

Not only does the FDA have limited resources to empower it against the virtually unlimited budgets of Big Food, but there are also legal limitations on its authority. The FDA has only as much power as Congress gives it, and it is also subject to review by the judicial branch through litigation (Piña & Pines, 2008). With some failures which might initially appear the fault of the FDA, closer examination reveals that it was in fact one of the other branches of government which limited the agency's authority. For example, after an early FDA attempt to regulate cigarettes, the Supreme Court ruled that Congress did not intend to give the FDA regulatory power over tobacco (FDA V. Brown & Williamson Tobacco Corp, 2000). To remedy this, Congress later passed the Family Smoking Prevention and Tobacco Control Act to explicitly authorize such oversight. The FDA again currently finds itself powerless in the regulation of e-cigarettes and vaping because these products do not meet the legal definition of tobacco products and therefore fall outside of the agency's regulatory purview. Similarly, the weak regulation of the supplement industry points not to a failure by the FDA itself, but to Congress's complicity with industry in its passage of DSHEA.

Along with limited authority, many of the FDA's enforcement strategies are fairly limited as well. While the agency has various means of enforcement such as recall, seizure, injunction, monetary penalties, and criminal prosecution, such strategies do not extend to every area of its reach (FDA, 1996). In particular, these measures generally are not used for food mislabeling unless the misbranding "will cause serious adverse health consequences of death" (21 US Code § 334). When the agency has determined that a manufacturer has violated a labeling regulation, but such misbranding would not cause serious adverse health consequences, its principal enforcement tool is a Warning Letter intended to achieve voluntary compliance. As you might imagine, without the threat of more serious action these Warning Letters amount to a slap on the wrist and are rarely effective in persuading companies to discontinue the use of misleading claims on food labels (Negowetti, 2014).

Weighing all of the evidence together leads me to conclude that consumerism *as advocacy* is the most impotent form of consumerism and that the market as religion has defeated any moral mandate to protect consumers from overconsumption. In many ways, we are probably complicit in that defeat. "The 'consumer spirit'… rebels against regulation. A society of consumers is resentful of all legal restrictions imposed on freedom of choice, of any delegalization of potential objects of consumption, and manifests its resentment by widespread support willingly offered to most 'deregulatory' measures" (Bauman, 1998, p. 29). Another way of thinking about this is that the culture of consumerism has effectively socialized us to subvert our psychological well-being for the well-being of the market. In the case of food and overeating, this socialization is bolstered by the neurologic hedonic reward offered by hyperpalatable foods. Just as nicotine addiction kept cigarette smokers from supporting tobacco regulation and increased taxes on cigarettes, so too the desire for hyperpalatable foods keeps us from supporting the very regulation that would protect our psychological and physiological health.

More importantly, framing food regulation as an issue of nanny state politics vs. personal responsibility is not only divisive, but it is a unidimensional framework. Such black and white thinking misses the bigger point that democracies function through checks and balances. There is no reason that consumer protection cannot coexist in healthy tension against industry. Increased regulation needn't mean socialism, communism, or a closed marketplace, but simply a fair playing field on which regulation and industry coexist.

In the concluding chapter, we will return to our proxy Allison and consider her future. For what happens to Allison is important as a barometer for what might happen to many of us in the culture of consumerism.

11

Conclusion

Like much of our culture, Allison is at a crossroads. She is hooked on spending, eating, drinking, and consuming; yet like all addicts she suffers profound ill-effects from that consumption. Over time, food, drinks, pills, and consumer products have come to populate her internal world, yet they fail to deliver purpose or meaning. Because the failure is experienced as a failure of the self, she turns to other forms of consumption to solve the ensuing hopelessness and dysphoria. This is the modern hedonism of desire, which ultimately creates a self bloated by sugar, fat, salt, and toxins, and a planet bloated by landfills, greenhouse gases, smog, and disease. In short, overconsumption is unsustainable at every level. At the current pace, we will kill ourselves and the planet in short order.

At the same time, however, we must consume or we will die. Every living organism must consume. Although much of this book has been an indictment of consumer culture and its psychological consequences, a wholesale rejection of that culture is not realistic nor desirable for most of us. If you are reading this book, you are almost certainly a citizen of consumer culture: you are fluent in its language, knowledgeable of its customs—its smells are familiar and the food tastes good. How then do we live within consumer culture, enjoying its innovation, prosperity, and leisure, while also protecting ourselves from the seduction and consequences of *over*consuming?

Recall that we began the book with five understandings of consumerism:

1 consumerism as *a moral doctrine*—consumer choice and acquisition are the vehicles for individual freedom, happiness, and power for developed countries.

2 consumerism as *a political ideology*—in contrast to the nanny state and its paternalism, the modern state protects transnational corporations and the consumerist ideology exalts choice and freedom for the consumer to acquire glamorous and stylish goods.

3   consumerism as *an economic ideology for global development*—in contrast to the austerity of communism, consumerism is seen as the driver of free trade and the nurturing of new consumers is seen as the key to developing economies.

4   consumerism as *a social ideology*—establishes class distinctions such that material commodities fix the social position and prestige of their owners.

5   consumerism as *a social movement*—consumer rights are characterized by advocacy for the protection of value and quality for the consumer often through regulation (Gabriel & Lang, 2006).

I have argued that the current states of consumerism as *moral doctrine, political ideology, economic ideology*, and *social ideology* have defeated consumerism *as a social movement*, ultimately undermining psychological well-being. This has created an Empty Self characterized by impulsivity, narcissism, and a diffuse and chronic emotional hunger (Cushman, 1990). Because we experience this emptiness as an individual deficiency rather than a cultural ill, we turn toward the consumption of pills, consumer goods, and food to "treat" ourselves. Yet one of the things that should be clear by now is that solving the problems of consumerism through new forms of consumption is self-defeating. This endless cycle only perpetuates the problems of the Empty Self. Instead, finding ways to consume less and consume more wisely are essential to rebalancing the five forms of consumerism and reversing the course of Empty Selfhood.

One of the many tensions inherent in rebalancing or moderating consumption, however, is that what's good for the individual is often bad for the economy. Many economists will reject the notion that individuals ought to better balance nutritional and financial budgets because the resulting reduction in consumption would restrict the economy (Krugman, 2014). The question that must be asked, though, is whether a flourishing free-market economy needs to be structured such that it inherently undermines the physical and psychological health of its citizens? Economists may answer this question differently than I do, but as a psychologist I come down on the side of collective physical and emotional well-being.

Rebalancing consumerism and pleasure

Many years ago I was with a group of female friends, one of whom had just lost twenty pounds and was receiving much praise from the group. Most of the women at the table were members of Weight Watchers, expensive gyms, and forever chasing the newest fad diet. The newly slender friend who happened to be a foreigner was peppered with questions: "What's your secret? How did you do it?" She looked puzzled and replied without guile, "Well……. I just didn't eat as much food as before." Eyes widened among everyone at the table as if it were the most revolutionary diet they'd heard of. These wide-eyed women were stunned by the simplicity of eating less because they were caught up in the culture of consumerism and consequently always searching for a magic bullet, a holy grail of thinness. Like Allison, these women perceive weight control as an individual issue of willpower and one that must be addressed through extreme self-control, restriction, and the disavowal of pleasure.

Yet good health shouldn't require asceticism or the disavowal of pleasure. From an evolutionary perspective, it is pleasure-seeking behavior that ensures the survival of the species. The pleasure of sex guarantees reproduction; the pleasure of taste guarantees energy and vitality. There are many other pleasures to be had in consumer culture: beautifully designed art and furnishings, sumptuous textiles, mobile devices that make life safer and more efficient. Where pleasure-seeking becomes self-defeating is when we become habituated to highly stimulating "supernormal" objects and experiences (Lorenz, 1974; Tinbergen, 1951; Wilson, 1975), such that we increasingly crave such stimulation and no longer find simple pleasures enjoyable. It is this tension between hedonism and asceticism that Daniel Bell identified as the central contradiction of late capitalism, that is, the discipline and asceticism required of production vs. the hedonism and waste of consumption (2008). This brings us to the vexing problem of overeating for a great many of us: How do we reverse the neurological and psychological habituation to hyperpalatable foods in order to locate pleasure in simpler tastes? To that end, the challenge of (re)training ourselves to find delicious the textures, flavors, and aromas beyond salt, sugar, and fat is daunting and complex. It will require not only widespread individual change, but also significant cultural shifts as well as systemic changes in the food landscape.

Individual change

Prosperity, desire, and unlimited consumer choice are powerful forces pushing us toward overeating, overspending, and the acquisition of material goods. Jean-Paul Sartre famously said that we are "condemned to freedom." It is with that in mind that I consider what people are up against in the desire to change. Although this book is not intended to be a self-help book nor a guide for clinicians, I am constantly asked about how I work with patients on behavioral change related to overeating and consumerism. I briefly address those approaches here, connecting them to existential psychology and the culture of consumerism. I caution the reader, however, not to view these strategies as a holistic solution to overeating. As discussed in earlier chapters, Americans have a tendency to overestimate the power of individual change and often fail to see themselves as actors in a complex web of interdependence. In weighing the potency of these behavioral strategies, it is important to remember the downward pressure exerted in the funnel of consumption (see Figure 3.1). Resisting consumerism on a psychological level still remains at odds with consumerism on political, economic, and cultural levels. To put it more simply, if I thought that willpower, discipline, and behavioral modification by themselves were enough to stop overeating I would have written a self-help book instead.

First, I always urge patients to consider that if they want to enact lasting behavioral change it is best to be slow and deliberate. There is no therapeutic gain in establishing Herculean goals that are likely to fail. Pick one thing at a time to start with and focus on that one behavior until it becomes habit before picking another. Much like hot milk must be tempered into eggs when making a custard, change must be done carefully and incrementally to succeed. A single behavioral change can be something as simple as switching from a muffin to oatmeal for breakfast, or from a vanilla latte to an unsweetened latte. The recommendations below include broad ways of thinking about consumerism, as well as behavioral strategies focused on taste, variety, and convenience. Note that these interventions speak more to the kinds of folks who populate the outpatient offices of American psychologists (that is, "the worried well") and they may not be useful or culturally appropriate to many other people struggling with overeating. In the future, I hope to see a great many more empirically validated treatments and interventions that represent a new integrative science of psychology and nutrition.

Taming consumerism

For those inclined to spend money, spending it on pro-health purchases and activities is a good strategy. One of my patients, a French man with a high income and a disinclination toward excessive spending, once told me that the store REI sold "outdoor porn." I liked that description because it captured the highly stimulating appeal of the gear, while also emphasizing that the items were for the pro-health purposes of being in nature. This patient, a newly divorced dad with a very high income, initially felt guilty after he spent hundreds of dollars at REI on camping and hiking equipment for a backpacking trip. He was looking for ways to spend quality time with his seven-year-old son and planned a week-long trip to the national forest. Although he first had misgivings about his expensive purchases, after his return, he couldn't have been happier at the investment. Watching his son learn outdoor skills, having safe and reliable camping equipment, and the prolonged opportunity to commune with nature after the grueling corporate daily grind represented money well spent.

Attending a dance class, joining a sports league, and shopping at farmers' markets are great ways to put money back in the economy. Moreover, research from the field of positive psychology consistently shows that spending money on experiences instead of material luxuries has long-lasting positive effects (Haidt, 2006). This is now so well established in the social sciences that many researchers have moved away from using GDP as a proxy measure for well-being and are developing more complex measures such as the UN's Human Development Index, the Organisation for Economic Co-operation and Development Better Life Index, and the Happy Planet Index (Marks, 2011), which accounts for citizens' life expectancy, experienced well-being, and ecological footprint instead of simple economic activity.

Taste, variety, and convenience

I generally discourage patients from purchasing diet foods or anything labeled "light" or "low-fat." They are false promises. Not only do these products taste like hell, but low-fat yogurts, packaged Jenny Craig foods, and Skinny Girl margaritas don't sate our appetite and are only a means to increase consumption. Moreover, because they contain highly stimulating manufactured flavors and are usually high in sugar, it is nearly impossible not to eat too much of them. For most of us in prosperous cultures with food surpluses and ready access to the global industrial diet, it is difficult to keep from overeating while eating these ultra-processed foods because of their high palatability and reward value. In fact, recent research has suggested that in the United States and other similar countries, a significant number of people simply cannot achieve self-regulation with refined carbohydrates in their diet (Lennerz et al., 2013).

Addressing variety is one of the more important strategies against overeating and any means of limiting our food and consumer choices is likely to be effective. Eating out is one of the single activities that has the biggest impact on the waistline and pocketbook because of the large variety of hyperpalatable foods. Of course it can be pleasant and convenient to eat out sometimes, but moderating this luxury behavior is one of the keys to taming the overconsumption that puts us in financial and caloric peril. Shopping at Costco and other warehouse stores also invites overconsuming because of the tremendous variety. Allison, for example, could benefit from reducing the frequency of her visits to Whole Foods Market because the overstimulation activates a powerful drive for her to consume and accumulate. We discussed the advantages of her shopping in smaller groceries where there are fewer choices and where the packaging is not as attractive or desirable as in luxury stores. A modest local grocery will have most of the things she needs. I also recommended that she consider an online grocery delivery service that would allow her to pick out what goes in her basket without the "hot" emotions of the labels, colors, smells, and sights of the store. Of course most people cannot afford grocery delivery so this is not a practical solution for others, but I offer it as an example of the small ways people can limit their consumer choices. In Allison's case, she already does all of her shopping at Whole Foods Market and has a considerable disposable income, so this is an appropriate recommendation and would probably even save her money.

Reckoning and regulation

Most of the aforementioned behavioral interventions could simply be thought of as strategies of "self-regulation," that is, a reflecting process of feedback control in which the individual makes self-corrective adjustments in order to achieve goals (Carver & Scheier, 2011). I think of self-regulation somewhat more broadly than is defined by psychology, such that it spans cognitive, moral, affective, nutritional, hormonal, and existential dimensions of the self. The culture of consumerism threatens self-regulation across all of these dimensions by creating distorted and insatiable desires, encouraging cultural superiority and labor exploitation, hijacking finely tuned hormonal and neurological processes, and directing us down a path of false selfhood in which branded products and constant consumption define our person.

For most of us, even vast improvements in self-regulation will not be powerful enough to curtail overeating if done in isolation. In my view, the complex determinants of overconsumption are such that there must be increased government regulation which protects consumers, *in addition to* robust self-regulation in the form of personal responsibility. Recall from Chapter 4 that history and accounting professor Jacob Soll (2014) argued that stable, sustainable capitalism requires "the [individual] mastery of accounting, accountability, and the ensuing struggle to successfully manage them" (p. xiv). He describes the historic practice known as *Oikonomia* as a policy of fiscal soundness for the stewardship of both households and governments. Originally an Aristotelian concept, *Oikonomia* meant that individuals and governments had a moral and financial responsibility to each other to remain accountable, transparent, and solvent (p. 4). If we broaden this concept of *Oikonomia* to include nutritional accountability and stewardship of the body, we then have a model in which regulation falls on both the individual and the government in a dynamic interdependence. By contrast, placing the locus of accountability for overeating squarely on the individual *or* the government misses the reality that humans exist within a political state, that is, there is a tandem of being, an organization of self that is mediated through the dyad of self-state. Putting this in more psychological terms, we could simply think of the balance between government regulation and self-regulation as perhaps a distribution of internal and external loci of control. In other words, caloric and financial reckoning work in tandem as a kind of reciprocal civic responsibility in the interest of health and solvency.

Final thoughts

I hope I have convinced you that overeating is not strictly a problem of food or eating—it is a problem of consuming. The constant and exclusive focus by the mass media on food, weight, and dieting ignores the larger systemic problem of how the culture of consumerism traps people in poverty, debt, nutritional confusion, metabolic dysfunction, and limitless desire. In a column last year on the link between obesity and poverty, *The New York Times* declared: "The articulated goal should not simply be to create a population of poor people who are thin, but to create a population of poor people who are less poor" (Bellafante, 2013). In other words, rather than simply putting poor people on diets, we should address the underlying systemic problems that make people poor *and* fat. I would broaden this logic to consumerism more generally and argue that our goal should not simply be to create a population of people that consumes less food, but a population that consumes less of everything. Addressing overconsumption so broadly is a far more direct way of stemming the tide of overweight, obesity, and metabolic dysfunction.

I've found that many of the movements trying to resist the forces of consumerism, such as Slow Living, Voluntary Simplicity, Slow Food, and Tiny House, are good resources for those seeking a community and specific strategies for simpler living. The Center for a New American Dream whose motto is "More fun, less stuff" is one of the most active and sensible organizations promoting these so-called pro-social values. Most of these movements are loosely informed by or compatible with an existential approach and they have emerged out of a desire to heal ourselves from the self-defeating tendencies of materialism and consumption. In previous chapters, I have also mentioned other ideas for stemming the tide of overconsumption, such as reinstating home economics and better integrating the clinical practices of psychology and nutrition. The scope of my imagination and expertise is limited, however, and it is a task that will require a great deal of innovation and creativity.

Finally, then, what will happen to Allison who has served as our proxy throughout this book? Will she be relegated to the life of a "fat and lonely spinster," all the while pursuing status and chasing the newest expensive fads and trends? Or will she find meaning, get healthy, and tether herself to a deeper purpose? Like Allison, we do not have much time to address the pressing issues related to overconsumption: pollution, climate change, overeating, obesity, diabetes, metabolic syndrome, labor exploitation, and income inequality, to name a few. I am not always optimistic, but I would not be working with Allison if I did not have hope for insight and change. Nor would I have written this book if I did not believe that cultures and governments, as well as individuals, have the capacity for insight and change.

Works Cited

Abbott, E. (2008). *Sugar: A bittersweet history.* Toronto: Penguin Canada.

ABC News. (2003). *How to get fat without really trying.* New York: ABC News Productions.

Adams, J. M., Hart, W., Gilmer, L., Lloyd-Richardson, E. E., & Burton, K. A. (2014). Concrete images of the sugar content in sugar-sweetened beverages reduces attraction to and selection of these beverages. *Appetite, 83C,* 10–18. doi: 10.1016/j.appet.2014.07.027

Adams, M. (2013, April 10). Soda companies rake in $4 billion a year of taxpayer money via the government food stamp program (SNAP). *Natural News.* Retrieved from http://www.naturalnews.com/039849_food_stamps_soda_subsidies_junk.html

Ahmed, S. (2012). Is sugar as addictive as cocaine? In K. D. Brownell & M. S. Gold (Eds.), *Food and addiction: A comprehensive handbook* (pp. 231–237). Oxford: Oxford University Press.

Aikman, S. N., Min, K. E., & Graham, D. (2006). Food attitudes, eating behavior, and the information underlying food attitudes. *Appetite, 47*(1), 111–114. doi: 10.1016/j.appet.2006.02.004

Allison, M. (2007, February 5). Seattle soda maker ends the sweet talk, opts for sugar. *Seattle Times.* Retrieved from http://seattletimes.com/html/businesstechnology/2003557096_sugar05.html

American Academy of Pediatrics. (2006). Children, adolescents, and advertising. *Pediatrics, 118*(6), 2563–2569. doi: 10.1542/peds.2006-2698

American Apparel and Footwear Association. (2008). *Trends: An annual statistical analysis of the U.S. apparel & footwear industries.* Retrieved from https://www.wewear.org/assets/1/7/Trends2008.pdf

American Beverage Association. (2014). Hydration. Retrieved from http://www.ameribev.org/nutrition-science/hydration/

American Psychiatric Association. (2013). *Diagnostic and statistical manual of mental disorders* (5th ed.). Arlington, VA: American Psychiatric Publications Incorporated.

American Psychiatric Association. (2013). Diagnostic and statistical manual of mental disorders. (5th ed.). Arlington: American Psychiatric Publications Incorporated.

American Society for Nutrition. (2014a). Mission and bylaws. Retrieved from http://www.nutrition.org/about-asn/mission-and-bylaws/

American Society for Nutrition. (2014b). Re: Docket No. FDA-2012-N-1210; Food labeling: Revision of the nutrition and supplement facts labels. Retrieved from http://www.regulations.gov/-!docketDetail;D=FDA-2012-N-1210

Angell, M. (2005). *The truth about the drug companies: How they deceive us and what to do about it.* New York: Random House Trade Paperbacks.

Arnold, J. E. (2012). *Life at home in the twenty-first century: 32 families open their doors.* Los Angeles, CA: Cotsen Institute of Archaeology Press.

Avena, N. M., Rada, P., & Hoebel, B. G. (2008). Evidence for sugar addiction: Behavioral and neurochemical effects of intermittent, excessive sugar intake. *Neuroscience & Biobehavioral Reviews, 32*(1), 20–39. doi: 10.1016/j.neubiorev.2007.04.019

Avena, N. (2015). *Hedonic eating: How the pleasurable aspects of food can affect our brains and behavior.* Oxford: Oxford University Press.

Averett, S., & Korenman, S. (1996). The economic reality of the beauty myth. *The Journal of Human Resources, 31*(2). doi: 10.2307/146065

Averett, S., Sikora, A., & Argys, L. M. (2008). For better or worse: Relationship status and body mass index. *Economics and Human Biology, 6*(3), 330–349. doi: 10.1016/j.ehb.2008.07.003

Avorn, J. (2007). Paying for drug approvals—who's using whom? *New England Journal of Medicine, 356*(17), 1697–1700.

Babiak, P. (2000). Psychopathic manipulation at work. In C. B. Gacono (Ed.), *The clinical and forensic assessment of psychopathy: A practitioner's guide* (pp. 287–311). Mahwah, NJ: Lawrence Erlbaum Associates Publishers.

Babiak, P., & Hare, R. D. (2009). *Snakes in suits: When psychopaths go to work.* New York: HarperCollins.

Baeyens, F., Eelen, P., Van den Bergh, O., & Crombez, G. (1990). Flavor-flavor and color-flavor conditioning in humans. *Learning and Motivation, 21*(4), 434–455.

Barrett, S. (2007). How the Dietary Supplement Health and Education Act of 1994 weakened the FDA. Retrieved from http://www.quackwatch.org/02ConsumerProtection/dshea.html

Bartoshuk, L. M. (1991). Sweetness – history, preference, and genetic variability. *Food Technology, 45*(11), 108–113.

Bartoshuk, L. M., Duffy, V. B., & Miller, I. J. (1994). PTC/PROP tasting: Anatomy, psychophysics, and sex effects. *Physiology & Behavior, 56*(6), 1165–1171.

Batte, M. T., Hooker, N. H., Haab, T. C., & Beaverson, J. (2007). Putting their money where their mouths are: Consumer willingness to pay for multi-ingredient, processed organic food products. *Food Policy, 32*(2), 145–159.

Baudrillard, J. (1970). Consumer society. In M. Poster (Ed.), *Jean Baudrillard: Selected writings.* Cambridge: Stanford University Press.

Bauman, Z. (1992). *Intimations of postmodernity.* London: Routledge.

Bauman, Z. (1998). *Work, consumerism and the new poor.* Buckingham: Open University Press.

Beaulac, J., Kristjansson, E., & Cummins, S. (2009). A systematic review of food deserts, 1966–2007. *Preventing Chronic Disease, 6*(3).

Belfiore, A., & Malaguarnera, R. (2011). Insulin receptor and cancer. *Endocrine Related Cancer, 18*(4), R125–147. doi: 10.1530/ERC-11-0074

Belk, R. W. (1988). Third world consumer culture. *Research in Marketing, 4*, 103.

Bell, D. (2008). *The cultural contradictions of capitalism: 20th anniversary edition.* New York: Basic Books.

Bellafante, G. (2013, March 16). In obesity epidemic, poverty is an ignored contagion. *New York Times.* Retrieved from http://www.nytimes.com/2013/03/17/nyregion/in-obesity-fight-poverty-is-patient-zero.html

Belli et al. v. Nestlé USA Inc. (2014). Case No. 14-cv-00283, N. D. CA.

Benton, D. (2010). The plausibility of sugar addiction and its role in obesity and eating disorders. *Clinical Nutrition, 29*(3), 288–303.

Bermudez, O. I., & Gao, X. (2010). Greater consumption of sweetened beverages and added sugars is associated with obesity among US young adults. *Annals of Nutrition and Metabolism, 57*(3–4), 211–218. doi: 10.1159/000321542

Berridge, K. (1995). Brain substances of liking and wanting. *Neuroscience & Biobehavioral Reviews, 20*, 1–25.

Bertino, M., Liska, D., Spence, K., Sanders, L., & Egan, V. (2014). Added-sugar labeling: Implications for consumers. *The FASEB Journal, 28*(1 Supplement).

Beverage Digest. (2014). *Dollar sales of liquid refreshment beverages (LRB) worldwide in 2012 and 2013 (in billion U.S. dollars)*. Retrieved from http://www.statista.com/statistics/307879/global-dollar-sales-of-lrb/

Beverage Institute for Health & Wellness. (2014). Retrieved from http://beverageinstitute.org/about-us/

Blendy, J. A., Strasser, A., Walters, C. L., Perkins, K. A., Patterson, F., Berkowitz, R., & Lerman, C. (2005). Reduced nicotine reward in obesity: Cross-comparison in human and mouse. *Psychopharmacology (Berl), 180*(2), 306–315. doi: 10.1007/s00213-005-2167-9

Block, J. P., & Roberto, C. A. (2014). Potential benefits of calorie labeling in restaurants. *JAMA, 312*(9), 887–888. doi: 10.1001/jama.2014.9239

Bloom, H. K. (2010). *The genius of the beast: A radical revision of capitalism*. Amherst, NY: Prometheus Books.

Blum, K., Bailey, J., Gonzalez, A. M., Oscar-Berman, M., Liu, Y., Giordano, J., … Gold, M. (2011). Neuro-genetics of reward deficiency syndrome (RDS) as the root cause of "addiction transfer": A new phenomenon common after bariatric surgery. *Journal of Genetic Syndromes & Gene Therapy, 2012*(1), S2–001.

Blumenthal, D. M., & Gold, M. S. (2010). Neurobiology of food addiction. *Current Opinion in Clinical Nutrition and Metabolic Care, 13*(4), 359–365. doi: 10.1097/MCO.0b013e32833ad4d4

Blüml, V., Kapusta, N., Vyssoki, B., Kogoj, D., Walter, H., & Lesch, O. M. (2012). Relationship between substance use and body mass index in young males. *The American Journal on Addictions, 21*(1), 72–77.

Bordo, S. (1986). Anorexia nervosa: Psychopathology as the crystallization of culture. *Philosophical Forum, 17*, 73–103.

Borgmann, A. (2000). The moral complexion of consumption. *Journal of Consumer Research, 26*(4), 418–422. doi: 10.1086/209572

Bosch, T. (2012, June 5). Bring back home ec! *Slate*. Retrieved from http://www.slate.com/articles/health_and_science/future_tense/2012/06/home_ec_or_family_and_consumer_sciences_should_be_mandatory_for_students_.html

Bottemiller Evich, H., & Parti, T. (2014, March 1). Food industry to make its own labeling splash. *Politico*. Retrieved from http://www.politico.com/story/2014/03/food-industry-labeling-104122.html

Bourdieu, P. (2010). *Distinction: A social critique of the judgement of taste*. London: Routledge.

Boyd, D. B. (2003). Insulin and cancer. *Integrative Cancer Therapies, 2*(4), 315–329. doi: 10.1177/1534735403259152

Bray, G. A., Nielsen, S. J., & Popkin, B. M. (2004). Consumption of high-fructose corn syrup in beverages may play a role in the epidemic of obesity. *The American Journal of Clinical Nutrition, 79*(4), 537–543.

Briers, B., & Laporte, S. (2013). A wallet full of calories: The effect of financial dissatisfaction on the desire for food energy. *Journal of Marketing Research, 50*(6), 767–781.

Brower, V. (1998). Nutraceuticals: Poised for a healthy slice of the healthcare market? *Nature Biotechnology, 16*, 728–732. doi: 10.1038/nbt0898-728

Brownell, K. D., & Gold, M. (2012). *Food and addiction: A comprehensive handbook*. Oxford: Oxford University Press.

Brownlee, S. (2007). *Overtreated: Why too much medicine is making us sicker and poorer*. New York: Bloomsbury.

Bureau of Labor Statistics. (2006). *100 years of U.S. consumer spending: Data for the nation, New York City, and Boston*. Retrieved from http://www.bls.gov/opub/uscs/

Burros, M. (2007, July 7). FDA inspections lax, Congress is told. *New York Times.* Retrieved from http://www.nytimes.com

Camejo, M. J., & Wilentz, A. (1990). *Harvesting oppression: Forced Haitian labor in the Dominican sugar industry*. New York: Human Rights Watch.

Cameron, J. D., Cyr, M., & Doucet, E. (2010). Increased meal frequency does not promote greater weight loss in subjects who were prescribed an 8-week equi-energetic energy-restricted diet. *British Journal of Nutrition, 103*(08), 1098–1101. doi: 10.1017/S0007114509992984

Campbell, C. (1987). *The romantic ethic and the spirit of modern consumerism*. Oxford: Blackwell.

Campbell, C. (1991). Consumption – the new wave of research in the humanities and social sciences. *Journal of Social Behavior and Personality, 6*(6), 57–74.

Campbell, D., & Chui, M. (2010). *Pharmerging shake-up: New imperatives in a redefined world*. Retrieved from http://www.imshealth.com/imshealth/Global/Content/IMS Institute/Documents/Pharmerging_Shakeup.pdf

Campbell, J. (2008). A growing concern: Modern slavery and agricultural production in Brazil and South Asia. In *Human Rights and Human Welfare*, 131–141.

Canadean. (2014, October 2). Beverage industry is wising up to an aging population. Retrieved from http://www.canadean.com/news/beverage-industry-is-wising-up-to-an-aging-population/

Canetti, L., Bachar, E., & Berry, E. M. (2002). Food and emotion. *Behavioural Processes, 60*(2), 157–164.

Carmalt, J. H., Cawley, J., Joyner, K., & Sobal, J. (2008). Body weight and matching with a physically attractive romantic partner. *Journal of Marriage and Family, 70*(5), 1287–1296. doi: 10.1111/j.1741-3737.2008.00566.x

Caro, J. F., Sinha, M. K., Kolaczynski, J. W., Zhang, P. L., & Considine, R. V. (1996). Leptin: The tale of an obesity gene. *Diabetes, 45*(11), 1455–1462.

Carpenter, D. (2014). *Reputation and power: Organizational image and pharmaceutical regulation at the FDA*. Princeton, NJ: Princeton University Press.

Carter, O. B., Patterson, L. J., Donovan, R. J., Ewing, M. T., & Roberts, C. M. (2011). Children's understanding of the selling versus persuasive intent of junk food advertising: Implications for regulation. *Social Science & Medicine, 72*(6), 962–968. doi: 10.1016/j.socscimed.2011.01.018

Carver, C., & Scheier, M. (2011). Self-regulation of action and affect. In K. D. Vohs & R. F. Baumeister (Eds.), *Handbook of self-regulation, second edition: Research, theory, and applications* (pp. 3–21). New York: Guilford Publications.

Cavadini, C., Siega-Riz, A. M., & Popkin, B. M. (2000). US adolescent food intake trends from 1965 to 1996. *Archives of Disease in Childhood, 83*(1), 18–24.

Center for a New American Dream. (September 2004). *New American dream survey report.* Retrieved from http://newdream.s3.amazonaws.com/19/e3/b/2268/ND2004Finalpollreport.pdf

Center for Science in the Public Interest. (2007). Nutrition review questions soda-obesity link… [Press release]. Retrieved from http://www.cspinet.org/integrity/press/200703121.html

Center for Science in the Public Interest. (2014a). CSPI supports proposed nutrition facts revisions. Retrieved from http://www.cspinet.org/new/201402271.html

Center for Science in the Public Interest. (2014b). Litigation project. Retrieved from https://www.cspinet.org/litigation/

Chandon, P., & Wansink, B. (2007). The biasing health halos of fast-food restaurant health claims: Lower calorie estimates and higher side-dish consumption intentions. *Journal of Consumer Research, 34*(3), 301–314.

Chang, H. J., Burke, A. E., & Glass, R. M. (2010). Food allergies. *JAMA, 303*(18), 1876–1876. doi: 10.1001/jama.303.18.1876

Chen, L., Appel, L. J., Loria, C., Lin, P. H., Champagne, C. M., Elmer, P. J., … Caballero, B. (2009). Reduction in consumption of sugar-sweetened beverages is associated with weight loss: The PREMIER trial. *American Journal of Clinical Nutrition, 89*(5), 1299–1306. doi: 10.3945/ajcn.2008.27240

Chilton, M., & Rose, D. (2009). A rights-based approach to food insecurity in the United States. *American Journal of Public Health, 99*(7), 1203–1211. doi: 10.2105/AJPH.2007.130229

Chiu, C. J., Liu, S., Willett, W. C., Wolever, T. M., Brand-Miller, J. C., Barclay, A. W., & Taylor, A. (2011). Informing food choices and health outcomes by use of the dietary glycemic index. *Nutrition Reviews, 69*(4), 231–242. doi: 10.1111/j.1753-4887.2011.00382.x

Clark, M. J., & Slavin, J. L. (2013). The effect of fiber on satiety and food intake: A systematic review. *Journal of the American College of Nutrition, 32*(3), 200–211. doi: 10.1080/07315724.2013.791194

Cleckley, H. (1941). *The mask of sanity: An attempt to reinterpret the so-called psychopathic personality.* St. Louis, MO: The C. V. Mosby Company.

Cline, E. L. (2012). *Overdressed: The shockingly high cost of cheap fashion.* New York: Portfolio/Penguin.

Cohen, D. (2012). The truth about sports drinks. *BMJ, 345*(e4737), 1–10. doi: 10.1136/bmj.e4737

Cohen, M. H. (2000). US dietary supplement regulation: Belief systems and legal rules. *Hastings Women's Law Journal, 11*, 3.

Cohen, P., & Cohen, J. (1996). *Life values and adolescent mental health.* Mahwah, NJ: L. Erlbaum Associates.

Coleman-Jensen, A., Gregory, C., & Singh, A. (2013). *Household food security in the United States. Economic Research Report No. (ERR-173).* Retrieved from http://www.ers.usda.gov/publications/err-economic-research-report/err173.aspx

Conason, A., Teixeira, J., Hsu, C.-H., Puma, L., Knafo, D., & Geliebter, A. (2013). Substance use following bariatric weight loss surgery. *JAMA Surgery, 148*(2), 145–150.

Conley, D., & Glauber, R. (2007). Gender, body mass, and socioeconomic status: New evidence from the PSID. *Advances in Health Economics and Health Services Research, 17*, 253–275. doi: 10.1016/S0731-2199(06)17010-7

Considine, R. V., & Caro, J. F. (1997). Leptin and the regulation of body weight. *International Journal of Biochemistry & Cell Biology, 29*(11), 1255–1272.

Considine, R. V., Considine, E. L., Williams, C. J., Hyde, T. M., & Caro, J. F. (1996). The hypothalamic leptin receptor in humans: Identification of incidental sequence polymorphisms and absence of the db/db mouse and fa/fa rat mutations. *Diabetes, 45*(7), 992–994.

Conus, F., Rabasa-Lhoret, R., & Peronnet, F. (2007). Characteristics of metabolically obese normal-weight (MONW) subjects. *Applied Physiology, Nutrition, and Metabolism, 32*(1), 4–12. doi: 10.1139/H07-926

Coontz, S. (1992). *The way we never were: American families and the nostalgia trap.* New York: BasicBooks.

Cooper, M. A., & Shlaes, D. (2011). Fix the antibiotics pipeline. *Nature, 472*(7341). doi: 10.1038/472032a

Cooper, M. L., Frone, M. R., Russell, M., & Mudar, P. (1995). Drinking to regulate positive and negative emotions: A motivational model of alcohol use. *Journal of Personality and Social Psychology, 69*(5), 990–1005. doi: 10.1037/0022-3514.69.5.990

Corsica, J. A., & Spring, B. J. (2008). Carbohydrate craving: A double-blind, placebo-controlled test of the self-medication hypothesis. *Eating Behaviors, 9*(4), 447–454. doi: 10.1016/j.eatbeh.2008.07.004

Corwin, R. L., & Grigson, P. S. (2009). Symposium overview—food addiction: Fact or fiction? *The Journal of Nutrition, 139*(3), 617–619.

Crawford, M. B. (2009). *Shop class as soulcraft: An inquiry into the value of work.* New York: Penguin Press.

Credit Suisse Research Institute. (2013). *Sugar consumption at a crossroads.* Retrieved from https://publications.credit-suisse.com/tasks/render/file/index.cfm?fileid=780BF4A8-B3D1-13A0-D2514E21EFFB0479

Crocker, D. (1996). Consumption, well being, and virtue. In N. R. Goodwin, F. Ackerman, & D. Kiron (Eds.), *The consumer society.* Washington, DC: Island Press.

Csikszentmihalyi, M., & Halton, E. (1981). *The meaning of things: Domestic symbols and the self.* Cambridge: Cambridge University Press.

Cushman, P. (1990). Why the self is empty: Toward a historically situated psychology. *American Psychologist, 45*(5), 599.

Cutler, D., Glaeser, E., & Shapiro, J. (2003). Why have Americans become more obese? *Journal of Economic Perspectives, 17*(3), 93–118. doi: 10.1257/089533003769204371

Cutright, K. M., Erdem, T., Fitzsimons, G. J., & Shachar, R. (2014). Finding brands and losing your religion? *Journal of Experimental Psychology: General, 143*(6), 2209–2222. doi: 10.1037/a0037876

Dahl, R. (1967). *Charlie and the chocolate factory.* London: Allen & Unwin.

Dahl, R. (1971). *Willy Wonka & the chocolate factory.* Burbank, CA: Warner Home Video.

Daly, K. (2011, March 31). The Fanjuls: Koch brothers of South Florida? *American Independent.* Retrieved from http://www.americanindependent.com

De Graaf, J., Wann, D., & Naylor, T. H. (2001). *Affluenza: The all consuming epidemic.* San Francisco, CA: Berrett-Koehler Publishers.

de la Monte, S. M., Re, E., Longato, L., & Tong, M. (2012). Dysfunctional pro-ceramide, ER stress, and insulin/IGF signaling networks with progression of Alzheimer's disease. *Journal of Alzheimers Disease, 30 Suppl 2*(0), S217–S229. doi: 10.3233/JAD-2012-111728

de la Monte, S. M., & Wands, J. R. (2005). Review of insulin and insulin-like growth factor expression, signaling, and malfunction in the central nervous system: Relevance to Alzheimer's disease. *Journal of Alzheimers Disease, 7*(1), 45–61.

de la Pena, C. (2010). *Empty pleasures: The story of artificial sweeteners from saccharin to Splenda.* Chapel Hill: University of North Carolina Press.

Delpeuch, F. (2009). *Globesity: A planet out of control?* London: Earthscan.

DeSilver, D. (2014/05/02/19:44:45 2013). *Obesity and poverty don't always go together.* Pew Research Center. Retrieved from http://www.pewresearch.org/fact-tank/2013/11/13/obesity-and-poverty-dont-always-go-together/

Dickson, S. L., Egecioglu, E., Landgren, S., Skibicka, K. P., Engel, J. A., & Jerlhag, E. (2011). The role of the central ghrelin system in reward from food and chemical drugs. *Molecular and Cellular Endocrinology, 340*(1), 80–87. doi: 10.1016/j.mce.2011.02.017

Dietary Supplement Health and Education Act. (1994). Public Law 103–417, 103rd Congress, 21 USC 301. October 25, 1994.

DiMeglio, D. P., & Mattes, R. D. (2000). Liquid versus solid carbohydrate: Effects on food intake and body weight. *International Journal of Obesity and Related Metabolic Disorders, 24*(6), 794–800.

DiNicolantonio, J. J., & Lucan, S. C. (2014). The wrong white crystals: Not salt but sugar as aetiological in hypertension and cardiometabolic disease. *Open Heart, 1*(1). doi: 10.1136/openhrt-2014-000167

Dobell, A. R. (1995). Environmental degradation and the religion of the market. In H. Coward (Ed.), *Population, consumption, and the environment: Religious and secular responses* (pp. 229–250). Albany: State University of New York Press.

Donohoe, C. L., Doyle, S. L., & Reynolds, J. V. (2011). Visceral adiposity, insulin resistance and cancer risk. *Diabetology & Metabolic Syndrome, 3*, 12. doi: 10.1186/1758-5996-3-12

Dorfman, L., & Wallack, L. (2007). Moving nutrition upstream: The case for reframing obesity. *Journal of Nutrition Education and Behavior, 39*(2), S45–S50. doi: 10.1016/j.jneb.2006.08.018

Drewnowski, A., & Greenwood, M. R. (1983). Cream and sugar: Human preferences for high-fat foods. *Physiology & Behavior, 30*(4), 629–633. doi: 10.1016/0031-9384(83)90232-9

Drewnowski, A., Krahn, D. D., Demitrack, M. A., Nairn, K., & Gosnell, B. A. (1995). Naloxone, an opiate blocker, reduces the consumption of sweet high-fat foods in obese and lean female binge eaters. *American Journal of Clinical Nutrition, 61*(6), 1206–1212.

Drewnowski, A., & Eichelsdoerfer, P. (2010). Can low-income Americans afford a healthy diet? *Nutrition Today, 44*(6), 246–249. doi: 10.1097/NT.0b013e3181c29f79

Drewnowski, A., Mennella, J. A., Johnson, S. L., & Bellisle, F. (2012). Sweetness and food preference. *Journal of Nutrition, 142*(6), 1142S–1148S. doi: 10.3945/jn.111.149575

Drewnowski, A., & Specter, S. E. (2004). Poverty and obesity: The role of energy density and energy costs. *American Journal of Clinical Nutrition, 79*(1), 6–16.

Drichoutis, A., Lazaridis, P., & Nayga Jr., R. M. (2006). Consumers' use of nutritional labels: A review of research studies and issues. *Academy of Marketing Science Review, 10*(9), 1–22.

Duffey, K. J., Huybrechts, I., Mouratidou, T., Libuda, L., Kersting, M., De Vriendt, T., … Hallström, L. (2011). Beverage consumption among European adolescents in the HELENA study. *European Journal of Clinical Nutrition, 66*(2), 244–252.

Duffey, K. J., & Popkin, B. M. (2008). High-fructose corn syrup: Is this what's for dinner? *American Journal of Clinical Nutrition, 88*(6), 1722S–1732S. doi: 10.3945/ajcn.2008.25825C

Duffy, V. B., & Anderson, G. (1998). Position of the American Dietetic Association: Use of nutritive and nonnutritive sweeteners. *Journal of the American Dietetic Association, 98*(5), 580.

Durning, A. (1997). Asking how much is enough. *Frontier Issues in Economic Thought, 2*, 11–13.

Dutton, K. (2012). *The wisdom of psychopaths.* New York: Scientific American/ Farrar, Straus and Giroux.

Ebbeling, C. B., Willett, W. C., & Ludwig, D. S. (2012). The special case of sugar-sweetened beverages. In K. D. Brownell & M. S. Gold (Eds.), *Food and addiction: A comprehensive handbook.* Oxford: Oxford University Press.

ElSohly, M. A., Ross, S. A., Mehmedic, Z., Arafat, R., Yi, B., & Banahan, B. F. (2000). Potency trends of delta9-THC and other cannabinoids in confiscated marijuana from 1980–1997. *Journal of Forensic Science, 45*(1), 24–30.

Ethisphere. (2015). The world's most ethical companies. Retrieved from http:// ethisphere.com/worlds-most-ethical/

Evans, D., Smith, M., & Willen, L. (2005, November 6). Human guinea pigs pay for lax FDA rules. *Bloomberg News.* Retrieved from http://seattletimes.com/ html/businesstechnology/2002606640_drugtesting06.html

Fanselow, M. S., & Birk, J. (1982). Flavor-flavor associations induce hedonic shifts in taste preference. *Animal Learning & Behavior, 10*(2), 223–228.

Farooqi, I. S., & O'Rahilly, S. (2005). Monogenic obesity in humans. *Annual Review of Medicine, 56*, 443–458. doi: 10.1146/annurev. med.56.062904.144924

FDA. (1993). Food labeling: Nutrient content claims, general principles, petitions, definition of terms; definitions of nutrient content claims for the fat, fatty acid, and cholesterol content of food. *Federal Register, 58*(3), 2302–2426.

FDA. (1996). Compliance policy guides manual. Retrieved from http://www. fda.gov/ICECI/ComplianceManuals/CompliancePolicyGuidanceManual/ ucm124048.htm

FDA. (2005). Prescription Drug User Fee Act (PDUFA): Adding resources and improving performance in FDA review of new drug applications. Retrieved from http://www.fda.gov/ForIndustry/UserFees/PrescriptionDrugUserFee/ ucm119253.htm

FDA. (2012). What is the meaning of 'natural' on the label of food? Retrieved from http://www.fda.gov/aboutfda/transparency/basics/ucm214868.htm

FDA. (2013). Front-of-package labeling initiative. Retrieved from http://www.fda. gov/Food/IngredientsPackagingLabeling/LabelingNutrition/ucm202726.htm

FDA. (2014). Foods must contain what label says. Retrieved from http://www.fda. gov/ForConsumers/ConsumerUpdates/ucm337628.htm

FDA v. Brown & Williamson Tobacco Corp. (2000). (98–1152) 529 U.S. 120 (2000) 153 F.3d 155, affirmed.

Fitch, C., Hamilton, S., Bassett, P., & Davey, R. (2011). The relationship between personal debt and mental health: A systematic review. *Mental Health Review Journals, 16*(4), 153–166. doi: 10.1108/13619321111202313

Flood-Obbagy, J. E., & Rolls, B. J. (2009). The effect of fruit in different forms on energy intake and satiety at a meal. *Appetite, 52*(2), 416–422. doi: 10.1016/j. appet.2008.12.001

Food and Drug Law Institute. (2014). *A natural solution: Why should FDA define "natural" foods?* Retrieved from http://www.fdli.org/resources/resources-order-box-detail-view/a-natural-solution-why-should-fda-define-natural-foods-

Food Marketing Institute. (2012). *Supermarket facts: Industry overview 2012.* Retrieved from https://www.fmi.org/research-resources/supermarket-facts

Food Research & Action Center. (2014). *Relationship between poverty and overweight or obesity.* Retrieved from http://frac.org/initiatives/hunger-and-obesity/are-low-income-people-at-greater-risk-for-overweight-or-obesity/

Forbes. (2013, February 13). PepsiCo pre-earnings: Snacking on emerging markets growth. Retrieved from http://www.forbes.com/sites/greatspeculations/2013/02/12/pepsico-pre-earnings-snacking-on-emerging-markets-growth/

Ford, M. R., & Widiger, T. A. (1989). Sex bias in the diagnosis of histrionic and antisocial personality disorders. *Journal of Consulting & Clinical Psychology, 57*(2), 301–305. doi: 10.1037/0022-006X.57.2.301

Fox News (Producer). (2014, February 14). Inspiring vs. insulting: New Cadillac ad sparks debate. Retrieved from http://video.foxnews.com/v/3204489936001/inspiring-vs-insulting-new-cadillac-ad-sparks-debate/

Frances, A. (2013). *Saving normal: An insider's revolt against out-of-control psychiatric diagnosis, DSM-5, Big Pharma, and the medicalization of ordinary life.* New York: HarperCollins.

Frank, J. D., Ascher, E., Margolin, J. B., Nash, H., Stone, A. R., & Varon, E. J. (1952). Behavioral patterns in early meetings of therapeutic groups. *American Journal of Psychiatry, 108*(10), 771–778.

Frank, R. H. (1999). *Luxury fever: Money and happiness in an era of excess.* Princeton, NJ: Princeton University Press.

Frankel, J. (2002). Exploring Ferenczi's concept of identification with the aggressor: Its role in trauma, everyday life, and the therapeutic relationship. *Psychoanalytic Dialogues, 12*(1), 101–139.

Frankl, V. E. (1963). *Man's search for meaning: An introduction to logotherapy.* Boston, MA: Beacon Press.

Frasca, F., Pandini, G., Sciacca, L., Pezzino, V., Squatrito, S., Belfiore, A., & Vigneri, R. (2008). The role of insulin receptors and IGF-I receptors in cancer and other diseases. *Archives of Physiology and Biochemistry, 114*(1), 23–37. doi: 10.1080/13813450801969715

Freedman, D. H. (2013, July/August). How junk food can end obesity. *The Atlantic.*

Freud, A. (1967). *The ego and the mechanisms of defense.* New York: International Universities Press.

Freud, S. (1930). *Civilization and its discontents.* New York: J. Cape & H. Smith.

Friedman, M. I., & Stricker, E. M. (1976). The physiological psychology of hunger: A physiological perspective. *Psychological Review, 83*(6), 409–431.

Fromm, E. (1955). *The sane society*. New York: Rinehart.

FTC. (1994). Enforcement policy statement on food advertising. Retrieved from http://www.ftc.gov/public-statements/1994/05/enforcement-policy-statement-food-advertising-5

Fu, H., & Goldman, N. (1996). Incorporating health into models of marriage choice: Demographic and sociological perspectives. *Journal of Marriage and the Family, 58*(3). doi: 10.2307/353733

Gabriel, Y., & Lang, T. (2006). *The unmanageable consumer*. New York: Sage Publications.

Gaesser, G. A., & Angadi, S. S. (2012). Gluten-free diet: Imprudent dietary advice for the general population? *Journal of the Academy of Nutrition and Dietetics, 112*(9), 1330–1333.

Gailey, J. A. (2012). Fat shame to fat pride: Fat women's sexual and dating experiences. *Fat Studies, 1*(1), 114–127.

Gallup. (2014). Student debt linked to worse health and less wealth. Retrieved from http://www.gallup.com/poll/174317/student-debt-linked-worse-health-less-wealth.aspx

Garn, S. M., Sullivan, T. V., & Hawthorne, V. M. (1989). Educational level, fatness, and fatness differences between husbands and wives. *American Journal of Clinical Nutrition, 50*(4), 740–745.

Garon, S. M. (2012). *Beyond our means: Why America spends while the world saves*. Princeton, NJ: Princeton University Press.

Garrison v. Whole Foods Market Inc. (2013). No. 13–05333 (N.D. Cal. Nov. 8, 2013).

Gearhardt, A., Corbin, W., & Brownell, K. (2009). Preliminary validation of the Yale Food Addiction Scale. *Appetite, 52*(2), 430–436. doi: 10.1016/j.appet.2008.12.003

Gearhardt, A., Davis, C., Kuschner, R., & Brownell, K. (2011a). The addiction potential of hyperpalatable foods. *Current Drug Abuse Reviews, 4*(3), 140–145.

Gearhardt, A., Grilo, C. M., DiLeone, R., Brownell, K., & Potenza, M. (2011b). Can food be addictive? Public health and policy implications. *Addiction, 106*(7), 1208–1212.

Gearhardt, A., White, M., & Potenza, M. (2011c). Binge eating disorder and food addiction. *Current Drug Abuse Reviews, 4*(3), 201.

Gearhardt, A., Yokum, S., Orr, P., Stice, E., Corbin, W., & Brownell, K. (2011d). Neural correlates of food addiction. *Archives of General Psychiatry, 68*(8), 808–816. doi: 10.1001/archgenpsychiatry.2011.32

Gearhardt, A., Roberts, M., & Ashe, M. (2013). If sugar is addictive what does it mean for the law? *The Journal of Law, Medicine & Ethics, 41*, 46–49.

Gibson, E. (2006). Emotional influences on food choice: Sensory, physiological and psychological pathways. *Physiology & Behavior, 89*(1), 53–61. doi: 10.1016/j.physbeh.2006.01.024

Gilmore, J., & Pine, B. (1997). The four faces of mass customization. *Harvard Business Review, 75*(1), 91–101.

Glasgow, L. (2001). Stretching the limits of intellectual property rights: Has the pharmaceutical industry gone too far? *Idea, 41*, 227.

Golan, E., Stewart, H., Kuchler, F., & Dong, D. (2008). Can low-income Americans afford a healthy diet. *Amber Waves, 6*(5), 26–33.

Gold, M. S., Frost-Pineda, K., & Jacobs, W. S. (2003). Overeating, binge eating, and eating disorders as addictions. *Psychiatric Annals, 33*(2), 117–122.

Goodwin, N. R., Ackerman, F., & Kiron, D. (1996). *The consumer society.* Washington, DC: Island Press.

Government Accountability Office. (2011). *Food labeling: FDA needs to reassess its approach to protecting consumers from false or misleading claims.* Report to congressional committees. Retrieved from http://purl.fdlp.gov/GPO/gpo11929

Graham, K. (2011, April 11). Conquistador who took on the world of fast fashion and won. *The Times (London).* Retrieved from http://www.lexisnexis.com.offcampus.lib.washington.edu/lnacui2api/api/version1/getDocCui?lni=52HH-FRF1-DYVC-J1VP&csi=10939&hl=t&hv=t&hnsd=f&hns=t&hgn=t&oc=00240&perma=true

Graham, R. (2013, October 13). Bring back home ec! *The Boston Globe.* Retrieved from http://www.bostonglobe.com/ideas/2013/10/12/bring-back-home/EJJi9yzjgJfNMqxWUIEDgO/story.html

Gregoire, C. (2014, February 16). Cadillac made a commercial about the American dream, and it's a nightmare. *Huffington Post.* Retrieved from http://www.huffingtonpost.com/2014/02/26/this-commercial-sums-up-e_n_4859040.html

Gregory, C., Rahkovsky, I., & Anekwe, T. (2014). Consumers' use of nutrition information when eating out. *USDA-ERS Economic Information Bulletin* (127).

Grimm, J. W. (2012). Incubation of sucrose craving in animal models. In K. D. Brownell & M. S. Gold (Eds.), *Food and addiction: A comprehensive handbook.* Oxford: Oxford University Press.

Guettabi, M., & Munasib, A. (2014). The impact of obesity on consumer bankruptcy. *Economics and Human Biology.* doi: http://dx.doi.org/10.1016/j.ehb.2014.11.003

Gulli, C. (2013, September 10). The dangers of going gluten-free. *Macleans.* Retrieved from http://www.macleans.ca/society/life/gone-gluten-free/

Haidt, J. (2006). *The happiness hypothesis: Finding modern truth in ancient wisdom.* New York: Basic Books.

Hajnal, A., Smith, G., & Norgren, R. (2004). Oral sucrose stimulation increases accumbens dopamine in the rat. *American Journal of Physiology. Regulatory, Integrative and Comparative, 286*(1), R31–R37. doi: 10.1152/ajpregu.00282.2003

Hall, K. D. (2012). Modeling metabolic adaptations and energy regulation in humans. *Annu Rev Nutr, 32*(1), 35–54. doi: 10.1146/annurev-nutr-071811-150705.

Haney, W., Rhodes, P., Grunebaum, E., Christopher, H., & Paul, N. (2007). The price of sugar. In Peter Rhodes (Ed.), *Uncommon productions.* New York: New Yorker Films.

Hanna, J. M., & Hornick, C. A. (1977). Use of coca leaf in southern Peru: Adaptation or addiction. *Bulletin on Narcotics, 29*(1), 63–74.

Harnack, L., Stang, J., & Story, M. (1999). Soft drink consumption among US children and adolescents: Nutritional consequences. *Journal of the American Dietetic Association, 99*(4), 436–441. doi: 10.1016/S0002-8223(99)00106-6

Harris, D., & Patrick, M. (2011). Is 'big food's' big money influencing the science of nutrition? *ABC News.* Retrieved from http://abcnews.go.com/US/big-food-money-accused-influencing-science/story?id=13845186

Harris, J. L. (2011). *Sugary drink FACTS: Evaluating sugary drink nutrition and marketing to youth*. Rudd Center for Food Policy and Obesity. Retrieved from http://www.sugarydrinkfacts.org/resources/sugarydrinkfacts_report.pdf

Harris, J. L. (2012). Is food advertising feeding Americans' sugar habit? An analysis of exposure to television advertising for high-sugar foods. In K. D. Brownell & M. S. Gold (Eds.), *Food and addiction: A comprehensive handbook*. Oxford: Oxford University Press.

Hartman Group. (2014). Should Whole Foods move downmarket? Retrieved from http://blog.hartman-group.com/2014/03/05/should-whole-foods-move-downmarket/

Haskins, K. M., & Ransford, H. (1999). The relationship between weight and career payoffs among women. *Sociological Forum, 14*(2), 295–318.

Havel, P. J., Townsend, R., Chaump, L., & Teff, K. (1999). High-fat meals reduce 24-h circulating leptin concentrations in women. *Diabetes, 48*(2), 334–341.

Hebebrand, J., Albayrak, Ö., Adan, R., Antel, J., Dieguez, C., de Jong, J., … Murphy, M. (2014). "Eating addiction", rather than "food addiction", better captures addictive-like eating behavior. *Neurosci Biobehav Rev, 47*, 295–306.

Heffernan, V. (2014, October 8). What if you just hate making dinner? *New York Times Magazine*.

Hellerstein, M. K. (1999). De novo lipogenesis in humans: Metabolic and regulatory aspects. *European Journal of Clinical Nutrition, 53*(Suppl 1), S53–S65.

Hellerstein, M. K. (2001). No common energy currency: De novo lipogenesis as the road less traveled. *The American Journal of Clinical Nutrition, 74*(6), 707–708.

Henry, J. (1963). *Culture against man*. New York: Random House.

Hill, R., & Chui, M. (2009). The pharmerging future. *Pharmaceutical Executive, 29*(7), 1–5.

Hilts, P. J. (2004). *Protecting America's health: The FDA, business, and one hundred years of regulation*. Chapel Hill: University of North Carolina Press.

Hollis, A. (2004). *Me-too drugs: Is there a problem?* World Health Organization. Retrieved from http://www.who.int/intellectualproperty/topics/ip/Me-tooDrugs_Hollis1.pdf

Horovitz, B. 2011. Marketers have a summer romance with packaging. USA Today, June 17-19, A1.

Hu, F. B., & Malik, V. S. (2010). Sugar-sweetened beverages and risk of obesity and type 2 diabetes: Epidemiologic evidence. *Physiology & Behavior, 100*(1), 47–54. doi: 10.1016/j.physbeh.2010.01.036

Hudson, J. I., Hiripi, E., Pope, H. G., Jr., & Kessler, R. C. (2007). The prevalence and correlates of eating disorders in the National Comorbidity Survey Replication. *Biological Psychiatry, 61*(3), 348–358. doi: 10.1016/j.biopsych.2006.03.040

Humphery, K. (1998). *Shelf life: Supermarkets and the changing cultures of consumption*. Cambridge: Cambridge University Press.

IEG. (2012, September). *Dollar sales of energy drink beverages and shots in the United States from 2011 to 2015 (in billion U.S. dollars)*. Retrieved from http://www.statista.com/statistics/275525/us-dollar-sales-of-energy-drink-beverages-and-shots/

Ifland, J., Preuss, H., Marcus, M., Rourke, K., Taylor, W., Burau, K., … Manso, G. (2009). Refined food addiction: A classic substance use disorder. *Medical Hypotheses, 72*(5), 518–526.

Inman, J. J. (2001). The role of sensory-specific satiety in attribute-level variety seeking. *Journal of Consumer Research, 28*(1), 105–120. doi: 10.1086/321950

Institute for American Values. (2008). *For a new thrift confronting the debt culture.* Institute for American Values Commission on Thrift. Retrieved from http://books.google.com/books?id=e79EAQAAIAAJ

Institute of Medicine. (2005). *Dietary reference intakes for energy, carbohydrate, fiber, fat, fatty acids, cholesterol, protein, and amino acids (macronutrients).* Washington, DC: National Academies Press.

International Food Information Council Information. (2014). Retrieved from http://www.foodinsight.org/about

IRI. (2010). *Times & trends: CPG 2010 year in review: Out of turmoil rises opportunity.* Retrieved from http://www.iriworldwide.com/Insights/ItemID/1231/View/Details.aspx

Jenkins, D. J., Wolever, T. M., Taylor, R. H., Barker, H., Fielden, H., Baldwin, J. M., ... Goff, D. V. (1981). Glycemic index of foods: A physiological basis for carbohydrate exchange. *American Journal of Clinical Nutrition, 34*(3), 362–366.

Jerome, N. (1977). Taste experience and the development of a dietary preference for sweet in humans: Ethnic and cultural variations in early taste experience. In Taste and Development: The Genesis of Sweet Preference. Washington DC: US Dep. HEW Pub. No. (NIH) Taste and Development, 235–248.

Johnson, R. K., Appel, L. J., Brands, M., Howard, B. V., Lefevre, M., Lustig, R. H., ... Wylie-Rosett, J. (2009). Dietary sugars intake and cardiovascular health: A scientific statement from the American Heart Association. *Circulation, 120*(11), 1011–1020. doi: 10.1161/CIRCULATIONAHA.109.192627

Johnston, J., & Szabo, M. (2011). Reflexivity and the Whole Foods Market consumer: The lived experience of shopping for change. *Agriculture and Human Values, 28*(3), 303–319. doi: 10.1007/S10460-010-9283-9

Jolliffe, D. (2011). Overweight and poor? On the relationship between income and the body mass index. *Economics and Human Biology, 9*(4), 342–355.

Judge, T. A., & Cable, D. M. (2011). When it comes to pay, do the thin win? The effect of weight on pay for men and women. *Journal of Applied Psychology, 96*(1), 95–112. doi: 10.1037/a0020860

Kaczka, K. A. (1999). From herbal Prozac to Mark McGwire's tonic: How the Dietary Supplement Health and Education Act changed the regulatory landscape for health products. *Journal of Contemporary Health Law and Policy, 16*, 463.

Kahn, B. E., & Wansink, B. (2004). The influence of assortment structure on perceived variety and consumption quantities. *Journal of Consumer Research, 30*(4), 519–533. doi: 10.1086/380286

Kasser, T. (2002). *The high price of materialism.* Cambridge: MIT Press.

Kasser, T., & Kanner, A. D. (2004). *Psychology and consumer culture: The struggle for a good life in a materialistic world.* Washington, DC: American Psychological Association.

Kasser, T., & Ryan, R. M. (1993). A dark side of the American dream: Correlates of financial success as a central life aspiration. *Journal of Personality and Social Psychology, 65*(2), 410–422. doi: 10.1037//0022-3514.65.2.410

Kasser, T., Ryan, R. M., Zax, M., & Sameroff, A. J. (1995). The relations of maternal and social environments to late adolescents materialistic and prosocial values. *Developmental Psychology, 31*(6), 907–914. doi: 10.1037/0012-1649.31.6.907

Kaza, S. (2005). *Hooked!: Buddhist writings on greed, desire, and the urge to consume*. Boston, MA: Shambhala.

Kefauver-Harris Drug Amendment of 1962, Pub. L. No. 87–781 (1962).

Kessler, D. A. (2001). *A question of intent: A great American battle with a deadly industry*. New York: Public Affairs.

Kessler, D. A. (2009). *The end of overeating: Taking control of the insatiable American appetite*. New York: Rodale.

Kessler, D. A. (2014). Toward more comprehensive food labeling. *New England Journal of Medicine, 371*(3), 193–195. doi: 10.1056/NEJMp1402971

Keyfitz, N. (1982). Development and the elimination of poverty. *Economic Development and Cultural Change, 30*(3), 649–670. doi: 10.1086/452579

Khan, A., Leventhal, R. M., Khan, S. R., & Brown, W. A. (2002). Severity of depression and response to antidepressants and placebo: An analysis of the Food and Drug Administration database. *Journal of Clinical Psychopharmacology, 22*(1), 40–45.

Khatchadourian, R. (2009, November 23). The taste makers: Inside the labs that flavor your food. *The New Yorker*.

Kiron, D. (1996). Perpetuating consumer culture: Media, advertising, and wants creation. In N. R. Goodwin, F. Ackerman, & D. Kiron (Eds.), *The consumer society* (pp. 229–268). Washington, DC: Island Press.

Kirsch, I. (2010). *The emperor's new drugs: Exploding the antidepressant myth*. New York: Basic Books.

Kirsch, I., Moore, T. J., Scoboria, A., & Nicholls, S. S. (2002). The emperor's new drugs: An analysis of antidepressant medication data submitted to the US Food and Drug Administration. *Prevention & Treatment, 5*(1), 23a.

Kirsch, I., & Sapirstein, G. (1998). Listening to Prozac but hearing placebo: A meta-analysis of antidepressant medication. *Prevention & Treatment, 1*(2), 2a.

Klein, D. F. (2005). The flawed basis for FDA post-marketing safety decisions: The example of anti-depressants and children. *Neuropsychopharmacology, 31*(4), 689–699.

Kleiner, K. D., Gold, M. S., Frostpineda, K., Lenzbrunsman, B., Perri, M. G., & Jacobs, W. S. (2004). Body mass index and alcohol use. *Journal of Addictive Diseases, 23*(3), 105–118.

Koehn, N. F. (2001). *Brand new: How entrepreneurs earned consumers' trust from Wedgwood to Dell*. Cambridge: Harvard Business Press.

Koerner, B. I. (2002). Disorders made to order. *Mother Jones, 27*(4), 58–81.

Kolaczynski, J., Ohannesian, J., Considine, R., Marco, C., & Caro, J. (1996). Response of leptin to short-term and prolonged overfeeding in humans. *Journal of Clinical Endocrinology and Metabolism, 81*(11), 4162–4165. doi: 10.1210/jcem.81.11.8923877

Kottler, J. (1999). *Exploring and treating acquisitive desire: Living in the material world*. Thousand Oaks, CA: Sage Publications.

Krugman, P. (2014, April 21). The economy is not like a household. *The New York Times*. Retrieved from http://krugman.blogs.nytimes.com/2014/04/21/the-economy-is-not-like-a-household/?_r=0

LaFerla, R. (2013, May 31). Such a doll. *New York Times*. Retrieved from http://runway.blogs.nytimes.com/2013/05/31/such-a-doll/?module=Search&mabReward=relbias%3Aw%2C%7B%221%22%3A%22RI%3A5%22%7D&_r=0

LaForgia, M., & Playford, A. (2012, January 1). Wikileaks: Fanjuls among 'sugar barons' who 'muscled' lawmakers to kill free trade deal. *Palm Beach Post*. Retrieved from http://www.palmbeachpost.com/news/news/wikileaks-fanjuls-among-sugar-barons-who-muscled-l/nL2wg/

Landman, A., Ling, P. M., & Glantz, S. A. (2002). Tobacco industry youth smoking prevention programs: Protecting the industry and hurting tobacco control. *American Journal of Public Health, 92*(6), 917–930.

Lappé, A. (2014, August 1). Big Food uses mommy bloggers to shape public opinion. *Al Jazeera America*. Retrieved from http://america.aljazeera.com/opinions/2014/8/food-agriculturemonsantogmoadvertising.html

Lasch, C. (1980). *The culture of narcissism: American life in an age of diminishing expectations*. New York: Warner Books.

Le Moal, M., & Simon, H. (1991). Mesocorticolimbic dopaminergic network: Functional and regulatory roles. *Physiological Review, 71*(1), 155–234.

Leiss, W. (1978). *The limits to satisfaction: On needs and commodities*. London: Boyars.

Lennerz, B. S., Alsop, D. C., Holsen, L. M., Stern, E., Rojas, R., Ebbeling, C. B., ... Ludwig, D. S. (2013). Effects of dietary glycemic index on brain regions related to reward and craving in men. *American Journal of Clinical Nutrition, 98*(3), 641–647. doi: 10.3945/ajcn.113.064113

Lenoir, M., Cantin, L., Serre, F., & Ahmed, S. (2008). *The value of heroin increases with extended use but not above the value of a non-essential alternative reward*. Paper presented at the 38th Annual Meeting of the Society for Neuroscience, Washington, DC.

Lenoir, M., Serre, F., Cantin, L., & Ahmed, S. H. (2007). Intense sweetness surpasses cocaine reward. *PLoS One, 2*(8), e698. doi: 10.1371/journal.pone.0000698

Lévi-Strauss, C. (1969). *The raw and the cooked*. New York: Harper & Row.

Lichtenstein, A. H., Appel, L. J., Brands, M., Carnethon, M., Daniels, S., Franch, H. A., ... Wylie-Rosett, J. (2006). Diet and lifestyle recommendations revision 2006: A scientific statement from the American Heart Association Nutrition Committee. *Circulation, 114*(1), 82–96. doi: 10.1161/circulationaha.106.176158

Liem, D. G., & Mennella, J. A. (2002). Sweet and sour preferences during childhood: Role of early experiences. *Developmental Psychobiology, 41*(4), 388–395. doi: 10.1002/dev.10067

Lilienfeld, S., Waldman, I., Landfield, K., Watts, A., Rubenzer, S., & Faschingbauer, T. (2012). Fearless dominance and the US presidency: Implications of psychopathic personality traits for successful and unsuccessful political leadership. *Journal of Personality and Social Psychology, 103*(3), 489–505. doi: 10.1037/a0029392

Lin, B.-H., Guthrie, J., & Frazão, E. (1999). *Away-from-home foods increasingly important to quality of American diet*. Washington, DC: United States Department of Agriculture Economic Research Service.

Linn, S. (2004). *Consuming kids: The hostile takeover of childhood*. New York: New Press.

Logue, A. W. (2004). *The psychology of eating and drinking*. New York: Brunner-Routledge/Taylor & Francis Group.

Lorenz, K. (1974). *Civilized man's eight deadly sins*. New York: Harcourt Brace Jovanovich.

Loy, D. (1997). The religion of the market + Religious responses to problems of population, consumption, and degradation of the global environment. *JAAR, 65*(2), 275–290.

Lukovitz, K. (2009, January 19). 'Natural' claims most common on new F&B products. *Marketing Daily*. Retrieved from http://www.mediapost.com/publications/article/98562/-axzz2YsPn6CWO

Lustig, R. H. (2010). Fructose: Metabolic, hedonic, and societal parallels with ethanol. *Journal of the American Dietetic Association, 110*(9), 1307–1321. doi: 10.1016/j.jada.2010.06.008

Lustig, R. H. (2013). *Sugar has 56 names: A shopper's guide.* New York: Penguin Group.

Macartney, S. E. (2011). *Child poverty in the United States 2009 and 2010: Selected race groups and Hispanic origin.* US Department of Commerce, Economics and Statistics Administration, US Census Bureau.

Macinnis, P. (2002). *Bittersweet: The story of sugar.* Sydney: Allen & Unwin.

Maillot, M., Darmon, N., & Drewnowski, A. (2010). Are the lowest-cost healthful food plans culturally and socially acceptable? *Public Health Nutrition, 13*(8), 1178–1185. doi: 10.1017/S1368980009993028

Malik, V. S., & Hu, F. B. (2011). Sugar-sweetened beverages and health: Where does the evidence stand? *American Journal of Clinical Nutrition, 94*(5), 1161–1162. doi: 10.3945/ajcn.111.025676

Malik, V. S., & Hu, F. B. (2012). Sweeteners and risk of obesity and type 2 diabetes: The role of sugar-sweetened beverages. *Current Diabetes Reports, 12*(2), 195–203. doi: 10.1007/s11892-012-0259-6

Malik, V. S., Popkin, B. M., Bray, G. A., Després, J.-P., & Hu, F. B. (2010a). Sugar-sweetened beverages, obesity, type 2 diabetes mellitus, and cardiovascular disease risk. *Circulation, 121*(11), 1356–1364. doi: 10.1161/CIRCULATIONAHA.109.876185

Malik, V. S., Popkin, B. M., Bray, G. A., Despres, J. P., Willett, W. C., & Hu, F. B. (2010b). Sugar-sweetened beverages and risk of metabolic syndrome and type 2 diabetes: A meta-analysis. *Diabetes Care, 33*(11), 2477–2483. doi: 10.2337/dc10-1079

Malik, V. S., Schulze, M. B., & Hu, F. B. (2006). Intake of sugar-sweetened beverages and weight gain: A systematic review. *American Journal of Clinical Nutrition, 84*(2), 274–288.

Maone, T. R., Mattes, R. D., Bernbaum, J. C., & Beauchamp, G. K. (1990). A new method for delivering a taste without fluids to preterm and term infants. *Developmental Psychobiology, 23*(2), 179–191. doi: 10.1002/dev.420230208

Marcason, W. (2011). Is there evidence to support the claim that a gluten-free diet should be used for weight loss? *Journal of the American Dietetic Association, 111*(11), 1786.

Margolskee, R. F., Dyer, J., Kokrashvili, Z., Salmon, K. S., Ilegems, E., Daly, K., … Shirazi-Beechey, S. P. (2007). T1R3 and gustducin in gut sense sugars to regulate expression of Na+-glucose cotransporter 1. *Proceedings of the National Academy of Sciences of the United States of America, 104*(38), 15075–15080. doi: 10.1073/pnas.0706678104

Marks, N. (2011). The happiness manifesto how nations and people can nurture well-being. Retrieved from http://www.contentreserve.com/TitleInfo.asp?ID={2F735A31-79E3-46C8-99FC-2D681BF24530}&Format=50

Martin, S. (Writer). (1991). *L.A. story*. Van Nuys: Carolco Home Video.

Martínez, S. (1995). *Peripheral migrants: Haitians and Dominican Republic sugar plantations*. Knoxville: University of Tennessee Press.

Mason, B., & Higley, A. (2012). Human laboratory models of addiction. In K. D. Brownell & M. S. Gold (Eds.), *Food and addiction: A Comprehensive handbook*. Oxford: Oxford University Press.

Mattes, R. D. (1996). Dietary compensation by humans for supplemental energy provided as ethanol or carbohydrate in fluids. *Physiology & Behavior, 59*(1), 179–187.

Mayes, S., Calhoun, S., & Crites, D. (2001). Does DSM-IV Asperger's disorder exist? *Journal of Abnormal Child Psychology, 29*(3), 263–271.

McCarthy, M. (2014, April 9). Cadillac clears up 'misconceptions' about contentious 'poolside' ad. *Ad Age*.

McKenna, M. (2014, August 15). Bring back home economics: Three food writers on teaching people to cook. *National Geographic*. Retrieved from http://theplate.nationalgeographic.com/2014/08/15/bring-back-home-ec-three-food-writers-on-teaching-people-to-cook/

McMillan, T., Cahana, K., Sinclair, S., & Toensing, A. (2014). The new face of hunger. *National Geographic, 226*, 66–89.

McWilliams, N. (2011). *Psychoanalytic diagnosis: Understanding personality structure in the clinical process*. New York: Guilford Press.

Medco. (2011). America's state of mind. Retrieved from http://apps.who.int/medicinedocs/documents/s19032en/s19032en.pdf

Mennella, J. A., & Beauchamp, G. K. (1998). Early flavor experiences: Research update. *Nutrition Reviews, 56*(7), 205–211.

Merton, R. K. (1957). *Social theory and social structure*. New York: Free Press.

Mintz, S. W. (1985). *Sweetness and power: The place of sugar in modern history*. New York: Penguin Books.

Mintz, S. W. (1996). *Tasting food, tasting freedom: Excursions into eating, culture, and the past*. Boston, MA: Beacon Press.

Moodie, R., Stuckler, D., Monteiro, C., Sheron, N., Neal, B., Thamarangsi, T., ... (NCD Action Group Lancet). (2013). Profits and pandemics: Prevention of harmful effects of tobacco, alcohol, and ultra-processed food and drink industries. *Lancet, 381*(9867), 670–679. doi: 10.1016/S0140-6736(12)62089-3

Moskowitz, H. R. (1981). Relative importance of perceptual factors to consumer acceptance: Linear vs quadratic analysis. *Journal of Food Science, 46*(1), 244–248.

Moss, M. (2013). *Salt sugar fat: How the food giants hooked us*. Toronto: McClelland & Stewart.

Moss, M. (2014, July 26). Coconut water changes its claims. *The New York Times*. Retrieved from http://www.nytimes.com/2014/07/30/dining/coconut-water-changes-its-claims.html

Mourao, D. M., Bressan, J., Campbell, W. W., & Mattes, R. D. (2007). Effects of food form on appetite and energy intake in lean and obese young adults. *International Journal of Obesity (Lond), 31*(11), 1688–1695. doi: 10.1038/sj.ijo.0803667

Moynihan, R., & Cassels, A. (2005). *Selling sickness: How the world's biggest pharmaceutical companies are turning us all into patients*. New York: Nation Books.

Mullainathan, S., & Shafir, E. (2013). *Scarcity: Why having too little means so much*. New York: Henry Holt and Company.

Münster, E., Rüger, H., Ochsmann, E., Letzel, S., & Toschke, A. M. (2009). Over-indebtedness as a marker of socioeconomic status and its association with obesity: A cross-sectional study. *BMC Public Health, 9*(1), 286.

Murphy, C. M., Stojek, M. K., & MacKillop, J. (2014). Interrelationships among impulsive personality traits, food addiction, and body mass index. *Appetite, 73*, 45–50.

Murray, C. A. (2013). *Coming apart: The state of white America, 1960–2010*. New York: Crown Forum.

Mustain, P. (2014). It is not true that kids won't eat healthy food: Why the new USDA school food guidelines are very necessary. Retrieved from http://blogs.scientificamerican.com/food-matters/2013/09/05/it-is-not-true-that-kids-wont-eat-healthy-food-why-the-new-usda-guidelines-are-very-necessary/

Myers, M., Cowley, M. A., & Münzberg, H. (2008). Mechanisms of leptin action and leptin resistance. *Annual Review of Physiology, 70*, 537–556. doi: 10.1146/annurev.physiol.70.113006.100707

Myers, M., Leibel, R., Seeley, R., & Schwartz, M. (2010). Obesity and leptin resistance: Distinguishing cause from effect. *Trends in Endocrinology & Metabolism, 21*(11), 643–651.

National Consumers League. (2012). Naturally misleading: Consumers' understanding of "natural" and "plant-derived" labeling claims. Retrieved from http://www.nclnet.org/

Navarro, V. J., Barnhart, H., Bonkovsky, H. L., Davern, T., Fontana, R. J., Grant, L., … Sherker, A. H. (2014). Liver injury from herbals and dietary supplements in the US Drug-Induced Liver Injury Network. *Hepatology, 60*(4), 1399–1408.

Negowetti, N. E. (2014). *Food labeling litigation: Exposing gaps in the FDA's resources and regulatory authority*. Brookings Institution. Retrieved from http://www.brookings.edu/research/papers/2014/06/26-food-labeling-litigation-fda-negowetti

Nestle, M. (2001). Food company sponsorship of nutrition research and professional activities: A conflict of interest? *Public Health Nutrition, 4*(05), 1015–1022.

Nestle, M. (2002). *Food politics: How the food industry influences nutrition and health*. Berkeley: University of California Press.

Ng, M., Fleming, T., Robinson, M., Thomson, B., Graetz, N., Margono, C., … Gakidou, E. (2014). Global, regional, and national prevalence of overweight and obesity in children and adults during 1980-2013: A systematic analysis for the Global Burden of Disease Study 2013. *Lancet, 384*(9945), 766–781. doi: 10.1016/S0140-6736(14)60460-8

Ng, S. W., Ni Mhurchu, C., Jebb, S. A., & Popkin, B. M. (2012). Patterns and trends of beverage consumption among children and adults in Great Britain, 1986–2009. *British Journal of Nutrition, 108*(03), 536–551.

Nickerson, L. A. (2013, November 24). Best beware of sugarless gummy bears and sweets!. *Examiner*. Retrieved from http://www.examiner.com/article/best-beware-of-sugarless-gummy-bears-and-sweets

Nielsen, S. J., & Popkin, B. M. (2004). Changes in beverage intake between 1977 and 2001. *American Journal of Preventive Medicine, 27*(3), 205–210. doi: 10.1016/j.amepre.2004.05.005

Nielsen, S. J., Siega-Riz, A. M., & Popkin, B. M. (2002). Trends in energy intake in US between 1977 and 1996: Similar shifts seen across age groups. *Obesity Research, 10*(5), 370–378.

Noakes, T. (2012a). *Waterlogged: The serious problem of overhydration in endurance sports*. Champaign, IL: Human Kinetics.

Noakes, T. D. (2012b). Commentary: Role of hydration in health and exercise. *BMJ, 345*(7866), e4171. doi: 10.1136/bmj.e4171

Nocera, J. (2013). *A piece of the action: How the middle class joined the money class*. New York: Simon and Schuster.

Nurkse, R. (1957). *Problems of capital formation in underdeveloped countries*. New York: Oxford University Press.

OED Online. (2014). *Oxford dictionary of English*. Oxford: Oxford University Press.

Offit, P., & Erush, S. (2013, December 14). Skip the supplements. *New York Times*. Retrieved from http://www.nytimes.com/2013/12/15/opinion/sunday/skip-the-supplements.html?_r=0

OED Online. (2015) "junk food". Oxford University Press. Retrieved from http://www.oed.com/viewdictionaryentry/Entry/11125

Okorodudu, D. O., Jumean, M. F., Montori, V. M., Romero-Corral, A., Somers, V. K., Erwin, P. J., & Lopez-Jimenez, F. (2010). Diagnostic performance of body mass index to identify obesity as defined by body adiposity: A systematic review and meta-analysis. *International Journal of Obesity, 34*(5), 791–799.

Oliver, G., Wardle, J., & Gibson, E. L. (2000). Stress and food choice: A laboratory study. *Psychosomatic Medicine, 62*(6), 853–865.

Olsen, D. P. (2014, June 16). Say no to natural on food labels. *Consumer Reports News*. Retrieved from http://www.consumerreports.org/cro/news/2014/06/say-no-to-natural-on-food-labels/index.htm

Oreffice, S., & Quintana-Domeque, C. (2010). Anthropometry and socioeconomics among couples: Evidence in the United States. *Economics and Human Biology, 8*(3), 373–384. doi: 10.1016/j.ehb.2010.05.001

Pan, A., & Hu, F. B. (2011). Effects of carbohydrates on satiety: Differences between liquid and solid food. *Current Opinion in Clinical Nutrition and Metabolic Care, 14*(4), 385–390. doi: 10.1097/MCO.0b013e328346df36

Park, K. H., Kim, J. Y., Ahn, C. W., Song, Y. D., Lim, S. K., & Lee, H. C. (2001). Polycystic ovarian syndrome (PCOS) and insulin resistance. *International Journal of Gynecology & Obstetrics, 74*(3), 261–267.

Patel, R. (2008). *Stuffed and starved: The hidden battle for the world food system*. Brooklyn, NY: Melville House.

Pearce, J. D. W. (1936). A Symposium on property and possessiveness. *The British Journal of Psychiatry, 82*(337), 187–188.

Pepino, M. Y., & Mennella, J. A. (2005). Sucrose-induced analgesia is related to sweet preferences in children but not adults. *Pain, 119*(1), 210–218.

Pfaffmann, C. (1977). Biological and behavioral substrates of the sweet tooth. In J. M. Weiffenbach (Ed.), *Taste and Development* (pp. 3–24). Bethesda, MD: US Department of Health, Education and Welfare.

Phipott, T. (2013, October 16). Why home economics should be mandatory. *Mother Jones*. Retrieved from http://www.motherjones.com/tom-philpott/2013/10/why-home-ec-class-should-be-mandatory

Piña, K. R., & Pines, W. L. (2008). *A practical guide to food and drug law and regulation.* Food and Drug Law Institute. Retrieved from http://www.fdli.org/resources/resources-order-box-detail-view/a-practical-guide-to-fda-s-food-and-drug-law-and-regulation–5th-edition

PLoS. (2012). Series on big food: The food industry is ripe for scrutiny. *PLoS Med, 9*(6), e1001246.

Pollack, A. (2010, November 5). Antibiotics research subsidies weighed by US. *The New York Times.*

Pollan, M. (2009, July 29). Out of the kitchen, Onto the couch. *New York Times Magazine.*

Popkin, B. M. (2010). Patterns of beverage use across the lifecycle. *Physiology & Behavior, 100*(1), 4–9. doi: 10.1016/j.physbeh.2009.12.022

Popkin, B. M. (2012). The changing face of global diet and nutrition. In K. D. Brownell & M. S. Gold (Eds.), *Food and addiction: A comprehensive handbook* (pp. 144–164). Oxford: Oxford University Press.

Popkin, B. M., & Duffey, K. J. (2010). Does hunger and satiety drive eating anymore? Increasing eating occasions and decreasing time between eating occasions in the United States. *American Journal of Clinical Nutrition, 91*(5), 1342–1347.

Popkin, B. M., & Nielsen, S. J. (2003). The sweetening of the world's diet. *Obes Res, 11*(11), 1325–1332. doi: 10.1038/oby.2003.179

Ramirez, I. (1990). Why do sugars taste good? *Neuroscience & Biobehavioral Reviews, 14*(2), 125–134. doi: 10.1016/s0149-7634(05)80213-1

Rappeport, A. (2012, Sep 10). Kraft warns on proposed cuts to US food stamps. *Financial Times*, p. 21. Retrieved from http://infoweb.newsbank.com/resources/doc/nb/news/1413AD3D941F4690?p=AWNB

Renehan, A. G., Tyson, M., Egger, M., Heller, R. F., & Zwahlen, M. (2008). Body-mass index and incidence of cancer: A systematic review and meta-analysis of prospective observational studies. *Lancet, 371*(9612), 569–578. doi: 10.1016/S0140-6736(08)60269-X

Repantis, D., Schlattmann, P., Laisney, O., & Heuser, I. (2010). Modafinil and methylphenidate for neuroenhancement in healthy individuals: A systematic review. *Pharmacological Research, 62*(3), 187–206. doi: 10.1016/j.phrs.2010.04.002

Richins, M. L. (1995). Social comparison, advertising, and consumer discontent. *American Behavioral Scientist, 38*(4), 593–607. doi: 10.1177/0002764295038004009

Rippe, J. M., & Angelopoulos, T. J. (2013). Sucrose, high-fructose corn syrup, and fructose, their metabolism and potential health effects: What do we really know? *Advances in Nutrition, 4*(2), 236–245. doi: 10.3945/an.112.002824

Robinson, J. (2013, May 25). Breeding the nutrition out of our food. *The New York Times.* Retrieved from http://www.nytimes.com/2013/05/26/opinion/sunday/breeding-the-nutrition-out-of-our-food.html

Robinson, N. (2014, October 3). Soft drink sales given boost from the elderly. *Food Manufacture.* Retrieved from http://www.foodmanufacture.co.uk/Ingredients/Target-the-elderly-soft-drinks-manufacturers-told-.VC7GPZmhOyg.twitter

Robinson-Jacobs, K. (2014, August 10). Soft drink makers have a powerful thirst for a new sweetener. *Dallas News.* Retrieved from http://www.dallasnews.

com/business/headlines/20140809-soft-drink-makers-have-a-powerful-thirst-for-a-new-sweetener.ece

Rock, C. (2005). *Chris Rock: Never scared*. New York: Home Box Office.

Rodwin, M. A. (2012). Conflicts of interest, institutional corruption, and Pharma: An agenda for reform. *Journal of Law, Medicine & Ethics, 40*(3), 511–522. doi: 10.1111/j.1748-720X.2012.00683.x

Roehling, M. V., Roehling, P. V., & Pichler, S. (2007). The relationship between body weight and perceived weight-related employment discrimination: The role of sex and race. *Journal of Vocational Behavior, 71*(2), 300–318.

Rolls, B. J., Rowe, E. A., Rolls, E. T., Kingston, B., Megson, A., & Gunary, R. (1981). Variety in a meal enhances food intake in man. *Physiology & Behavior, 26*(2), 215–221.

Romero-Corral, A., Somers, V. K., Sierra-Johnson, J., Thomas, R. J., Collazo-Clavell, M. L., Korinek, J., … Lopez-Jimenez, F. (2008). Accuracy of body mass index in diagnosing obesity in the adult general population. *International Journal of Obesity, 32*(6), 959–966.

Rosenberg, R. E., Daniels, A. M., Law, J. K., Law, P. A., & Kaufmann, W. E. (2009). Trends in autism spectrum disorder diagnoses: 1994–2007. *Journal of Autism and Developmental Disorders, 39*(8), 1099–1111. doi: 10.1007/s10803-009-0723-6

Rotter, J. B. (1966). Generalized expectancies for internal versus external control of reinforcement. *Psychological Monographs, 80*(1), 1–28.

Royte, E. (2008, May 23). A fountain on every corner. *The New York Times*. Retrieved from http://www.nytimes.com/2008/05/23/opinion/23royte.html

Ruderman, N. B., Schneider, S. H., & Berchtold, P. (1981). The "metabolically-obese," normal-weight individual. *American Journal of Clinical Nutrition, 34*(8), 1617–1621.

Rydell, S. A., Harnack, L. J., Oakes, J. M., Story, M., Jeffery, R. W., & French, S. A. (2008). Why eat at fast food restaurants: Reported reasons among frequent consumers. *Journal of the American Dietetic Association, 108*(12).

Sahlins, M. (1974). The original affluent society. *Ecologist, 4*(5), 5–41.

Schlosser, E. (2004, January 2). The cow jumped over the USDA. *New York Times*. Retrieved from http://www.nytimes.com/2004/01/02/opinion/the-cow-jumped-over-the-usda.html

Schor, J. B. (1999). *The overspent American: Why we want what we don't need*. New York: HarperCollins.

Schwartz, B. (2004). *The paradox of choice: Why more is less*. New York: Ecco.

Schwartz, B. (Producer). (2014). Is the famous paradox of choice a myth? *PBS Newshour*. Retrieved from http://www.pbs.org/newshour/making-sense/is-the-famous-paradox-of-choic/

Schwartz, L. M., & Woloshin, S. (2011). Communicating uncertainties about prescription drugs to the public: A national randomized trial. *Archives of Internal Medicine, 171*(16), 1463–1468.

Schwartz, L. M., Woloshin, S., & Welch, H. G. (2009). Using a drug facts box to communicate drug benefits and harms: Two randomized trials. *Annals of Internal Medicine, 150*(8), 516–527.

Sclafani, A. (2007). Sweet taste signaling in the gut. *Proceedings of the National Academy of Sciences of the United States of America, 104*(38), 14887–14888. doi: 10.1073/pnas.0707410104

Scott-Thomas, C. (2012). FDA offers support in industry roll-out of Facts Up Front labeling. *Food Navigator.* Retrieved from http://www.foodnavigator-usa.com/content/view/print/616127

Seabrook, J. (2011, November 21). Crunch. *New Yorker, 87.*

Segato, F. N., Castro-Souza, C., Segato, E. N., Morato, S., & Coimbra, N. C. (1997). Sucrose ingestion causes opioid analgesia. *Brazilian Journal of Medical and Biological Research, 30*(8), 981–984.

Senak, M. (2005). *Bringing a drug or device to market: Public relations implications.* Drugs and Biologics. Retrieved from http://www.eyeonfda.com

Shank, F. R. (1992). The Nutrition Labeling and Education Act of 1990. *Food & Drug Law Journal, 47,* 247.

Sharma, L. L., Teret, S. P., & Brownell, K. D. (2010). The food industry and self-regulation: Standards to promote success and to avoid public health failures. *American Journal of Public Health, 100*(2), 240. doi: 10.2105/AJPH.2009.160960

Shell, E. R. (2009). *Cheap: The high cost of discount culture.* New York: Penguin Press.

Sicherer, S. H. (2011). Epidemiology of food allergy. *Journal of Allergy and Clinical Immunology, 127*(3), 594–602. doi: 10.1016/j.jaci.2010.11.044

Silcoff, M. (2014, August 15). A mother's journey through the unnerving universe of 'unboxing' videos. *The New York Times.* Retrieved from http://www.nytimes.com/2014/08/17/magazine/a-mothers-journey-through-the-unnerving-universe-of-unboxing-videos.html

Silverglade, B., & Heller, I. R. (2010). *Food labeling chaos: The case for reform.* Center for Science in the Public Interest. Retrieved from http://www.cspinet.org/new/pdf/food_labeling_chaos_report.pdf

Simmons, D. (2010). Structural violence as social practice: Haitian agricultural workers, anti-Haitianism, and health in the Dominican Republic. *Human Organ, 69*(1), 10–18.

Simon, G. E., Von Korff, M., Saunders, K., Miglioretti, D. L., Crane, P. K., van Belle, G., & Kessler, R. C. (2006). Association between obesity and psychiatric disorders in the US adult population. *Archives of General Psychiatry, 63*(7), 824–830.

Simon, M. (2012). *Food stamps, follow the money: Are corporations profiting from hungry Americans?* Eat Drink Politics. Retrieved from http://www.eatdrinkpolitics.com/wp-content/uploads/FoodStampsFollowtheMoneySimon.pdf

Sisson, M. (2013, September 5). This gluten-free thing is a really overblown fad! *Huffington Post.* Retrieved from http://www.huffingtonpost.com/mark-sisson/gluten-free-fad_b_3873157.html

Slater, D. (1997). Consumer culture and the politics of need. In M. Nava (Ed.), *Buy this book: Studies in advertising and consumption* (pp. 51–63). New York: Psychology Press.

Slavin, J. L. (2005). Dietary fiber and body weight. *Nutrition, 21*(3), 411–418. doi: 10.1016/j.nut.2004.08.018

Slavin, J. L., & Lloyd, B. (2012). Health benefits of fruits and vegetables. *Advances in Nutrition: An International Review Journal, 3*(4), 506–516. doi: 10.3945/an.112.002154

Smith, A. F. (2009). *Eating history: 30 turning points in the making of American cuisine.* New York: Columbia University Press.

Soll, J. (2014). *The reckoning: Financial accountability and the rise and fall of nations*. New York: Basic Books.

Stafford, R. S. (2008). Regulating off-label drug use–rethinking the role of the FDA. *New England Journal of Medicine, 358*(14), 1427–1429. doi: 10.1056/NEJMp0802107

Stanhope, K. L., & Havel, P. J. (2008). Endocrine and metabolic effects of consuming beverages sweetened with fructose, glucose, sucrose, or high-fructose corn syrup. *American Journal of Clinical Nutrition, 88*(6), 1733S–1737S. doi: 10.3945/ajcn.2008.25825D

Stanhope, K. L., & Havel, P. J. (2009). Fructose consumption: Considerations for future research on its effects on adipose distribution, lipid metabolism, and insulin sensitivity in humans. *Journal of Nutrition, 139*(6), 1236S–1241S. doi: 10.3945/jn.109.106641

Stanhope, K. L., & Havel, P. J. (2010). Fructose consumption: Recent results and their potential implications. *Annals of the New York Academy of Sciences, 1190*(1), 15–24. doi: 10.1111/J.1749-6632.2009.05266.X

Starbucks. (2014). Salted Caramel Mocha Frappuccino® Blended Beverage. Retrieved from http://www.starbucks.com/menu/drinks/frappuccino-blended-beverages/salted-caramel-mocha-frappuccino-blended-beverage-size=11015675&milk=67&whip=125

Starbucks UK. (2014). Espresso Beverages. Retrieved from http://www.starbucks.co.uk/menu/beverage-list/espresso-beverages

Starling, S. (2014, August 26). Energy category brushes up against toothpaste. *NutraIngredients*. Retrieved from http://www.nutraingredients.com/Manufacturers/Energy-category-brushes-up-against-toothpaste

Starr, K. (1998). *The Starr report: The findings of independent counsel Kenneth W. Starr on President Clinton and the Lewinsky affair*. New York: PublicAffairs.

Steen, E., Terry, B. M., Rivera, E. J., Cannon, J. L., Neely, T. R., Tavares, R., … de la Monte, S. M. (2005). Impaired insulin and insulin-like growth factor expression and signaling mechanisms in Alzheimer's disease-is this type 3 diabetes? *Journal of Alzheimers Disease, 7*(1), 63–80.

Steiner, J. E. (1977). Facial expressions of the neonate infant indicating the hedonics of food-related chemical stimuli. In H. van Goudoever, S. Guandalini, & R. E. Kleinman (Eds.), *Taste and development: The genesis of sweet preference* (pp. 173–188). Basel: Karger Medical and Scientific Publishers.

Stevens, B., Yamada, J., & Ohlsson, A. (2004). Sucrose for analgesia in newborn infants undergoing painful procedures. *Cochrane Database of Systematic Reviews, 3*(3). doi: 10.1002/14651858.CD001069.pub2

Stewart, H., Blisard, N., & Jolliffe, D. (2006). *Let's eat out: Americans weigh taste, convenience and nutrition*. United States Department of Agriculture Economic Research Service. Retrieved from http://www.ers.usda.gov/media/860870/eib19.pdf

Stigler, G. J. (1971). The theory of economic regulation. *Bell Journal of Economics and Management Science, 2*(1), 3–21.

Stokes, C. (2012). Artificial sweetness: A survey of the harmful effects caused by the US sugar program and possibilities for reform. *Geo Journal of Law & Public Policy, 10*, 589.

Strom, S. (2014, August 8). Cashew juice, the apple of Pepsi's eye. *The New York Times*. Retrieved from http://www.nytimes.com/2014/08/09/business/international/cashew-juice-the-apple-of-pepsis-eye.html

Suez, J., Korem, T., Zeevi, D., Zilberman-Schapira, G., Thaiss, C. A., Maza, O., ... Elinav, E. (2014). Artificial sweeteners induce glucose intolerance by altering the gut microbiota. *Nature, 514*(7521), 181–186. doi: 10.1038/nature13793

Swithers, S. E. (2013). Artificial sweeteners produce the counterintuitive effect of inducing metabolic derangements. *Trends in Endocrinology & Metabolism, 24*(9), 431–441. doi: 10.1016/j.tem.2013.05.005

Swithers, S. E. (2014). A paucity of data, not robust scientific evidence: A response to Johnston and Foreyt. *Trends in Endocrinology & Metabolism, 25*(1), 2–4. doi: 10.1016/j.tem.2013.09.003

Swithers, S. E., Baker, C. R., & Davidson, T. L. (2009). General and persistent effects of high-intensity sweeteners on body weight gain and caloric compensation in rats. *Behavioral Neuroscience, 123*(4), 772–780. doi: 10.1037/a0016139

Swithers, S. E., & Davidson, T. L. (2008). A role for sweet taste: Calorie predictive relations in energy regulation by rats. *Behavioral Neuroscience, 122*(1), 161–173. doi: 10.1037/0735-7044.122.1.161

Sylvetsky, A. C., Welsh, J. A., Brown, R. J., & Vos, M. B. (2012). Low-calorie sweetener consumption is increasing in the United States. *American Journal of Clinical Nutrition, 96*(3), 640–646. doi: 10.3945/ajcn.112.034751

Taubes, G. (2007). *Good calories, bad calories.* New York: Random House.

Taylor, M. (2010, July 19). How the FDA is picking its food label battles. *The Atlantic.*

Taylor, M. C., & Saarinen, E. (1994). *Imagologies: Media philosophy.* New York: Routledge.

Tellez, L. A., Ren, X., Han, W., Medina, S., Ferreira, J. G., Yeckel, C. W., & de Araujo, I. E. (2013). Glucose utilization rates regulate intake levels of artificial sweeteners. *Journal of Physiology, 591*(Pt 22), 5727–5744. doi: 10.1113/jphysiol.2013.263103

The Onion. (2014, August 15). FDA recommends at least 3 servings of foods with word 'fruit' on box. Retrieved from http://www.theonion.com/articles/fda-recommends-at-least-3-servings-of-foods-with-w,36699/

Thomas, E. L., Frost, G., Taylor-Robinson, S. D., & Bell, J. D. (2012). Excess body fat in obese and normal-weight subjects. *Nutrition Research Reviews, 25*(01), 150–161. doi: 10.1017/S0954422412000054

Thompson, G. D. (1998). Consumer demand for organic foods: What we know and what we need to know. *American Journal of Agricultural Economics, 80*(5), 1113–1118.

Tian, K. T., & McKenzie, K. (2001). The long-term predictive validity of the consumers' need for uniqueness scale. *Journal of Consumer Psychology, 10*(3), 171–193.

Tinbergen, N. (1951). *The study of instinct.* New York: Clarendon Press/Oxford University Press.

Traister, R. (2014, May 28). Feminists killed home ec. Now they should bring it back—for boys and girls. *The New Republic.*

Turner-McGrievy, G., Tate, D. F., Moore, D., & Popkin, B. (2013). Taking the bitter with the sweet: Relationship of supertasting and sweet preference with metabolic syndrome and dietary intake. *Journal of Food Science, 78*(2), S336–S342. doi: 10.1111/1750-3841.12008

Union of Concerned Scientists. (2014). Comments to proposed rulemaking; Docket no. FDA-2012-N-1210; Food labeling: Revision of the nutrition and supplement facts labels, 79 Federal Register 11880. Retrieved from http://www.ucsusa.org/assets/documents/center-for-science-and-democracy/ucs-sugar-label-comment-signers.pdf

Urala, N., & Lähteenmäki, L. (2007). Consumers' changing attitudes towards functional foods. *Food Quality and Preference, 18*(1), 1–12.

USDA. (2000). *Nutrition and your health: Dietary guidelines for Americans.* Retrieved from http://www.health.gov/dietaryguidelines/dga2000/dietgd.pdf

USDA. (2002). *Agriculture Fact Book 2001–2002.* Retrieved from http://www.usda.gov/documents/usda-factbook-2001-2002.pdf

USDA. (2014). *What's in food?* Retrieved from http://www.nutrition.gov/whats-food/commonly-asked-questions-faqs

Vanderschuren, L., & Everitt, B. J. (2004). Drug seeking becomes compulsive after prolonged cocaine self-administration. *Science, 305*(5686), 1017–1019. doi: 10.1126/science.1098975

Veblen, T. (1899). *The theory of the leisure class.* New York: The New American Library.

Ventola, C. L. (2011). Direct-to-consumer pharmaceutical advertising: Therapeutic or toxic? *Pharmacy and Therapeutics, 36*(10), 669.

Verebey, K., & Gold, M. S. (1988). From coca leaves to crack: The effects of dose and routes of administration in abuse liability. *Psychiatric Annals, 18*(9), 513–520.

Visser, S. N., Danielson, M. L., Bitsko, R. H., Holbrook, J. R., Kogan, M. D., Ghandour, R. M.,... Blumberg, S. J. (2014). Trends in the parent report of health care provider diagnosed and medicated Attention-Deficit/Hyperactivity Disorder: United States, 2003–2011. *Journal of the American Academy of Child & Adolescent Psychiatry.* doi: 10.1016/j.jaac.2013.09.001

Volkow, N. D., Wang, G.-J., Fowler, J. S., & Telang, F. (2008). Overlapping neuronal circuits in addiction and obesity: Evidence of systems pathology. *Philosophical Transactions of the Royal Society of London Series B: Biological Science, 363*(1507), 3191–3200. doi: 10.1098/rstb.2008.0107

Volkow, N. D., Wang, G. J., Tomasi, D., & Baler, R. D. (2013). The addictive dimensionality of obesity. *Biological Psychiatry, 73*(9), 811–818. doi: 10.1016/j.biopsych.2012.12.020

Wachtel, P. (1983). *The poverty of affluence: A psychological portrait of the American way of life.* New York: Free Press.

Wachtel, P. (2003). Full pockets, empty lives: A psychoanalytic exploration of the contemporary culture of greed. *American Journal of Psychoanalysis, 63*(2), 103–122.

Wagmiller, R. L. (2003). *Debt and assets among low-income families.* National Center for Children in Poverty. Retrieved from http://www.nccp.org/publications/pdf/text_534.pdf

Wakefield, M., Terry-McElrath, Y., Emery, S., Saffer, H., Chaloupka, F. J., Szczypka, G., ... Johnston, L. D. (2006). Effect of televised, tobacco company–funded smoking prevention advertising on youth smoking-related beliefs, intentions, and behavior. *American Journal of Public Health, 96*(12), 2154. doi: 10.2105/AJPH.2005.083352

Wallsten, P., & Hamburger, T. (2013, December 7). Sugar protections prove easy to swallow for lawmakers on both sides of aisle. *The Washington Post.* Retrieved from http://www.washingtonpost.com/politics/2013/12/07/f5959c06-5ac4-11e3-bf7e-f567ee61ae21_story.html

Wang, D., Leung, C. W., Li, Y., Ding, E., Chiuve, S., Hu, F. B., & Willett, W. C. (2014a). Trends in dietary quality among adults in the United States, 1999 through 2010. *JAMA Internal Medicine.* doi: 10.1001/jamainternmed.2014.3422

Wang, G., Simone, K., & Palmer, R. (2014b). *Description of edible marijuana products, potency ranges, and similarities to mainstream foods.* Paper presented at the Clinical Toxicology Conference, New York.

Wang, J., Obici, S., Morgan, K., Barzilai, N., Feng, Z., & Rossetti, L. (2001). Overfeeding rapidly induces leptin and insulin resistance. *Diabetes, 50*(12), 2786–2791.

Wang, S. S. (2011, August 16). Psychiatric drug use spreads. *Wall Street Journal.* Retrieved from http://online.wsj.com/articles/SB10001424052970203503204577040431792673066

Wang, Y. C., Ludwig, D. S., Sonneville, K., & Gortmaker, S. L. (2009). Impact of change in sweetened caloric beverage consumption on energy intake among children and adolescents. *Archives of Pediatrics & Adolescent Medicine, 163*(4), 336–343.

Wansink, B. (2006). *Mindless eating: Why we eat more than we think.* New York: Bantam Books.

Warner-Cohen, K. (2014, April 16). Coca-Cola sees growth in non-soda and emerging markets. *WallStreetCheatSheet.* Retrieved from http://wallstcheatsheet.com/business/coca-cola-sees-growth-in-non-soda-and-emerging-markets.html/?a=viewall-ixzz3GuDsViNZ

Warren, M., Frost-Pineda, K., & Gold, M. (2005). Body mass index and marijuana use. *Journal of Addictive Diseases, 24*(3), 95–100.

Watson, E. (2014, January 8). FDA 'respectfully declines' judges' plea for it to determine if GMO's belong in all natural products. *Food Navigator.* Retrieved from http://www.foodnavigator-usa.com/Regulation/FDA-respectfully-declines-judges-plea-for-it-to-determine-if-GMOs-belong-in-all-natural-products

Watson, J. L. (2006). *Golden arches East: McDonald's in East Asia* (2nd ed.). Stanford, CA: Stanford University Press.

Webley, P., & Nyhus, E. K. (2001). Life-cycle and dispositional routes into problem debt. *British Journal of Psychology, 92*(3), 423–446.

Wei, W., & Miao, L. (2013). Effects of calorie information disclosure on consumers' food choices at restaurants. *International Journal of Hospitality Management, 33*(0), 106–117. doi: 10.1016/j.ijhm.2012.06.008

Welch, H. G., Schwartz, L., & Woloshin, S. (2011). *Overdiagnosed: Making people sick in the pursuit of health.* Boston, MA: Beacon Press.

Werle, C., Wansink, B., & Payne, C. (2014). Is it fun or exercise? The framing of physical activity biases subsequent snacking. *Marketing Letters,* 1–12. doi: 10.1007/s11002-014-9301-6.

Wilson, E. (1975). *Sociobiology: The new synthesis.* Cambridge, MA: Harvard University Press.

White, J. S. (2008). Straight talk about high-fructose corn syrup: What it is and what it ain't. *The American Journal of Clinical Nutrition, 88*(6), 1716S–1721S. doi: 10.3945/ajcn.2008.25825B

White, J. S. (2009). Misconceptions about high-fructose corn syrup: Is it uniquely responsible for obesity, reactive dicarbonyl compounds, and advanced glycation endproducts? *The Journal of Nutrition, 139*(6), 1219S–1227S. doi: 10.3945/jn.108.097998

White House Archives. (2001, September 27). At O'Hare, President says "get on board". Retrieved from http://georgewbush-whitehouse.archives.gov/news/releases/2001/09/20010927-1.html

WikiLeaks. (2007). Evaluating the enforcement of Dominican labor law in the agricultural sector. Retrieved from http://www.wikileaks.org/plusd/cables/07SANTODOMINGO1119_a.html

Wilkinson, R., & Pickett, K. (2014, February 2). How inequality hollows out the soul. *New York Times*. Retrieved from http://opinionator.blogs.nytimes.com/2014/02/02/how-inequality-hollows-out-the-soul/

Williams, R. (2009). Advertising: The magic system. In J. Turow & M. McAllister (Eds.), *The advertising and consumer culture reader*. Oxford: Routledge.

Williams, R. (2011). *Keywords: A vocabulary of culture and society*. Oxford: Routledge.

Winson, A. (2013). *The industrial diet: The degradation of food and the struggle for healthy eating*. Vancouver: UBC Press.

Woloshin, S., & Schwartz, L. M. (2011). Communicating data about the benefits and harms of treatment: A randomized trial. *Annals of Internal Medicine, 155*(2), 87–96.

World Cancer Research Fund/American Institute for Cancer Research. (2007). *Food, nutrition, physical activity, and the prevention of cancer: A global perspective*. American Institute for Cancer Research. Retrieved from http://www.aicr.org/assets/docs/pdf/reports/Second_Expert_Report.pdf

Wrangham, R. W. (2009). *Catching fire: How cooking made us human*. New York: Basic Books.

Wysocki, C. J., & Preti, G. (2004). Facts, fallacies, fears, and frustrations with human pheromones. *The Anatomical Record. Part A: Discoveries in Molecular, Cellular, and Evolutionary, 281*(1), 1201–1211. doi: 10.1002/ar.a.20125

Yudkin, J. (1972). *Pure, white and deadly: The problem of sugar*. London: Davis-Poynter Ltd.

Zellner, D. A., Rozin, P., Aron, M., & Kulish, C. (1983). Conditioned enhancement of human's liking for flavor by pairing with sweetness. *Learning and Motivation, 14*(3), 338–350.

Zhang, Y., Proenca, R., Maffei, M., Barone, M., Leopold, L., & Friedman, J. M. (1994). Positional cloning of the mouse obese gene and its human homologue. *Nature, 372*(6505), 425–432. doi: 10.1038/372425a0

Index